Bis Edmund Hillary und Tenzing Norgay den Gipfel des Mount Everest bezwungen hatten, wollten sie

Warum sollte Ihre Bank sich Tenzing Norgay zum *Vorbild* nehmen?

Man sagt, dass Genialität zu einem Prozent
aus Inspiration und zu 99 Prozent aus Fleiß besteht.

Wir denken, es gibt eine dritte Komponente.

Teamwork.

Wie Edmund Hillary und Tenzing Norgay
der Welt bewiesen haben, brauchen auch die
außergewöhnlichsten Talente Unterstützung,
um absolute Höchstleistungen zu erbringen.

Das gilt für die Finanzwelt selbstverständlich
genauso wie fürs Bergsteigen.

Weil wir alle wissen, dass das Klima an
den Finanzmärkten ebenso launisch sein kann
wie das im Himalaja.

Dass die Folgen von Ignoranz und Leichtsinn
verheerend sein können.

Aber die Belohnung für den Erfolg
ebenso atemberaubend.

Bis Sie Ihren finanziellen Zielen
ein Stück näher sind,
dürfen Sie sich auf eines verlassen:

Wir werden nicht ruhen   ❉ UBS

Wealth Management · Asset Management · Investment Banking   www.ubs.com/wirwerdennichtruhen

Armin Heinzl • Peter Buxmann • Oliver Wendt
Tim Weitzel
Editors

Theory-Guided Modeling and Empiricism in Information Systems Research

Physica-Verlag

Editors
Prof. Dr. Armin Heinzl
Universität Mannheim
Fak. Betriebswirtschaftslehre
LS ABWL und
Wirtschaftsinformatik I
Schloss, S 220
68131 Mannheim
Germany
heinzl@uni-mannheim.de

Prof. Dr. Peter Buxmann
TU Darmstadt
Fachgebiet Wirtschaftsinformatik
Hochschulstr. 1
64289 Darmstadt
Germany
buxmann@is.tu-darmstadt.de

Oliver Wendt
University of Kaiserslautern
Business Information Systems
and Operations Research
Gottlieb-Daimler-Str.
67663 Kaiserslautern
Germany
wendt@wiwi.uni-kl.de

Dr. Tim Weitzel
Universität Bamberg
Fak. Wirtschaftsinformatik und
Angewandte Informatik
Feldkirchenstr. 21
96045 Bamberg
Germany
tim.weitzel@uni-bamberg.de

ISBN 978-3-7908-2780-4   e-ISBN 978-3-7908-2781-1
DOI 10.1007/978-3-7908-2781-1
Springer Heidelberg Dordrecht London New York

Library of Congress Control Number: 2011939220

Printed on acid-free paper

Physica-Verlag is a brand of Springer
Springer is part of Springer Science+Business Media (www.springer.com)

Preface

In the age of important journal and conference rankings, anniversary publications have become slightly out of fashion. Contributing authors usually offer only manuscripts that were not accepted in or even targeted at high quality outlets with a peer-review process. This would, of course, embarrass the modern jubilee. In order to circumvent such a phenomenon, we asked the authors of this editorial book to first submit their research papers to internationally and nationally well-established and accepted conferences with a transparent peer-review process to prove the quality of the respective research. As a consequence, ten submissions have been accepted at venues like the European Conference on Information Systems (ECIS), the Americas' Conference on Information Systems (AMCIS), the Pacific-Asian Conference on Information Systems (PACIS) as well as the conference of German Academic Association for Business Research (VHB-Tagung) in 2010 and 2011. These contributions are accompanied by two invited papers that frame the book. The first one opens the series of articles by looking at an academic family in the field of IS research conducting a publication network analysis. The second closes this book by asking the programmatic question "where is the "I" in IS research?" and calling for a coherent research stream in the context of Human Information Behavior.

All contributions have two things in common. First, they contain pieces of research which explicitly focus on theory guided modeling and empiricism in the field of IS research. Second, they all have been written by scholars who are academic descendants of Prof. Dr. Wolfgang König. His accomplishments through the last three decades have spawned off a considerably growing academic family. This family has been contributing to the internationalization of the Wirtschaftsinformatik through the development of theoretical models and artefacts which have been either validated by empirical, experimental or field testing. Thus, in the name of all authors and beyond, we would like to dedicate this editorial book to our academic teacher Wolfgang König. His entrepreneurial spirit as well as his dauntless demand for high quality has helped to further develop our academic discipline as well as our personal careers.

From the perspective of the editors of this book, we thank all the authors for their contributions and cooperation. It has been a pleasure to make this project happen in such a short time. While we are grateful to the authors of the chapters of the book, we take responsibility for the content and any errors in the book. Since all articles - except the invited ones - have been published in conferences, all rights remain with the authors. Nevertheless, we will provide a reference in each chapter at which conference the respective paper had been presented. Our special thanks go to Christoph Schmidt and Lea Offermann from the Institute of Enterprise Systems and the Business School of the University of Mannheim for their efforts and support in crafting the manuscript.

As the honoree in particular and Wirtschaftsinformatik in general have always been engaged in both, the intellectual advancement of what we know and what we can, we are indebted to the contributions to this book from highly appreciated industry partners who have provided the tangible resources for this endeavour. Our deepest gratitude belongs to Axel Hoerger, UBS Deutschland AG, Dr. Jochen Malinowski, Accenture GmbH, Josef Pfeiffer, DZ Bank AG, Stephan Wolf, Interactive Data, Dr. Norman Hoppen, Deutsche Leasing AG as well as Matthias Uhrig, Intargia GmbH. Without their valuable support, we would have not been able to accomplish this project. Many thanks go also to Christian Rauscher, Springer Publishers, who was very open to a novel form of reviving an anniversary publication.

We hope you find the reading of this editorial book "Theory guided Modeling and Empiricism in IS research" to be valuable as well as insightful and furthermore, that you realize that the revival of this anniversary publication is going into the right direction in order to appropriately honor our admired jubilee Prof. Dr. Wolfgang König.

Armin Heinzl   Peter Buxmann   Oliver Wendt   Tim Weitzel

Mannheim   Darmstadt   Kaiserslautern   Bamberg

INTARGIA

INTARGIA sincerely congratulates

Professor Dr. Wolfgang König

on his 60th birthday

Thank you, Wolfgang,

for more than 30 years of

amity, spirit and successful cooperation !

Matthias Uhrig   Dr. Thomas Jurisch   Martin Hentschel

on behalf of the entire INTARGIA Team

INTARGIA Managementberatung GmbH, Max-Planck-Str. 20, 63303 Dreieich, www.intargia.com

Contents

Publication Network Analysis of an Academic Family in Information Systems

Dr. Jörn Grahl

Information Systems and Business Administration, Johannes Gutenberg-University Mainz, Jacob-Welder-Weg 9, 55128 Mainz, Germany, grahl@uni-mainz.de

Bastian Sand

Business Information Systems & Operations Research, University of Kaiserslautern, Erwin-Schrödinger-Straße 42-420, 67653 Kaiserslautern, Germany, sand@bisor.de

Michael Schneider

Business Information Systems & Operations Research, University of Kaiserslautern, Erwin-Schrödinger-Straße 42-420, 67653 Kaiserslautern, Germany, schneider@bisor.de

Dr. Michael Schwind

IT-based Logistics, Goethe-University Frankfurt, Campus Westend Grüneburg-platz 1, 60323 Frankfurt, schwind@wiwi.uni-frankfurt.de

1   Introduction

The study of scientific collaboration through network analysis can give interesting conclusions about the publication habits of a scientific community. Co-authorship networks represent scientific collaboration as a graph: nodes correspond to authors, edges between nodes mark joint publications (Newman 2001a,b). Scientific publishing is decentralized. Choices of co-authors and research topics are seldomly globally coordinated. Still, the structure of co-authorship networks is far from random. Co-authorship networks are governed by principles that are similar in

A. Heinzl et al. (eds.), *Theory-Guided Modeling and Empiricism in Information Systems Research*, DOI 10.1007/978-3-7908-2781-1_1, © Springer-Verlag Berlin Heidelberg 2011

other complex networks such as social networks (Wasserman and Faust 1994), networks of citations between scientific papers (Egghe and Rousseau 1990), the World Wide Web (Albert and Barabási 1999, Kleinberg et al. 1999) or power grids (Watts and Strogatz 1998). It is therefore not astounding that scholars have studied co-authorship networks in considerable detail and in a variety of contexts, such as physics (Newman 2001a), evolutionary computation (Cotta and Merelo 2007) or computer supported cooperative work (Horn et al. 2004).

A significant share of publications emerges inside the boundaries of "academic families". These groups are often founded by one or few senior scholars and evolve through the training of academic offspring. This paper studies the academic family founded by Wolfgang König. It includes him and his academic offspring: assistant and tenured professors with current and former graduate students. For the remainder of this paper, it is referred to as "the group". We construct the group's co-authorship network and the co-authorship network of the German speaking Information Systems community (GIS). We then analyze the relation between the two networks. We discuss author centrality on an individual level and on a group level as well as the role the group plays in stabilizing the larger network. We detect the community structure of GIS and locate the group inside the resulting network of research communities.

Section 2 describes the data collection process and introduces required notation and symbols. The global structure of the GIS co-authorship network is studied in Section 3.1. The group's author centralities are computed and interpreted in Section 3.2. Group level centrality is discussed in Section 3.3 and some results on connectivity and resilience to author removal are given in Section 3.4. The community structure of GIS is detected in Section 3.5. The paper ends with concluding remarks.

2   Data Retrieval and Notation

The raw data for our study is the complete Digital Bibliography & Library Project (DBLP) as of December 2010. DBLP clearly does not list every paper published by IS scholars, but the data should be comprehensive enough to be suitable for our study. The scope of DBLP is broader than required, including computer science and related fields. To select only relevant authors and publications, we crawled DBLP for publications written by IS scholars from Germany, Austria or Switzerland. An author list was assembled from two publicly available sources. The German Academic Association for Business Research maintains a scientific committee for IS research. Its members were merged with the IS scholars listed in Kurbel et al. (2008). The resulting list contains 340 visibly active authors from GIS. All available publications by these authors are selected from DBLP. Non-research articles such as editorial introductions, calls for papers, interviews, conference reports, book reviews and acknowledgments to referees were removed manually. The remaining publications form the basis of the co-authorship networks.

We denote networks with uppercase letters. Network G has a set of nodes n^G and an edge set e^G. Edges are undirected. If edge length is required in an analysis, we assume it to be one. Edges do not carry other information. Operator $\|$ denotes set cardinality, i.e. G has $|n^G|$ nodes and $|e^G|$ edges.

The co-authorship network constructed from the collected, complete data is denoted as W. A node corresponds to an author, an edge between two nodes marks that these authors have published at least one paper together. W has $|n^W|=6.409$ nodes (authors), $|e^W|=21.342$ edges (collaborations) and represents coauthorship in GIS. The number of nodes is larger than the initial set of 340 researchers as it contains coauthors outside this set.

The group of authors founded by König consists of himself and his academic offspring, including tenured and assistant professors and current or former graduate students. Membership is also determined based on attendance of a yearly scientific colloquium. Beside W, we constructed a co-authorship network K which is a subgraph of W. Nodes in K correspond to authors who are both in the König group and in n^W. Edges in K mark co-authorship between authors in n^K. K has $|n^K|=49$ nodes, $|e^K|=83$ edges and represents collaboration in König's "scientific family".

The remainder of this paper explores the group's centrality and that of its members, K's importance for W's integrity and whether we can discover K by inspecting W.

3   Network Analysis

3.1   Topology: Degree Distribution, Path Lengths, Clustering

W's degree distribution is depicted in Figure 1. In this and the remaining figures, König's position is marked by a "▲". The degree distribution is skewed. While most of the authors have few co-authors, a minority publishes with dozens. Approximating the tail with a power law fits the distribution well, and yields a degree exponent of 2.2. This is inside the characteristic range for degree exponents of co-authorship networks (Wagner and Leydesdorff 2005) and of scale-free networks

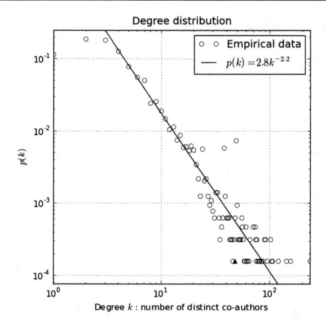

Figure 1:   Degree distribution of W in log-log scale. Straight lines indicate power laws.

formed by preferential attachment (Barabási and Albert 1999). The scale-free degree distribution is likely caused by new authors who, upon entering the IS community, prefer to publish with more experienced, better-connected scholars. With this degree exponent, numerous well-connected authors serve as hubs and we expect the size of the giant component to be robust against random removal of authors (Cohen et al. 2000).

W consists of 68 connected components, but a single giant component contains 94.8% of the nodes. The network formed by nodes of the giant component and their adjacent edges is denoted by C.

C's average shortest path length is 5.39 and the average cluster coefficient is 0.77. The average cluster coefficient is an indicator $\in[0;1]$ for local clustering around nodes. The cluster coefficient of a node is 1, if all nodes adjacent to it are neighbors themselves. When edges between the neighbors are removed, the coefficient progresses towards 0. In contrast, the average shortest path length is a global indicator measuring the average number of edges between any two nodes in the network. When comparing these results to connected *random* graphs with $|n^C|$ nodes and $|e^C|$ edges one finds that their average shortest path length is quite similar (≈ 4.72), but that the average cluster coefficients is only ≈ 0.00125. Thus, W's giant component shows much higher clustering than these equivalently sized random graphs. This phenomenon is common in small world networks (Watts and Strogatz 1998) whose nodes are apart by just 'six degrees of separation' (Milgram 1967).

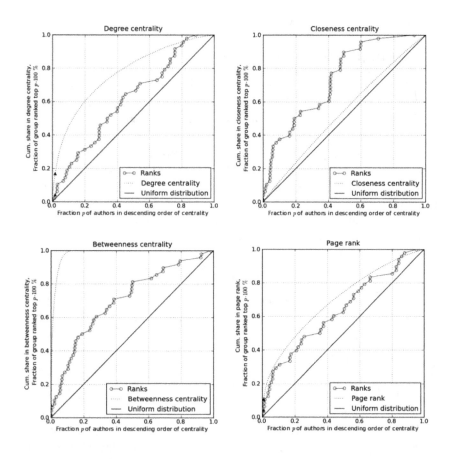

Figure 2:   Author centrality according to degree-, closeness-, betweenness-centrality and page rank. The straight 45° line marks a uniform distribution of centrality or ranks. The dotted lines are Lorenz curves for the distribution of centrality. Straight lines with circles mark the distribution of the group members' ranks in the context of GIS

C exhibits a scale-free distribution of node degrees, strong local clustering and short paths. Note that pure scale-free networks obtained from Barabási and Albert's (1999) preferential attachment model do not exhibit strong clustering. The distribution of node degrees in most small world models like that of Watts and Strogatz (1998) is not scale-free. We observe both features simultaneously in graphs that have a hierarchical community structure (Ravasz and Barabási 2003).

This fact motivated the application of a community detection algorithm in Section 3.5. to reveal the community structure of the publication network.

3.2   Centrality Measures on Actor Level

Social network analysis has developed a variety of measures to interpret the position of a node in a network (Wasserman and Faust 1994). Centrality measures are frequently used to assess whether a node has a central position or not. The detailed meaning of "central" depends highly on the context of the study and the measure used. We computed degree centrality, closeness centrality, betweenness centrality, and the page rank for authors inside C. The degree centrality (Shaw 1954, Nieminen 1974) of a node is the number of edges connected to it. In our study, the degree centrality of an author is simply the number of her distinct co-authors. It is intuitively appealing to define those authors with many direct co-authors to be central.

Closeness centrality (Beauchamp 1964) considers the distance of a node to all other nodes. We compute closeness centrality of node i as the inverse sum of the shortest paths from i to all other nodes. The rationale behind closeness centrality is that nodes with a short distance to all other nodes can take a central position in the network due to their potential efficiency in spreading information. Authors who can reach other authors via few intermediaries might be able to spread their ideas more quickly and thus be less dependent on the remaining network.

Betweenness centrality (Freeman 1977) of node i considers the control that i might exercise on information passing through the network. Betweenness centrality is the share of shortest paths between any two nodes $\neq i$ passing through i. The higher a node's betweenness centrality, the more information passes through i, assuming that information flow follows the shortest possible paths.

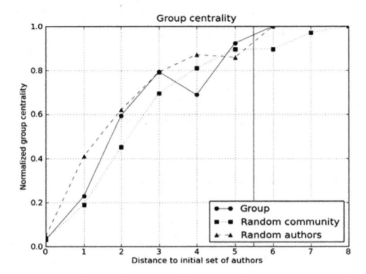

Figure 3:   K's normalized group centrality (circles) compared to that of random authors
            (squares) and random communities with same component structure (triangles).
            The vertical line marks the average shortest path length.

Page rank (Brin and Page 1998) is based on the idea that an author connected to central authors is central himself. This is a recursive view on degree centrality which dates back to (Katz 1953) and shares some similarity with eigenvector centrality (Bonacich and Lloyd 2001). The page rank of a node i in a network can be interpreted as the long-run steady state probability that a random walk along the network topology ends in i. For a detailed discussion of centrality measures see (Landherr et al. 2010).

We are not interested in absolute centrality values but instead study how evenly centrality is distributed in the network and how the group members compare to the remaining authors on individual level and on group level (presented in Section 3.3). The Lorenz curves from Figure 2 (dotted lines) show that closeness centrality is almost evenly distributed, followed by page rank, degree centrality and betweenness centrality. The lengths of shortest paths between pairs of authors are rather evenly distributed and center around 5.4. The shortest paths do not cover the complete network well. The hubs are traversed in most of the shortest paths while the majority of nodes are not visited at all.

Next, we considered the author *ranks* according to their individual centrality. The results are plotted in Figure 2 with straight lines and circles. Specifically, we computed the top 1,2,…100% of all authors in C ordered by centrality (horizontal axes) and counted how many members of the König group were among this share (vertical axes, normalized to group size). For comparison, the 45° lines in Figure 2 represent uniform distributions of ranks. The König group lies above this line for all considered centrality measures. This means that their ranks are not evenly spread over all possible ranks, but the rank distribution is skewed towards smaller ranks. As an example, consider closeness centrality. Half of the group is among the top 20% of all authors. Similar observations for the other centrality measures let us conclude that the members of the König network tend to be more central than the average author in the overall network W.

3.3   Centrality Measures on Group Level

Everett and Borgatti (1999) extend actor-level centrality to groups. This allows addressing questions like "How central is a group of authors in the publication network, compared to other groups?" We consider the normalized variant of group degree centrality. This measure computes for a group g of authors the number of its distinct direct neighbors $\notin g$. This number is normalized by the number of authors outside the group. Put differently, normalized group degree centrality of group g is the share of remaining actors that g is connected to. Note that we can add the neighbors to the group, compute group centrality again, and repeat these steps until the whole network has been included in g. We have computed this iterative variant for K. Results are compared to group centrality of (1) groups that contain the same number of authors but the authors are randomly selected, and (2) randomly picked subgraphs in C that have the same number and sizes of components as K. The comparison groups did not include members of K. Results are averaged over 100 independent trials.

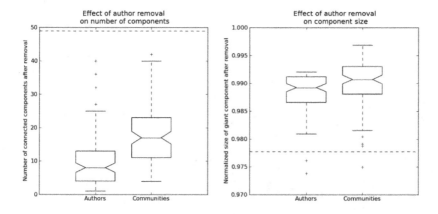

Figure 4:   Effect of author removal on number of resulting components (left) and size of
              the largest resulting components (right). The vertical line marks the result from
              removing the König group. In each subfigure, the left (right) box-plot is
              obtained from removing random authors (random communities with same
              component structure). The boxes cover the data from the lower to the upper
              quantiles, the central lines mark medians. Whiskers extending from the box
              cover data within 1.5 times the interquartile range. Points are potential outliers.

Consider the results in Figure 3. About 25% of the German speaking IS community is connected to the König group while an identical number of random authors
reaches more than 40% of the network. Random authors are distributed over the
network, covering it more evenly. Further, the probability that two random authors
have identical neighbors is much smaller compared to two authors from the same
connected subgraph. Second-order neighbors cover ≈60% of the network for both
random authors and K. The König group's group centrality is larger than the one
of randomly pitioned subgraphs with equal component structure.

The vertical line marks the average shortest path length. When the distance to the
initial set approaches the average shortest path length, the complete graph should
be almost covered. This plausibility check is clearly met by the results. Further,
each curve rises up to a certain distance, followed by a sharp drop in group centrality. This drop appears when the enlarged author set approaches the network's
periphery. Here, some gateway nodes which act as funnels must be passed. The
plot shows normalized group centrality. When passing a funnel, only few of the
remaining authors can be reached, causing the drop that is visible in the figures.
Funnels slow down the coverage process. Once the gateway nodes are passed, W
is quickly covered in entirety. In summary, group centrality of König's academic
family is high. It approaches that of randomly positioned authors and surpasses
that of randomly positioned communities with identical structure.

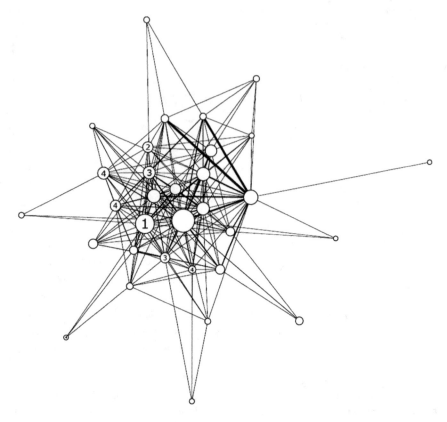

Figure 5:   Network of communities obtained from applying the community detection algo-
             rithm from Blondel et al. (2008) to *C*. Each community is represented by a node.
             Node size is proportional to community size. The thickness of an arc between
             two communities is proportional to the number of collaborations between the
             communities.

3.4   Network Resilience to Removal of Authors

We are interested in K's importance to maintain C's integrity. We removed K
from C and study the remains of C. The results are compared to removing $|K|$
random authors, and to removing random subgraphs with component structures
equal to that of K. Figure 4 depicts the results in the form of box-plots. The additional horizontal lines mark the results from removing K.

Removing K from C breaks C into 49 parts. Removing $|K|$ random authors breaks
it into 9.5 parts. This is in accordance with Cohen et al. (2000) who show that
removing random nodes from scale-free networks does not split the network in
many parts, but removing the hubs does. Removing random subgraphs with K's

component structure breaks C into 17.9 parts (randomized results were averaged over 100 trials). It is intuitive to state that K has a significant influence on C's integrity. Now consider the sizes of the largest components after author removal. Although C is broken into many parts, the largest component after removal still contains 97% of C's nodes. Therefore, although the effect is larger than for random removal of authors and communities, K is not large enough to be C's "backbone".

3.5   Community Detection in GIS

Scale-free degree distributions, short paths and high local clustering let us conjecture that W is organized in communities connected by hubs (Ravasz and Barabasi 2003). Not only are we interested in the community structure of the GIS but we also investigate whether König's academic family is discovered as a community inside C. Community detection is an active research area, with the method by Blondel et al. (2008) being one of the prominent algorithms to cluster connected graphs into modular parts. We use this method to detect author communities in C. The result from applying the method is a partitioning of authors. Each partition holds some authors and represents a community. Figure 5 is a visualization of C's community graph. Each community is a node, its size proportional to the number of community members. C is fully connected, so that there will be arcs between community subgraphs. The number of collaborations between any two communities is represented by arc thickness.

K is formed by organizational membership. Is this affiliation mirrored in the network of publications? To this end we were interested in which of the communities the members of the group can be found. It turns out that they are present in some of these subgroups, indeed 70.8% (12.5%, 4.2%, 2.1%) of the group members are member of the community marked 1 (2,3,4).

4   Concluding Remarks

We have studied how the academic family of German IS scholar Wolfgang König integrates into the German speaking IS community. The academic family consists of König himself and his academic offspring, including tenured and assistant professors as well as graduate students. Our approach was based on coauthorship network analyses.

The results show that most 'family members' exhibit above-average centrality on their *individual* level. Further, the group is remarkably central *as a whole*. It has evolved to a position that allows higher outreach than groups with identical sizes and structure, but different locations in the network. The König group reaches almost the same number of authors like authors that we distribute evenly in whole German speaking IS. The group might not be large enough to form the stability backbone of the whole IS community. Yet we clearly recognize König and his academic offspring even from a bird's-eye view on the publication network and the ties therein.

As a final note, we conjecture that simple preferential attachment models are not very useful in explaining why König has become a central 'hub'. These models take a rather passive view on hub behavior. They do not consider node attributes and attitudes. They neither consider König's long lasting commitment to highest standards in IS research nor his far-reaching influence on the field.

References

Albert, R., Jeong, H. and Barabási, A.-L. "Internet: Diameter of the world-wide web", *Nature* (401), 1999, pp. 130–131.

Barabási, A.-L. and Albert, R. "Emergence of scaling in random networks", *Science* (286), 1999, pp. 509–512.

Beauchamp, M. A. "An improved index of centrality", *Behavioral Science* (10:2), 1965, pp. 161–163.

Blondel, V. D., Guillaume, J.-L., Lambiotte, R. and Lefebvre, E. "Fast unfolding of communities in large networks", *Journal of Statistical Mechanics: Theory and Experiment* (10), 2008, P10008.

Bonacich, P. and Lloyd, P. "Eigenvector-like measures of centrality for asymmetric relations", *Social Networks* (23:3), 2001, pp. 191–201.

Brin, S. and Page, L. "The anatomy of a large-scale hypertextual web search engine", *Computer networks and ISDN systems* (30), 1998, pp. 107–117.

Cohen, R., Erez, K., Ben Avraham, D. and Havlin, S. "Resiliance of the internet to random breakdowns", *Physical Review Letters* (85:21), 2000, pp. 4626–4628.

Cotta, C. and Merelo, J. J. "Where is evolutionary computation going? A temporal analysis of the EC community", *Genetic programming and evolvable machines* (8:3), 2007, pp. 239–253.

Egghe, L., and Rousseau, R. *Introduction to Infometrics*, Elsevier, Amsterdam, 1990.

Everett, M. G. and Borgatti, S. P. "The centrality of groups and classes", *Journal of Mathematical Sociology* (23:3), 1999, pp. 181–201.

Freeman. L. C. "A set of measures of centrality based on betweenness", *Sociometry* (40:1), 1977, pp. 35–41.

Horn, D. B., Finholt, T. A., Birnholtz, J. P., Motwani, D. and Jayaraman, S. "The six degrees of Jonathan Grudin: A social network analysis of the evolution and impact of CSCW research", In *Proceedings of the 2004 ACM Conference on Computer supported cooperative work (CSCW '04)*, 2004, pp. 582–591.

Katz, L. "A new status index derived from sociometric analysis", *Psychometrika* (18:1), 1953, pp. 39–43.

Kleinberg, J. M., Kumar, S. R., Raghavan, P., Rajagopalan, S. and Tomkins A. "The Web as a graph: Measurements, models and methods", In *Lecture Notes in Computer Science* (1627), 1999, pp. 1–18.

Kurbel, K., Brenner, W., Chamoni, P., Frank, U., Mertens, P. and Roithmayr, F. *Studienführer Wirtschaftsinformatik 2009/2010. Studieninhalte-Anwendungsfelder-Berufsbilder*. Universitäten in Deutschland/Österreich/Schweiz. Gabler, 2008.

Landherr, A., Friedl, B. and Heidemann, J. "A critical review of centrality measures in social networks", *Business & Information Systems Engineering* (2:6), 2010, pp. 371–385.

Milgram. S. "The Small World Problem", *Psychology Today* (2), 1967, pp. 60-67.

Newman, M. E. J. "Scientific collaboration networks. I. Network construction and fundamental results", *Physical Review E* (64:1), 2001a, pp. 06131–1 – 06131–8.

Newman, M. E. J. "Scientific collaboration networks. II. Shortest paths, weighted networks, centrality", *Physical Review E* (64:1), 2001b, pp. 06132–1 – 06132–7.

Nieminen, J. "On the centrality in a graph", *Scandinavian Journal of Psychology* (15:1), 1974, pp. 332–336.

Ravasz, E. and Barabási, A.-L. "Hierarchical organization in complex networks", *Physical Review E* (67:2), 2003, pp. 026112–1 – 026112–7.

Shaw, M. E. "Group structure and the behavior of individuals in small groups", *Journal of Psychology* (38), 1954, pp. 139–149.

Wagner, C. S. and Leydesdorff, L. "Network structure, self-organization, and the growth of international collaboration in science", *Research Policy* (34:10), 2005, pp. 1608–1618.

Wasserman, S. and Faust, K. *Social network analysis: Methods and applications*, Cambridge University Press, 1994.

Watts, D. J. and Strogatz, S. H. "Collective dynamics of small-world networks", *Nature* (393), 1998, pp. 440–442.

Compatibility of Software Platforms[1]

Dr. Thomas Widjaja

Chair of Information Systems, Technische Universität Darmstadt,
Hochschulstraße 1, 64289 Darmstadt, Germany, widjaja@is.tu-darmstadt.de

Prof. Dr. Peter Buxmann

Chair of Information Systems, Technische Universität Darmstadt,
Hochschulstraße 1, 64289 Darmstadt, Germany, buxmann@is.tu-darmstadt.de

1 Introduction

In the software industry, as well as in numerous other IT industries, products are often offered as systems consisting of complementary components (Gawer and Henderson 2007). In this context, specific components take on the role of software platforms, and around these platforms so-called ecosystems evolve. Evans et al. (2006) describe a software platform as "a software program that makes services available to other software programs through Application Programming Interfaces (APIs)".[2] Jansen et al. (2009) define such an ecosystem around a platform as "a set of actors functioning as a unit and interacting with a shared market for software and services, together with the relationships among them. These relationships are frequently underpinned by a common technological platform or market and operate through the exchange of information, resources, and artifacts." The idea of offering software systems, which are based on platforms, in combination with complementary products from an "ecosystem" is applied throughout the software industry. This is not a new phenomenon: Around the first operating systems, "ecosystems" of applications had already evolved. Current examples for developing ecosystems are both Apple, with the AppStore, and Google, with the Android Marketplace. A similar constellation can be found in the area of service-oriented architectures (SOA): SOA services from different vendors can be integrated on the

---

[1] Another version of this paper appeared as: Widjaja, Thomas and Peter Buxmann, "Kompatiblität von Softwareplattformen", Corsten, H. et al.: 73. Jahrestagung des Verbandes der Hochschullehrer für Betriebswirtschaft e.V., Kaiserlautern 2011.

[2] In this article, we concentrate on software platforms which provide infrastructure services to other software programs.

A. Heinzl et al. (eds.), *Theory-Guided Modeling and Empiricism in Information Systems Research*, DOI 10.1007/978-3-7908-2781-1_2, © Springer-Verlag Berlin Heidelberg 2011

basis of SOA platforms. Moreover, the evolvement of ecosystems is observable in the Software-as-a-Service (SaaS) market (Cusumano 2010a; Cusumano 2010b).

If several competing software platforms and their corresponding ecosystems exist in an industry, the users must decide which platform they want to use. This question is of especially great importance, because a change of platform often can only be realized with high switching costs. Likewise, the producers of software components resp. "apps" must decide for which platforms they should provide their products.

The goal of this article is to evaluate the optimal degree of compatibility between a software platform and the components of competing ecosystems. Therefore, we take the platform vendors perspective. If a vendor facilitates the integration of applications from competitors' ecosystems with his platform, on the one hand, the attractiveness of his platform is increased. On the other hand, the complementary products of the vendor's ecosystem have no advantages over complementary products offered by competitive ecosystems. Note that the degree of compatibility varies considerably among ecosystems: while, for example, an application implemented for an Android cellular phone cannot be used on an Apple iPhone, it is possible to use ERP components developed for the SAP ecosystem in combination with a platform provided by a different vendor (e.g., IBM or Oracle). In this article, we focus on situations where competing ecosystems exist and users are able to combine components (out of the different ecosystems) to individual systems.

After a short overview of the literature regarding the openness of software platforms (Chapter 2), a binary linear optimization problem is introduced in order to model the users' trade-off between the higher functional coverage and the additional costs of heterogeneous solutions from the viewpoint of the standardization economy (Chapter 3). Assuming that the users decide based on the modeled aspects, this model can be utilized (from the platform vendor's perspective) in order to anticipate the effects of changes in compatibility of the platform. On the basis of a simulation experiment, in which the effect of a change in compatibility on the structure of the optimal solution of the optimization problem is analyzed, recommendations for action for the vendors are derived (Chapter 4). The article concludes with a short summary and the outlook on future research (Chapter 5).

2   Openness of Software Platforms

On the one hand, existing literature examines the motives of platform vendors as well as those of vendors of complementary products to participate in an ecosystem (Arndt et al. 2008a; Arndt et al. 2008b; Hilkert et al. 2010; Kude and Dibbern 2009). On the other hand, competitive platform vendors have to take specific design decisions, including especially "openness and control", price setting, and innovation strategy, as discussed in the literature (Gawer and Henderson 2007; Rysman 2009; West 2003).

In this article, we focus on the compatibility of a platform with complementary components of competitors and thus, on an aspect of the openness of a platform. Especially for large and established vendors, incompatibility can be a way to establish and preserve a competitive advantage. However, openness, and particularly the compatibility of a platform, facilitates the integration of niche vendors and thus helps to extend their ecosystem. When assembling a platform-based product, the user makes decisions based not only on the performance of the individual components, but also on whether and to what extent components of different vendors are compatible. Therefore, compatibility has advantages for the customers as well: it simplifies the integration of complementary products of different ecosystems and hence, the realization of best-of-breed systems.

In this article, we understand best-of-breed systems as software systems formed by the combination of components that offer the user the highest functional coverage for the particular functions, which generally leads to heterogeneous systems (in terms of utilized vendors and ecosystems). As a result, the user is confronted with the following optimization problem (cf. Chapter 3): on the one hand, the components of a single ecosystem often do not cover all of the user's requirements, while, on the other hand, the combination of components from different ecosystems typically results in increased cost due to incompatibility. The compatibility decision of the vendor thus has an immense effect on the selection decision of potential users (Köster 1999). If incompatibility additionally raises the risk for the user to "strand" with an inferior vendor (or an inferior standard, respectively), he might even decide himself against adoption (Katz and Shapiro 1994). These considerations emphasize the role of the platform: often times, this infrastructure component is established in line with the first projects and thus constitutes a lasting advantage for the chosen vendor when further selection decisions are made by the user.

The analysis presented in this article is based on the perspective of the standardization economy. Farrell and Saloner (1992) describe the relationship between compatibility standards and compatibility as follows: "Compatibility may be achieved through standardization" (Farrell and Saloner 1992). Accordingly, we understand a "compatibility standard" in this article as a standard that is used to realize interaction between elements of a system. In this context, we consider the interaction between the platform and complementary products, as well as the information relationships between complementary components.

An important characteristic of communication standards is that they show so-called "network effects".[3] Katz and Shapiro (1985) define the concept of network effects as follows: "The utility that a given user derives from the good depends upon the number of other users who are in the same 'network' as is he or she" (Katz and Shapiro 1985; Liebowitz and Margolis 1994). Several articles provide a sound overview of the network effect theory (David and Greenstein 1990; Gandal 2002; Koski and Kretschmer 2004; Matutes and Regibeau 1996; Weitzel et al. 2000).

3 Modeling the Decision of the Platform Users

In this chapter, we present a model to support the simultaneous selection of plat-forms and services from the user's perspective. In this article, the term "service" is understood as a component which implements functionality through software. The granularity of services can vary – in this context, the term includes the CRM mod-ule of an ERP standard software as well as an "app" for a cellular phone. The presented model displays the trade-off between the potentially better functional coverage of software systems composed of components from different vendors and the typically increased cost inherent to such heterogeneous systems. This is relevant for the selection of platforms and services in the business-to-consumer sector, as well as in the business-to-business sector. For instance, companies have to decide which platform vendor they choose in the context of „Software as a Service" (SaaS) (Buxmann et al. 2008). In this field, vendors like SAP and sales-force.com offer corresponding platforms as well as an ecosystem of associated services (Cusumano 2010a; Cusumano 2010b). A similar constellation can be found in the area of service-oriented architectures (SOA): here, SOA services from different vendors can be integrated on the basis of SOA platforms. The main principle is therefore comparable to the AppStore and the Android Marketplace. However, a significant difference lies in the information relationships between the services. While apps are usually independent from each other in the previously mentioned marketplaces, information exchange is necessary in the business-to-business sector. For example, project management and finance services exchange payment information on the basis of a CRM platform. As a consequence, we must not only consider the cost of potential incompatibility in the integration of services and platforms, but also the costs resulting from information exchange between services of different vendors. In the following model formulation, we will concen-trate on the business-to-business field. This consideration constitutes the general

---

[3]   Note that we refer in this article to "system-internal" network effects. The usage of components of a vendor becomes (from this perspective) more and more favorable, as more components of this vendor are already in use.

case, i.e., the selection decision in the sector of business-to-consumer platforms can be regarded as a special case of the selection decision modeled here. The special case in which single services are obtained from other service vendors, for example as in SaaS, and where integration into the company's platform plays a minor role, is thereby considered as well.

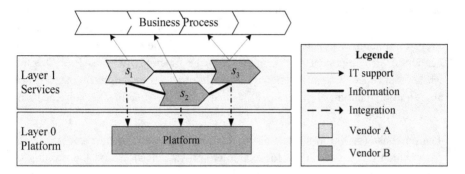

Figure 1:   Two layers of a platform-based software system

When establishing a software system based on a platform, the user must decide which services he will purchase from which vendor, and which he wants to develop on his own in order to support his business processes. As displayed in Figure 1, we assume in this article that platform-based software systems can be structured into two layers. According to this model, the service layer (Layer 1) involves all services used which provide IT functions (e.g., for the business process). However, in order to use the services, an additional infrastructure component – the platform – is needed in Layer 0. In the SOA case, such platforms are developed and sold by big software vendors, such as IBM, Oracle, or SAP, but also by smaller vendors, like Software AG.

Based on the business processes that are to be supported by the system, the set of IT functions to be modeled and $i \in N^{Service}$ can be identified. Depending on the business process to be supported, it may be necessary that the IT functions $i, j \in N^{Service}$ with $i \neq j$ exchange information, i.e. information relationships exist. The set $E^{com} \subseteq \{(i,j) | i, j \in N^{Service}$ and $i < j\}$ [4] of unsigned[5] edges represents these information relationships. Thus, the service graph can be defined as $G^{Service} := (N^{Service}, E^{com})$. Not every IT function $i \in N^{Service}$ must necessarily exchange information with all other IT functions $j \in N^{Service} / \{i\}$ – the service graph therefore does not need to be fully meshed. Platform F_0 is a special IT function

---

[4]   In the article, the elements of the set N are denoted with F_{index} with $index \in \mathbb{N}$. The used relation $<$ is defined as: $F_{index_1} < F_{index_2} \Leftrightarrow index_1 < index_2$.

[5]   Cf., e.g., Domschke et al. (2002) for an analogous approach.

which is connected to all IT functions $i \in N^{Service}$ by integration relationships. The set of IT functions is defined as $N := N^{Service} \cup \{F_0\}$. In this way, the IT functions graph can be defined as $G := (N, E)$ with $E := E^{Com} \cup \{\{F_0\} \times N^{Service}\}$.

We assume that every IT function $i \in N^{Service}$ can be implemented by services $s \in R^{Service}$ ($R^{Service}$ therefore is the set of services) and that the IT function F_0 can be implemented through a platform $p \in R^{Plattform}$ (set of platforms). In the following, we denote $R := R^{Service} \cup R^{Plattform}$ as set of components. In a feasible solution, every IT function $i \in N$ is implemented by exactly one component $r \in R$. Some vendors offer components for a multitude of IT functions (e.g., SAP or Oracle), while others specialize in functional niches. In order for a component $r \in R$ to be able to implement an IT function i, it must fulfill the functional requirements of the IT function i.

The purchase (or the in-house implementation) of a component $r \in R$ results in costs which are the result of, for example, software licenses and the training of employees. These costs are represented by the parameter $\tilde{a}^r \in \mathbb{R}_+$ and are referred to as *implementation costs* in the following. Dependent on their ability to meet the user requirements, components also provide utility, which will be denoted by $\tilde{b}^r \in \mathbb{R}$ in the following. The *net utility* $b^r \in \mathbb{R}$ can be defined as follows:[6]

$$b^r := \tilde{b}^r - \tilde{a}^r \,|\, \forall r \in R \qquad [1]$$

In some cases, the user has the option to implement all IT functions through components from one single vendor. Such a homogenous solution usually carries the advantage of a smooth interaction between components. Nevertheless, a single vendor only succeeds in completely (or even optimally) meeting all user requirements in rare instances. Therefore, open standards are used to simplify the integration of services from different vendors and therefore, best-of-breed systems tend to become more attractive. However, many vendors extend open standards by proprietary additions. Due to this, it can be concluded that heterogeneous systems usually come with the problem of incompatibility. This incompatibility is a reason for the increased cost of information exchange between services from different vendors on the one hand, and the higher cost of the integration of services and platforms of different vendors on the other hand.

To model the higher costs for the information exchange between services of different vendors, we introduce *information costs* for every pair of nodes with $(i, j) \in E^{com}$ and every pair (s,t) of service candidates with $s \in R_i^{Service}$ and $t \in R_j^{Service}$. The information costs are defined as the sum of the one-time costs and

---

[6]   Note that, if the costs associated with the component exceed the corresponding utility, it is possible that $b^r < 0$.

the discounted operating costs for the information transmission between two services, where the costs directly connected to the information exchange, as well as the opportunity costs of suboptimal decisions which could be prevented by the use of standards, are taken into account. Examples for information costs are costs for pre- and post-processing of the transmitted data (which are partly caused by the incompatibility of communication standards).[7]

In the case that services and a platform from different vendors are used in a company's software system, the user must consider possible compatibility problems in the integration of the services with the platform. Proprietary additions made by platform vendors to open integration standards are a possible reason for incompatibility. Such extensions provide for example a higher data capacity or a better security level. The services of the platform vendor often use these extensions without further adjustment and usually run much more easily on this particular vendor's platform as integration is typically prepared, well documented, and partially supported by tools. Vendors that exclusively offer services often certify these services for the use of the platform of a certain platform vendor and, in this way, become part of the corresponding ecosystem. In the following, we account for this by weighting the integration relationships between the service $s \in R^{Service}$ and the platform $p \in R^{Plattform}$ with *integration costs*. The integration costs are defined as sum of the one-time and the discounted operating costs, that occur when making a service $s \in R^{Service}$ executable on a platform $p \in R^{Plattform}$, i.e., costs directly connected to the integration. Costs for installation and configuration of a service are examples of integration costs.

We assume that every vendor uses exactly one integration standard and one communication standard and that every component fulfills exactly one integration and communication standard. With this assumption, communication and integration standards for component $r \in R$ can be combined in parameter $k^r \in K$. Hence, $k^r \in K$ can also be interpreted as a vendor of component $r \in R$. Taking into account the assumption that each component can only implement one IT function and that each vendor offers at most one component for each IT function, each component is uniquely identified by the tuple (i,k).

---

[7]   Note that, for example, in a service-oriented architecture, the information exchange is technically realized via the platform. Since, in most cases, no "semantic" enterprise-wide standards exist (which would enable a "semantic" hub and spoke architecture), it is nevertheless necessary to model direct communication relationships between the services.

For purposes of simplification, the IT function graph is not modeled bi-directional, since the reciprocal information costs between service candidates of two IT functions i and j with $i < j$ can be aggregated into one parameter:[8]

$$c_{ij}^{kk'} \in \mathbb{R} \,|\, \forall (i,j) \in E \text{ and } k \in K^i \text{ and } k' \in K^j \qquad [2]$$

Therefore, $c_{ij}^{kk'}$ for $(i,j) \in E^{com}$ represents the corresponding information costs and $c_{ij}^{kk'}$ for $(i,j) \in \{\{F_0\} \times N^{Service}\}$ refers to the corresponding integration costs. In the following, we assume that $c_{ij}^{kk} \le c_{ij}^{kk'} \,|\, \forall (i,j) \in E$ holds, i.e., the information costs (and integration costs respectively) between components of the same vendor are at most equal to the corresponding costs between components of two different vendors. K^i denotes the set of the available standards for the respective IT function. In this way, the model presented here can be understood as a standardization problem (Buxmann 2002; Domschke et al. 2002) with a special graph structure (the IT function F_0 is connected to all other IT functions by an edge).

	Symbol	Definition
Set	$G(N,E)$	IT functions graph.
	$i, j \in N$	Set of IT functions.
Parameter	$b_i^k \in \mathbb{R} \,|\, \forall i \in N \text{ and } k \in K^i$	Net utility that the component with standard $k \in K^i$ provides, if it is implemented by the IT function $i \in N$.
	$c_{ij}^{kk'} \in \mathbb{R} \,\begin{vmatrix} \forall (i,j) \in E \text{ and} \\ k \in K^i \text{ and} \\ k' \in K^j \end{vmatrix}$	Combined information and integration costs for $(i,j) \in E$ that occur if IT function $i \in N$ implements the component with standard $k \in K^i$ and the IT function $j \in N$ implements the component with standard $k' \in K^j$.

Table 1   Notation for the mathematical model

---

[8]   Cf. for an analogous approach (Domschke et al. 2002).

	Symbol	Definition
Variable	$x_i^k \in \{0,1\} \mid i \in N \text{ and } k \in K^i$	The binary variable equals one if the IT function $i \in N$ implements the component with standard $k \in K$; otherwise it is zero.
	$y_{ij}^{kk'} \in \{0,1\}$ $\begin{vmatrix} (i,j) \in E \\ \text{and } k \in K^i \\ \text{and } k' \in K^j \end{vmatrix}$	The binary variable takes the value one if the IT function $i \in N$ implements the component with standard $k \in K$ and the IT function $j \in N$ implements the component with standard $k' \in K$; otherwise it takes the value zero. This binary variable is only defined for pairs of IT functions $(i,j) \in E$.

Table 1(cont.)   Notation for the mathematical model

With the notation summarized in Table 1, the decision problem can be formulated as follows:

$$\textit{Maximize } F(\mathbf{x},\mathbf{y}) = \underbrace{\sum_{i \in N} \sum_{k \in K^i} b_i^k x_i^k}_{\text{net utility}} - \underbrace{\sum_{(i,j) \in E} \sum_{k \in K^i} \sum_{k' \in K^j} c_{ij}^{kk'} y_{ij}^{kk'}}_{\text{information costs and integration costs}}$$

[3]

subject to

$$\sum_{k \in K^i} x_i^k = 1 \qquad \left| \forall i \in N \right.$$

[4]

$$y_{ij}^{kk'} - x_i^k \leq 0 \qquad \left| \forall (i,j) \in E \text{ and } k \in K^i \text{ and } k' \in K^j \right.$$

[5]

$$y_{ij}^{kk'} - x_j^{k'} \leq 0 \qquad \left| \forall (i,j) \in E \text{ and } k \in K^i \text{ and } k' \in K^j \right.$$

[6]

$$\sum_{k \in K^i} \sum_{k' \in K^j} y_{ij}^{kk'} = 1 \qquad \left| \forall (i,j) \in E \right.$$

[7]

$$x_i^k \in \{0,1\} \qquad \left| \forall i \in N \text{ and } k \in K^i \right.$$

[8]

$$y_{ij}^{kk'} \in \{0,1\} \qquad \left| \forall (i,j) \in E \text{ and } k \in K^i \text{ and } k' \in K^j \right.$$

[9]

The objective function F maximizes the net utility with respect to the information costs and integration costs. The first term of the objective function represents the total net utility of the components and the second term corresponds to the occurring information and integration costs of the feasible solution. The set of constraints [4] guarantees that every function implements exactly one standard (and therefore one component). The sets of constraints [5] and [6] guarantee that the information and integration costs $c_{ij}^{kk'}$ occur only if function i implements the component with standard k and function j implements the component with standard k'. The set of constraints in [7] is necessary because we assume $c_{ij}^{kk'} > 0$ in many cases and therefore, it must be guaranteed that the respective information and integration costs are considered in the objective function. The sets of constraints [8] and [9] guarantee the binary domain of the decision variables x_i^k and $y_{ij}^{kk'}$.

4 Compatibility of the Platform from the Vendors' Perspective

It is the goal of the following study to analyze the structure of the optimal solution of the optimization problem presented above. On this basis, recommendations for action for platform and service vendors are developed.[9]

We assume that only two vendors (A and B) exist, that each of these vendors offers one component for each IT function, information exchange takes place between the IT functions, and that the users can combine components of those two vendors to best-of-breed systems. In the random experiment described below, for each of the $\bar{m} \in \mathbb{N}$ scenario types $\bar{n} \in \mathbb{N}$[10], random scenarios are generated. The resulting deterministic linear optimization problems are subsequently solved and selected characteristic indexes of the optimal solution for all random scenarios of a scenario type are aggregated with the arithmetic mean. Thus, the effect of the variation of the parameter values among the scenario types on the statistic distribution of the index for the optimal solution within a simulation experiment can be investigated.

The simulation experiment is executed according to the following process (cf. Weitzel (2004) for a similar approach): first, the graph structure and the parameters for the information and integration costs as well as the net utility are generated (Step 1). After that, the random scenario is solved (Step 2) and the corresponding indexes for the optimal solution are determined (Step 3). In the next step, single parameters of the random scenario are adjusted systematically in $\bar{m}$ steps (Step 4). Then, a new random scenario is generated (Step 5). The final step is the interpretation of the aggregated indexes (Step 6).

---

[9] We assume $|N| \geq 2$ and $|E| \geq 1$ – otherwise, the resulting optimization problem is trivial.

[10] In this article, all experiments are based on 250 random scenarios.

4.1 Parameter Generation: Graphs, Information Costs, Integration Costs, and Net Utility

In the following, three topologies for the $|N|-1$ nodes[11] of the service graph E^{Com} are analyzed: A) Erdős, P. and A. Renyi random graph (Erdős and Rényi 1959), algorithms by B) Albert, R. and A. Barabási (Albert and Barabási 2000) and by C) Watts and Strogatz (Newman and Watts 1999; Watts and Strogatz 1998). Three random graphs, in particular for $p^{ZG}=0.1$, $p^{ZG}=0.5$ resp. $p^{ZG}=1$ are analyzed. In the following, these will be labeled "RG01", "RG05" resp. "RG10". Analogous to IT function graphs, in which the service graph is a scale-free graph (according to Albert & Barabási (2000)) with $p^{SF}=q^{SF}=0$ and $m_0^{SF}=m^{SF}=2$ resp., a graph with small-world properties (according to Watts & Strogatz (1998)) with $k^{SW}=4$, $p^{SW}=0.05$, are labeled as "SF" resp. "SW". The parameters for the generation of the service graphs were chosen in order to ensure comparability with similar studies (Schade et al. 2007; Weitzel et al. 2006).

A random scenario is determined by the two parameter types net utility b_i^k and information and integration costs $c_{ij}^{kk'}$. In order to generate the information and integration costs $c_{ij}^{kk'}$ for the pairings of standards in two IT functions, a base value c_{ij} for all pairs of IT functions $(i,j)\in E$ is determined. The base values $c_{ij}|\forall(i,j)\in E$ for the information and integration costs are drawn from a normal distribution $c_{ij}\sim N(\mu_c,\sigma_c^2)|\forall(i,j)\in E$ with $\mu_c>0$. Thus, it is assumed that there are differences in communication intensity, but the distribution for each pair of IT functions is identical (cf., e.g., Weitzel et al. (2006) for a similar approach).

For simplification, it is assumed that only positive base values for the information and integration costs can occur. Accordingly, the normal distribution is "cut" at the zero point. This results in a truncated normal distribution (Johnson and Thomopoulos 2002), and for the adjusted expected value $\mu_{korr}(c_{ij})$ holds (Arzideh 2008):

$$\mu_{korr}(c_{ij}):=\mu_c+\sigma_c\underbrace{\frac{\phi\left(-\frac{\mu_c}{\sigma_c}\right)}{1-\Phi\left(-\frac{\mu_c}{\sigma_c}\right)}}_{\text{adjusting term}} \qquad [10]$$

Here, ϕ denotes the density function and Φ denotes the cumulative distribution function of the standard normal distribution. The correction term [10] becomes more relevant the closer $\mu_c>0$ is to zero and especially the bigger σ_c becomes.

---

[11]   In order to ensure comparability to prior studies, we assume $|N|=35$.

In order to model the fact that there are higher information and integration costs among different vendors, a percental premium is added to the information and integration costs of these pairings. The premium between the two standards k and k' is modeled with the aid of the compatibility factor $1 \le f^{kk'} < \infty$. The compatibility factor indicates how much additional effort (in relation to the base value) is necessary in order to establish compatibility between the components, and thus determines the extent of the network effects.

$$c_{ij}^{kk'} = c_{ij} \cdot f^{kk'} = c_{ij} + \underbrace{c_{ij} \cdot \left(f^{kk'} - 1 \right)}_{\text{premium term}}$$ [11]

In the following, it is assumed that $f^{kk'} = f^{k'k} | \forall k,k' \in K$ and $f^{kk} = 1 | \forall k,k' \in K$ with $k \ne k'$ applies. Here, $f^{kk'} = 1$ corresponds to "complete compatibility", whereas $f^{kk'} = \infty$ expresses "complete incompatibility". For a premium of 0 (i.e., $f^{kk'} = 1$), this results in a non-consideration of the information and integration relations. The compatibility factor $f^{kk'}$ is defined among standard combinations, i.e., the compatibility factor is identical for two standards and independent from the IT functions, which are implemented. In the following, an initial compatibility factor of $f^{AB} = f^{BA} = 1.5$ is chosen.

The net utility b_i^k for each component is drawn from the normal distribution $N(0, \sigma_b^2)$. Therefore, the two vendors A and B on average provide the same net utility. For the net utility, negative values are possible as well. These can be interpreted as "under fulfillment" of the expectations of the users.

In the simulation experiments presented in the following two sections, all compatibility factors between 1 (inclusive) and 2.5 (inclusive) are analyzed in steps of 0.125 as well as 3 and 4, beginning with $f^{AB} = 1.5$ (as the initial compatibility factor).

4.2   Strengths of the Network Effect

In this section, the net utility benefit (*NUB*) and the information and integration costs benefit (*IICB*) are defined in order to determine the expected strength of the network effects for each random scenario. The *NUB* is the monetary advantage with respect to the net utility that can be maximally reached by employing a complete "best-of-breed" solution (i.e., a feasible solution where for each IT function the component with the highest net utility is chosen) in a random scenario compared to the solution where for each IT function the component with the lowest net utility is chosen. The difference between the net utility of the components of vendors A and B for an IT function i is $\left| b_i^A - b_i^B \right|$. This results in:

$$NUB := \sum_{i \in N} \left| b_i^A - b_i^B \right| \qquad [12]$$

$$\mu(NUB) := \underbrace{\mu\left(\left| b_i^A - b_i^B \right| \right)}_{\substack{\text{expected difference of} \\ \text{net utiltiy per node}}} \cdot \underbrace{|N|}_{\text{number of nodes}} \qquad [13]$$

As $\left(b_i^A - b_i^B \right) \sim N\left(0, 2\sigma_b^2 \right)$, $\left| b_i^A - b_i^B \right|$ is distributed semi-normally, and for the expected value applies: (Leone et al. 1961)

$$\mu\left(\left| b_i^A - b_i^B \right| \right) = \sqrt{2} \cdot \sigma_b \cdot \sqrt{\frac{2}{\pi}} = 2 \cdot \sigma_b \cdot \frac{1}{\sqrt{\pi}} \qquad [14]$$

This implies that:

$$\mu(NUB) = \mu\left(\left| b_i^A - b_i^B \right| \right) \cdot |N| = 2 \cdot \sigma_b \cdot \frac{1}{\sqrt{\pi}} \cdot |N| \qquad [15]$$

In case of an implementation through components of different vendors, for each IT function pair $(i,j) \in E$, the following additional information and integration costs arise:

$$\left(c_{ij}^{AB} - c_{ij}^{AA} \right) = \left(c_{ij} \cdot f^{AB} - c_{ij} \cdot f^{AA} \right) = c_{ij} \cdot \left(f^{AB} - f^{AA} \right) = c_{ij} \cdot \lambda \qquad [16]^{12}$$

with $\lambda := f^{AB} - f^{AA} = f^{AB} - 1$.[13] With this, the IICB can be defined as:

$$IICB := \sum_{(i,j) \in \hat{E}} \hat{c}_{ij} \cdot \lambda \qquad [17]$$

The IICB corresponds to the monetary advantage of a completely homogenous solution (i.e., of "complete standardization") in comparison to a potential solution in which for each edge, the maximum possible information and integration costs arise. With $\overline{\text{deg}}$, the average degree, the number of edges of the graph, can be calculated and $\mu(IICB)$ can be defined as:

$$\mu(IICB) := \underbrace{\mu_{korr}\left(c_{ij} \right) \cdot \lambda}_{\substack{\text{expected difference of information} \\ \text{and integration costs per edge}}} \cdot \underbrace{\frac{\overline{\text{deg}}}{2} \cdot |N|}_{\text{number of edges}} \qquad [18]$$

---

[12]   Based on the assumptions (cf. [11]), the following holds: $c_{ij}^{AB} = c_{ij}^{BA}$ and $c_{ij}^{AA} = c_{ij}^{BB}$ and also $\left(c_{ij}^{BA} - c_{ij}^{BB} \right) = c_{ij} \cdot \lambda$.

[13]   Note that, since $1 \le f^{kk'} < \infty | \forall k, k' \in K$ and $f^{kk} = 1 | \forall k \in K$, the following holds: $\lambda \ge 0$.

The index $\mu(Q)$ defined in [19]:[14]

$$0 \leq \mu(Q) := \frac{\mu(IICB)}{\mu(IICB) + \mu(NUB)} \leq 1 \qquad [19]$$

For $\mu(Q) = 0\%$ resp. $\mu(Q) = 100\%$ the NUB resp. IICB dominates and it must be assumed that in nearly all of the cases, a "best-of-breed" solution resp. a "complete standardization" will arise. Thus, the value of Q can be used as a first decision rule to assess whether it is "useful" to apply the model. For extreme values of Q, only the component with the highest net utility for each IT function can be chosen, or as another extreme case, only the two single-vendor solutions (i.e., fully standardized) solutions must be compared to obtain the optimal solution. In the following, random scenarios with a particular value of $\mu(Q)$ are generated. This ensures parameter constellations in the "interesting" area and that the extreme cases are typically avoided. Note that [15] and [18] yield [19]:

$$\mu(Q) = \frac{\left(\mu_c + \sigma_c \dfrac{\phi\left(-\dfrac{\mu_c}{\sigma_c}\right)}{1 - \Phi\left(-\dfrac{\mu_c}{\sigma_c}\right)}\right) \cdot \lambda \cdot \dfrac{\overline{deg}}{2} \cdot |N|}{\left(\left(\mu_c + \sigma_c \dfrac{\phi\left(-\dfrac{\mu_c}{\sigma_c}\right)}{1 - \Phi\left(-\dfrac{\mu_c}{\sigma_c}\right)}\right) \cdot \lambda \cdot \dfrac{\overline{deg}}{2} \cdot |N|\right) + \left(2 \cdot \sigma_b \cdot \dfrac{1}{\sqrt{\pi}} \cdot |N|\right)} \qquad [20]$$

In the following experiments, $\mu_c = 10$ and $\sigma_c = 2$ are assumed (Weitzel et al. 2006). Therefore, the correction term μ_c takes (relatively) very low values (for the chosen values, the correction term takes the value $2.9734 \cdot 10^{-6}$) and the equation is simplified by ignoring the correction term:

$$\mu(Q) \approx \frac{\mu_c \cdot \lambda \cdot \dfrac{\overline{deg}}{2} \cdot |N|}{\left(\mu_c \cdot \lambda \cdot \dfrac{\overline{deg}}{2} \cdot |N|\right) + \left(2 \cdot \sigma_b \cdot \dfrac{1}{\sqrt{\pi}} \cdot |N|\right)} \qquad [21]$$

The $\overline{deg}$ can be determined after generating the graphs and $|N|$ is known for all experiments and fixed. Since $f^{AB} = f^{BA} = 1.5$ and thus $\lambda = 0.5$, $\mu(Q)$ can be determined by σ_b. This results for a chosen $\mu(Q)$ to:

---

[14]   Cf. Buxmann (2002) and Wiese (1990) for a similar approach.

$$\sigma_b \approx \frac{(1-\mu(Q)) \cdot \mu_c \cdot \lambda \cdot \frac{\overline{\text{deg}}}{4}}{\mu(Q) \cdot \frac{1}{\sqrt{\pi}}} \qquad [22]$$

A value of $\mu(Q)$ near 0% means that the IICB is typically not crucial and the individual IT functions are in each case implemented with those components which cause the highest net utility. Therefore, it tends to be a best-of-breed solution. Analogously, the IICB dominates if $\mu(Q)$ is near 100 % and there is typically a single-vendor solution (i.e., "full standardization"). This is investigated in the following, using two indexes $\kappa_{\Delta h}$ and κ_b.

For the optimal solutions, the degree of standardization for supplier A κ_h^A indicates which part of the IT functions is implemented by components of supplier A.[15] If $\mathbf{x}^*$ is the set of binary variables x_i^k of an optimal solution, then κ_h^A is defined as:

$$\kappa_h^A := \frac{\sum\limits_{i \in N \text{ and } x_i^A \in \mathbf{x}^*} x_i^A}{|N|} \qquad [23]$$

Because components of supplier A implement minimally zero IT functions and maximally all $|N|$ IT functions, $0 \leq \kappa_h^A \in \mathbb{R} \leq 1$ applies. Since every IT function must be implemented by a component of a vendor and in each of the following simulation experiments, exactly two suppliers, A and B, are examined, the degree of standardization of supplier B in the optimal solution is: $\kappa_h^B = 1 - \kappa_h^A$. In the simulation experiments, it is assumed that a vendor aims to maximize the degree of standardization by the examined methods. A high level of standardization does not always lead to high profits for the vendor. A simple example is an extreme price cut (e.g., to zero monetary units) for all components.

The index $\kappa_{\Delta h} = |\kappa_h^A - \kappa_h^B| = |\kappa_h^A - 1 + \kappa_h^A| = |2 \cdot \kappa_h^A - 1|$ equals the difference between the standardization degrees of supplier A and B in an optimal solution $\mathbf{x}^*$ and $0 \leq \kappa_{\Delta h} \in \mathbb{R} \leq 1$ holds. A value of $\mu(Q)$ close to 100 % results in $\hat{\mu}(\kappa_{\Delta h}) = 100\%$, i.e., one of the suppliers implements 100 % of the components and full standardization (i.e., single-vendor solution) is achieved. In cases in which $\mu(Q)$ is close to 0 %, $\hat{\mu}(\kappa_{\Delta h})$ approaches the value 0 %, but does not reach it (in Figure 2 $\hat{\mu}(\kappa_{\Delta h}) = 13.78\%$). A value of $\kappa_{\Delta h} = 0\%$ implies that both suppliers reach an identical degree of standardization. At $\kappa_{\Delta h} \approx 14\%$, this implies for $\kappa_{\max h} \approx (\kappa_{\Delta h} + 1)/2 \approx (0.14 + 1)/2 \approx 0.57$. In these cases – as already described –

---

[15]   If more than one „optimal" configuration of components exists, we chose an arbitrarily yet fixed solution.

the *IICB* is nearly irrelevant to the decision and the respective IT functions are implemented with those components that result in a higher net utility (a combinatory derivation of this value can be found in the Appendix).

The index $0 \leq \kappa_b \in \mathbb{R} \leq 1$ puts the realized net utility benefit reached in an optimal solution $\mathbf{x}^*$ (as compared to the worst alternative) into relation with the highest possible net utility benefit (as compared to the worst alternative):

$$0 \leq \kappa_b := \frac{\sum\limits_{\substack{i \in N \text{ and} \\ x_i^A, x_i^B \in \mathbf{x}^*}} \left((b_i^A \cdot x_i^A + b_i^B \cdot x_i^B) - \min(b_i^A, b_i^B) \right)}{\sum\limits_{i \in N} \left(\max(b_i^A, b_i^B) - \min(b_i^A, b_i^B) \right)} \leq 1 \qquad [24]$$

Figure 3 shows the arithmetic average of the indicators $\hat{\mu}(\kappa_b)$ and $\hat{\mu}(\kappa_{\Delta h})$ dependent on $\mu(Q)$ for (RG10). For the other investigated graph types, the results have a similar structure.

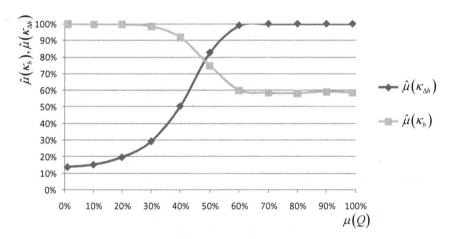

Figure 2:   Average of the standardization degree $\hat{\mu}(\kappa_{\Delta h})$ and average of the degree of
realized net utility benefit $\hat{\mu}(\kappa_b)$ dependent on $\mu(Q)$. Graph type = RG10.

For small values of $\mu(Q)$, i.e., when optimum solutions occur in which the component with the highest net utility is chosen for each IT function, $\hat{\mu}(\kappa_b)$ reaches values close to 100 %. For values of $\mu(Q)$ close to 100 %, i.e., when optimum solutions typically lead to a single-vendor solution, a $\hat{\mu}(\kappa_b)$ of slightly more than 50 % is reached. This can partly be explained by the fact that in such situations, the single-vendor solution, which yields the higher net utility, is optimal.

Based on these results, three different strengths of network effects are simulated in the following: "weak", "balanced", and "strong".[16] In the case of "balanced network effects", for the random scenarios examined in a simulation experiment should hold in average: $\mu(NUB) = \mu(IICB)$, i.e., $\mu(Q) = 0.5$. The values for the low and strong network effects were set at $\mu(Q) = 0.4$ and $\mu(Q) = 0.6$.

The development of efficient methods for solving the presented decision problem was not the focus of this investigation. Therefore, the standard implementation of a branch-and-bound-algorithm was used.

4.3   Results of the Simulation experiments: Diffusion of the Platform vs. Effect on the Choice of Services

The simulation experiments show that, in particular, two effects should be considered when a vendor changes the compatibility of his own platform to services of competitors. On the one hand, this compatibility change affects the expected distribution of the platform: the more services that can be well integrated with the platform, the more often the platform is used. On the other hand, the impact of the platform on the choice of services changes: the more compatible a platform is with the services of competitors, the lower the positive effect is on the choice of their own services.

In this section, these two effects are first analyzed separately. Here, the perspective of Vendor A is considered (w.l.o.g.). From the perspective of Vendor A, the compatibility level (i.e., a reduction of information and integration costs) may increase, if either Vendor B "converges" to the standard of Vendor A, or vice versa. In this simulation experiment, the compatibility factor $\tilde{f}^{kk'}$ is used and the following applies to information and integration costs (cf. also Formula [11]):

$$c_{ij}^{kk'} = \begin{cases} c_{ij} \cdot \tilde{f}^{kk'} \,|\, \forall (i,j) \in E \text{ with } i \in N^{Service} \text{ and } i = F_0 \text{ and } k = A \text{ and } k' = B \\ c_{ij} \cdot f^{kk'} \,|\, \text{otherwise} \end{cases} \qquad [25]$$

In this formula $1 \le \tilde{f}^{kk'} \in \mathbb{R} < \infty \,|\, \forall (i,j) \in E \text{ with } i \in N^{Service} \text{ and } j = F_0$ holds. In the simulation experiment, only $\tilde{f}^{kk'}$ varies and $f^{kk'} = 1.5$ remains constant.

In the following, the first of the two effects described above is examined, i.e., the effect of the compatibility change of the platform of Vendor A with the services of Vendor B on the adoption of the platform of Vendor A. Figure 3 (the results of the other graph types show a similar structure) shows the average degree of standardization of the platform of Vendor A dependent on the compatibility factor $\tilde{f}^{kk'}$ (in the following $0 \le \kappa_{h_p}^A \in \mathbb{R} \le 1$ resp. $\hat{\mu}\left(\kappa_{h_p}^A\right)$).

---

[16]   Note that we refer in this article to "system internal" network effects (cf. Chapter 2).

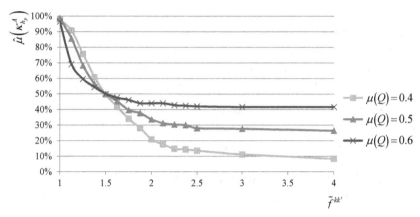

Figure 3:   Average degree of standardization of the platform of vendor A $\hat{\mu}\left(\kappa_{h_p}^A\right)$ dependent on $\tilde{f}^{kk'}$. Graph type = RG01.

If $\tilde{f}^{kk'} = f^{kk'} = 1.5$, the result $\kappa_{h_p}^A \approx 50\%$ arises for all graph types and for $\mu(Q) \in \{0.4; 0.5; 0.6\}$ respectively (as expected). Based on $\tilde{f}^{kk'} = 1.5$, a reduction of $\tilde{f}^{kk'}$ (i.e., increasing the compatibility level of the platform of Vendor A with the services of Vendor B) causes the platform of Vendor A to become more "attractive". This compatibility change may be interpreted as an extension of the ecosystem of this platform. If the platform of Vendor A is fully compatible with the services of Vendor B (i.e. $\tilde{f}^{kk'} = 1$), identical costs are incurred for the integration of the services of Vendor A and B with this platform. In these cases, for RG01, SF, and SM, the index $\kappa_{h_p}^A$ reaches values near 100 % – for graphs (RG05 and RG10) with higher $\overline{deg}$ – values of about 80 %. Note that, in the case of RG10, each IT function has the same degree. The lower $\mu(Q)$, i.e., as lower the share of IICB of the total benefit is, the lower $\kappa_{h_p}^A$ is with high $\tilde{f}^{kk'}$. The smaller $\mu(Q)$, the less homogeneous solutions are optimal (cf. Figure 2 and in particular, the shape of the curve for $\hat{\mu}(\kappa_{\Delta h})$).[17] With an increase in $\tilde{f}^{kk'}$, solutions in which the platform of Vendor A and services of Vendor B are used become more and more inefficient. Nevertheless, the optimal solutions which are completely provided by Vendor A remain unaffected.

As described above, the change in compatibility of the platform of Vendor A with the services of Vendor B has an impact on the service layer. Figure 4 (the results of the other graph types show a similar structure) shows the average degrees of standardization of Vendor A for the service layer (in the following $0 \leq \kappa_{h_s}^A \in \mathbb{R} \leq 1$ resp. $\hat{\mu}\left(\kappa_{h_s}^A\right)$) dependent of $\tilde{f}^{kk'}$. The higher the typical degree of standardization of the platform node of Vendor A, the greater the advantage (for constant informa-

---

[17]   Note that, for RG01 at $\mu(Q) = 0.6$, the index $\hat{\mu}(\kappa_{\Delta h})$ is as high as 90 %.

tion and integration costs) of implementing the services of Vendor A, from a user's point of view. For complete compatibility (i.e., $\tilde{f}^{kk'}=1$) of the platform of Vendor A with the services of Vendor B, platform A has no influence on the service layer and $\hat{\mu}(\kappa_{h_s}^A)$ is near 50 %. With increasing incompatibility, $\hat{\mu}(\kappa_{h_s}^A)<50\%$ holds (cf. Figure 4). For higher values of $\mu(Q)$, this effect, however, loses its strength; this can be justified as analogous to the development of $\hat{\mu}(\kappa_{h_p}^A)$ for varying $\mu(Q)$.

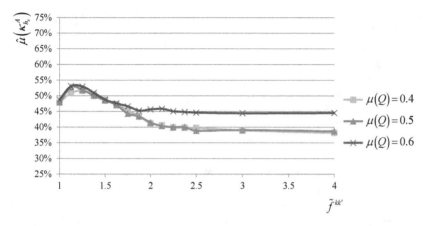

Figure 4:   Average degree of standardization of the services of Vendor A $\hat{\mu}(\kappa_{h_s}^A)$ dependent of $\tilde{f}^{kk'}$. Graph type = RG01.

In the following, the above described effect of platform choice on the selection decision on the service layer and thus on $\hat{\mu}(\kappa_{h_s}^A)$ is examined. For this purpose, $\Delta_p \kappa_{h_s}^A$ is defined, i.e., the difference between $\kappa_{h_s}^A$ in the case of a platform implemented by Vendor A and $\kappa_{h_s}^A$ in the case of a platform implemented by Vendor B are examined (cf. Figure 5). It should be noted that the negative effect of the change in platform $\hat{\mu}(\kappa_{h_s}^A)$ results from two effects:

Effect 1: The disappearance of the benefit of services from Vendor A due to lower integration costs. (If $\tilde{f}^{kk'}>1$)

Effect 2: Benefit of services from Vendor B in the selection decision due to lower integration costs.

The variation of $\tilde{f}^{kk'}$ influences only the first effect; this is an explanation for the fact that, even in complete compatibility and $\mu(Q)=0,4$, the value of $\Delta_p \kappa_{h_s}^A$ to RG01 is located at about 13 % (cf. Figure 5). For increasing network effects, the impact of the choice of platform on $\kappa_{h_s}^A$ increases as well because both Effect 1 (for all $\tilde{f}^{kk'}>1$) and Effect 2 are reinforced. Figure 5 shows that for increasing

$\tilde{f}^{kk'}$, the value of $\hat{\mu}\left(_{\Delta_p}\kappa^A_{h_s}\right)$ increases as well – this is especially interesting because the impact of Effect 2 remains constant.

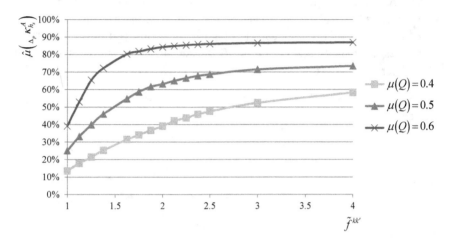

Figure 5:   Average difference in the degree of standardization for the platform of Vendor A $\hat{\mu}\left(_{\Delta_p}\kappa^A_{h_s}\right)$ dependent of $\tilde{f}^{kk'}$. Graph type = RG01.

For complete compatibility, as well as for increasing incompatibility, the value of $\hat{\mu}\left(_{\Delta_p}\kappa^A_{h_s}\right)$ for RG05 and RG10 is lower than for RG01. This can be explained by the fact that, for these closely matched graphs, the average degree of nodes is not (substantially) smaller than the degree of nodes of the platform. If $\tilde{f}^{kk'}$ is > 1.5, $\kappa^A_{h_p}$ decreases for all types of graphs and strengths of network effects (cf. Figure 3). However, if it can be assumed that a vendor can predetermine a specific platform or the platform is already implemented, the following applies for high $\tilde{f}^{kk'}$: an implemented and incompatible platform typically has a high impact on $\kappa^A_{h_s}$.

In the course of an increasing compatibility of Vendor A's platform ($\tilde{f}^{kk'}$), $\hat{\mu}\left(\kappa^A_{h_p}\right)$ increases (cf. Figure 3). The impact on the service layer (i.e., on $\hat{\mu}\left(\kappa^A_{h_s}\right)$) of an implemented platform decreases (cf. Figure 5). In the following, this trade-off is investigated further (cf. Table 2) in order to determine which value for $\tilde{f}^{kk'}$ maximizes κ^A_h.

Compatibility between the platform of Vendor A and the services of Vendor B ($\tilde{f}^{kk'}$) is ...

... increased.	... reduced.
+ The ecosystem of vendor A grows (in relation to the ecosystem of vendor B) – i.e., a positive effect on $\hat{\mu}\left(\kappa_h^A\right)$.	– The ecosystem of vendor A gets smaller (in relation to the ecosystem of vendor B) – i.e., a negative effect on $\hat{\mu}\left(\kappa_h^A\right)$.
– The effect of the platform provided by vendor A on the selection of services is reduced – i.e. a negative effect on $\hat{\mu}\left(_{\Delta_p}\kappa_{h_s}^A\right)$.	+ The effect of the platform provided by vendor A on the selection of services is reinforced – i.e., a positive effect on $\hat{\mu}\left(_{\Delta_p}\kappa_{h_s}^A\right)$.

Table 2   Diffusion of the platform vs. effect on the choice of services

Figure 6 shows that $\hat{\mu}\left(\kappa_h^A\right)$ is dependent of $\tilde{f}^{kk'}$. For RG01, in the case of $\tilde{f}^{kk'} > 1.5$, for all analyzed strengths of network effects, $\hat{\mu}\left(\kappa_h^A\right)$ is below 50 % (the value that is reached for an unchanged $\tilde{f}^{kk'} = 1.5$). The positive effect (the increased impact of the platform on the selection of services) is always overcompensated by the negative effect (the reduction of the ecosystem and the resulting decrease in $\hat{\mu}\left(\kappa_{h_p}^A\right)$). Figure 6 for RG01 implies that, for an increase in compatibility (i.e., $\tilde{f}^{kk'} < 1.5$), first the positive effect (increase in the ecosystem of Vendor A) prevails, but is overcompensated with increasing $\tilde{f}^{kk'}$. As derived earlier, in the case of complete compatibility $\left(\tilde{f}^{kk'} = 1\right)$, it holds that in nearly all cases, the platform of Vendor A is implemented, but this fact has hardly any impact on the selection decision of the service layer.

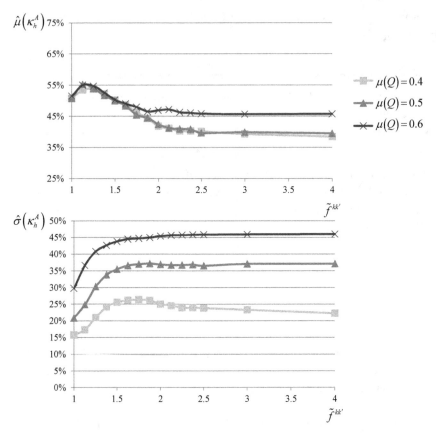

$\hat{\mu}\left(\kappa_h^A\right)$

Figure 6:   Average degree of standardization of Vendor A $\hat{\mu}\left(\kappa_h^A\right)$ and the respective standard deviation $\hat{\sigma}\left(\kappa_{h_p}^A\right)$ dependent of $\tilde{f}^{kk'}$. Graph type = RG01.

In Figure 6, the standard deviation $\hat{\sigma}\left(\kappa_h^A\right)$ is also depicted. Dependent of the risk preference, the following "risk optimal" $\tilde{f}^{kk'}$ can be derived as a result of the corresponding preference function $\tau_\kappa(m)$.

$$\tau_{\kappa_h^A}(m) = \hat{\mu}_m\left(\kappa_h^A\right) + q_{\kappa_h^A} \cdot \hat{\sigma}_m\left(\kappa_h^A\right) \qquad |\forall m \in \{1...\bar{m}\} \qquad [26]$$

The parameter $q_{\kappa_h^A}$ describes the risk preference of the decision maker: for, $q_{\kappa_h^A} > 0$, the decision maker is risk averse resp. prepared to take risks (for this, it is assumed that κ is to be maximized). For $q_{\kappa_h^A} = 0$, the decision maker is risk neutral. Figure 6 shows that a risk neutral decision maker would choose a value higher than 0 and lower than 1.5 for $\tilde{f}^{kk'}$, i.e., the platform should be more compatible with the services of the competitor.

5   Limitations

The presented mathematical model considers the user's decision from the network effect theory and standardization perspective. It must be noted that besides this, further aspects exist that can also be relevant to the users' decision (but which are typically hard to quantify). An example would be the aversion of some decision makers to rely on a single-vendor solution due to the possibility of a "vendor-lock-in". Furthermore, the presented model is static and therefore does not allow for the analysis of dynamic aspects. The analysis is based on the assumption that all necessary parameters are known at the time of the decision, but in some cases of application, this data is typically not ex ante and exactly determinable (respectively only with high financial effort). Another simplifying assumption is the identical weighting of the information and integration costs. A possible extension of the simulation model is the introduction of a factor that allows the purposeful variation of the relations among the base values of the information costs and the base values of the integration costs in the course of the random scenario generation.

In the simulation-based investigation, only selected topologies of the service graph were considered. Even though the three analyzed algorithms for graph generation (and the parameters used) are utilized in comparable investigations in the literature, limitations arise due to restricted information about the (especially future) topology and of service graphs. Thus, for instance, the (future) average service granularity has an effect on the number of information connections, and thus on the topology of the service graph. Due to these restrictions, the simulation proto-type was implemented in a modular and extendable way – thus, further types of graphs can be considered in future investigations.

6   Summary and Avenues for Further Research

In this article, the optimal degree of compatibility of a vendor's platform with the complementary components of competitors is analyzed. The user perspective is modeled on the basis of a binary linear optimization problem in order to model the trade-off between the higher functional coverage of heterogeneous solutions and the lower costs of homogenous solutions. The user's decision is analyzed from the perspective of the standardization economy. Assuming that user's decision is based on this model, a simulation experiment for the analysis of the optimal degree of compatibility of a vendor's platform with the complementary components of a competitor is introduced. In comparison to most approaches in the standardization economy, it is possible to model the different strengths of (system internal) network effects, as well as the structure of the integration and information relationships among services and platforms. Utilizing the simulation model, and especially the method of the systematic generation of simulation instances, the following results were derived:

- An increase in compatibility of the platform with the complementary products of competitors results in a higher diffusion of the platform.

- An increase in compatibility of the platform with the complementary products of competitors reduces the effect of a platform implemented on the user's side on the choice of complementary services.

The simulation experiments show that, under the assumptions made above, slightly increased – but not complete – compatibility results in maximization of the degree of diffusion (i.e., the amount of components used in the optimal solution) of the acting vendor. This increase in compatibility can be achieved in various ways, for instance through changes in extension and quality of interface documentation, the provision of tools supporting the integration of services and platforms, the facilitation of certification processes for service vendors, and the usage of open standards. In addition, these results have implications for the business models of the vendors: a high degree of compatibility is advisable for vendors whose main source of revenue is the offering of platform licenses. For vendors focusing on the distribution of services, slightly increased compatibility is recommendable.

The goal of this investigation was to analyze the structure of the optimal solutions for the presented decision problem. It would be interesting to integrate these results in a simulation of the market of complementary products and platforms. To this end, it is among other things necessary to model the interaction and anticipation possibilities among the different groups of actors. In this context, for vendors and users especially, the interactions within and among the groups of actors must be considered (that is, possible interactions among user-user, user-vendor, and vendor-vendor). These considerations build the starting point for an investigation applying game theory. In addition, the characteristics of a two sided-market (Rochet and Tirole 2003) should be considered in the course of a market simulation.

In the simulation experiments presented above, the net utility of both vendors is generated from an identical distribution – by utilizing different distributions, strategies for, e.g., qualitatively "weaker" resp. "stronger" vendors could be analyzed. In the simulation experiment, exactly two vendors are considered. One possibility for further investigation is the consideration of niche vendors, i.e., of vendors who only provide components for a fraction of IT functions.

Appendix

The extreme case, in which the *IICB* is not relevant for the decision ($\mu(Q)$ is close to 0 %), can be modeled as follows: let k be the number of IT functions in which w. l. o. g. Vendor A provides the highest net utility, then in this case (dependent of k) the value of $\kappa_{\Delta h}$ is:

$$\left| \underbrace{\frac{k}{|N|}}_{\kappa_h^A} - \underbrace{\frac{|N|-k}{|N|}}_{\kappa_h^B} \right| \qquad [27]$$

For $|N|$ IT functions,

$$\binom{|N|}{k} \qquad [28]$$

combinations exist to distribute k IT functions (i.e., the IT functions in which Vendor A is predominant). Thus, in this case, for the expectancy value of $\kappa_{\Delta h}$, the following results:

$$\frac{\sum_{k=0}^{|N|} \left(\binom{|N|}{k} \cdot \overbrace{\left| \frac{k}{|N|} - \frac{|N|-k}{|N|} \right|}^{\kappa_{\Delta h}} \right)}{\sum_{k=0}^{|N|} \binom{|N|}{k}} \qquad [29]$$

For $|N| = 35$, this term takes the value ≈ 13.58 %.

References

Albert, R., and Barabási, A. 2000. "Topology of Evolving Networks: Local Events and Universality", *Physical Review Letters* (85:24), pp. 5234–5237.

Arndt, J.-M., Kude, T., and Dibbern, J. 2008a. "The Emergence of Partnership Networks in the Enterprise Application Development Industry - a Global Corporation Perspective", in: *20th World Computer Congress (WCC)*. Mailand, Italien.

Arndt, J.-M., Kude, T., and Dibbern, J. 2008b. "The Emergence of Partnership Networks in the Enterprise Application Software Industry – an SME Perspective", in: *Multikonferenz Wirtschaftsinformatik 2008 (PRIMIUM)*. Garching, Deutschland.

Arzideh, F. 2008. *Estimation of Medical Reference Limits by Truncated Gaussian and Truncated Power Normal Distributions*. Bremen: Universität Bremen (Dissertation).

Buxmann, P. 2002. "Strategien Von Standardsoftware-Anbietern: Eine Analyse Auf Der Basis Von Netzeffekten", *Zeitschrift für betriebswirtschaftliche Forschung* (54), pp. 442–457.

Buxmann, P., Hess, T., and Lehmann, S. 2008. "Software as a Service", *Wirtschaftsinformatik* (50:6), pp. 500–503.

Cusumano, M. 2010a. "Cloud Computing and SaaS as New Computing Platforms", *Commun. ACM* (53:4), pp. 27-29.

Cusumano, M.A. 2010b. "Will SaaS and Cloud Computing Become a New Industry Platform?", in *Software-as-a-Service,* A. Benlian, T. Hess and P. Buxmann (eds.). Gabler, pp. 3-13.

David, P.A., and Greenstein, S. 1990. "The Economics of Compatibility Standards: An Introduction to Recent Research", *Economics of Innovation and New Technology* (1:1), pp. 3–41.

Domschke, W., Mayer, G., and Wagner, B. 2002. "Effiziente Modellierung Von Entscheidungsproblemen: Das Beispiel Des Standardisierungsproblems", *Zeitschrift für betriebswirtschaftliche Forschung* (72:8), pp. 847–863.

Erdős, P., and Rényi, A. 1959. "On Random Graphs", *Publicationes Mathematicae Debrecen* (6), pp. 290–297.

Evans, D.S., Hagiu, A., and Schmalensee, R. 2006. *Invisible Engines: How Software Platforms Drive Innovation and Transform Industries*. Boston: MIT Press.

Farrell, J., and Saloner, G. 1992. "Converters, Compatibility, and the Control of Interfaces", *The Journal of Industrial Economics* (40:1), pp. 9–35.

Gandal, N. 2002. "Compatibility, Standardization, and Network Effects: Some Policy Implications", *Oxford Review of Economic Policy* (18:1), pp. 80–91.

Gawer, A., and Henderson, R. 2007. "Platform Owner Entry and Innovation in Complementary Markets: Evidence from Intel", *Journal of Economics and Management Strategy* (16), pp. 1 – 34.

Hilkert, D., Benlian, A., and Hess, T. 2010. "Motivational Drivers to Develop Apps for Social Software-Platforms: The Example of Facebook", in: *16th Americas Conference on Information Systems (AMCIS 2010)*. Lima, Peru.

Jansen, S., Brinkkemper, S., and Finkelstein, A. 2009. "Business Network Management as a Survival Strategy: A Tale of Two Software Ecosystems", *First International Workshop on Software Ecosystems*, Virginia, pp. 34-48.

Johnson, A., and Thomopoulos, N. 2002. "Characteristics and Tables of the Left-Truncated Normal Distribution", in: *Midwest Decision Sciences*. San Diego, California: pp. 133–139.

Katz, M.L., and Shapiro, C. 1985. "Network Externalities, Competition, and Compatibility", *The American Economic Review* (75:3), pp. 424–440.

Katz, M.L., and Shapiro, C. 1994. "Systems Competition and Network Effects", *Journal of Economic Perspectives* (8:2), pp. 93–115.

Koski, H., and Kretschmer, T. 2004. "Survey on Competing in Network Industries: Firm Strategies, Market Outcomes, and Policy Implications", *Journal of Industry, Competition and Trade* (4:1), pp. 5–31.

Köster, D. 1999. *Wettbewerb in Netzproduktmärkten*. Gabler, Wiesbaden.

Kude, T., and Dibbern, J. 2009. "Tight Versus Loose Organizational Coupling within Inter-Firm Networks in the Enterprise Software Industry – the Perspective of Complementors", in: *Americas Conference on Information Systems (AMCIS)*. San Francisco, USA.

Leone, F.C., Nelson, L.S., and Nottingham, R.B. 1961. "The Folded Normal Distribution", *Technometrics* (3:4), pp. 543-550.

Liebowitz, S.J., and Margolis, S.E. 1994. "Network Externality: An Uncommon Tragedy", *The Journal of Economic Perspectives* (8:2), pp. 133–150.

Matutes, C., and Regibeau, P. 1996. "A Selective Review of the Economics of Standardization: Entry Deterrence, Technological Progress and International Competition", *European Journal of Political Economy* (12:2), pp. 183–209.

Newman, M.E.J., and Watts, D.J. 1999. "Scaling and Percolation in the Small-World Network Model", *Physical Review E* (60:6), p. 7332.

Rochet, J.-C., and Tirole, J. 2003. "Platform Competition in Two-Sided Markets", *Journal of the European Economic Association* (1:4), pp. 990–1029.

Rysman, M. 2009. "The Economics of Two-Sided Markets", *The Journal of Economic Perspectives* (23:3), pp. 125-143.

Schade, S., Strube, J., and Buxmann, P. 2007. "Simulation of the Impact of Network Topologies on Standardization Decisions", in: *Proceedings of the 5th International Conference on Standardization, Innovation and Information Technology (SIIT)*, P.M. Fen, Dan; Hawkings, Richard (ed.). Calgary, Kanada pp. 59–70.

Watts, D., and Strogatz, S. 1998. "Collective Dynamics of 'Small-World' Networks", *Nature* (393), pp. 440–442.

Weitzel, T. 2004. *Economics of Standards in Information Networks*. Heidelberg: Physica.

Weitzel, T., Beimborn, D., and König, W. 2006. "A Unified Economic Model of Standard Diffusion: The Impact of Standardization Cost, Network Effects, and Network Topology", *Management Information Systems Quarterly* (30:Special Issue on Standard Making), pp. 489–514.

Weitzel, T., Wendt, O., and Westarp, F. 2000. "Reconsidering Network Effect Theory", in: *8th European Conference on Information Systems (ECIS)*. Wien, Österreich.

West, J. 2003. "How Open Is Open Enough? Melding Proprietary and Open Source Platform Strategies", *Research Policy* (32:7), pp. 1259-1285.

Wiese, H. 1990. *Netzeffekte Und Kompatibilität: Ein Theoretischer Und Simulationsgeleiteter Beitrag Zur Absatzpolitik Für Netzeffekt-Güter*. Stuttgart: Poeschel.

Impact of Grid Assimilation on Operational Agility in Turbulent Environments: An Empirical Investigation in the Financial Services Industry

Jens Vykoukal

Goethe University Frankfurt, Grüneburgplatz 1, 60323 Frankfurt, Germany,
jvykoukal@wiwi.uni-frankfurt.de

Immanuel Pahlke

Goethe University Frankfurt, Grüneburgplatz 1, 60323 Frankfurt, Germany,
pahlke@wiwi.uni-frankfurt.de

Prof. Dr. Roman Beck

Goethe University Frankfurt, Grüneburgplatz 1, 60323 Frankfurt, Germany,
rbeck@wiwi.uni-frankfurt.de

1 Introduction

Enterprises increasingly adopt value chain improving technologies to retain a competitive position in a rapidly changing, uncertain, and demanding environment. Due to its hyper-competitive market, especially the financial services industry is exposed to a high level of environmental turbulence and resulting uncertainty (Ang and Cummings 1997). The ongoing need to realize and adapt to these environmental changes is reflected by the concept of agility which describes one of the key success factors for organizations striving to stay competitive, even in uncertain and turbulent markets (Dove 2001). Moreover, the financial services industry exhibits information-intensive business processes, high demand for large computing and data processing capacities, as well as fast changing customer needs (Teubner 2007). These industrial characteristics are reflected by the above-average annual IT investments (~ 8% of the annual revenues) which are more than twice as high as the average IT spending across all industries (Zhu et al. 2004). One way to

A. Heinzl et al. (eds.), *Theory-Guided Modeling and Empiricism in Information Systems Research*, DOI 10.1007/978-3-7908-2781-1_3, © Springer-Verlag Berlin Heidelberg 2011

address arising environmental turbulence and computational challenges is the organizational assimilation of a Grid-based IT infrastructure that provides users and applications with immediate access to a large pool of interconnected IT resources (i.e., computing and storage devices). Grid technology provides several benefits, including seamless computing power achieved by exploiting under-utilized IT resources and a more reliable, resilient, and scalable IT infrastructure with autonomic management capabilities and on-demand aggregation of resources from multiple sites to meet unforeseen demand (Foster and Kesselman 1999).

In this article, we especially focus on the assimilation of Grid technology for the purpose of facilitating two business processes that are of significant importance for financial services providers to gain and maintain sustainable competitive advantage in the highly competitive and dynamic financial market: *risk management* and *new product development*. Risk management is an essential and vital task to improve sensing capabilities and is mainly driven by (1) the pressure from regulators for a better control of financial risks, (2) the globalization of financial markets that has led to exposure to more sources of risk, and (3) technological advances which have made enterprise-wide risk management possible (Jorion 2006). The need for the continuous enhancement of the new product development process as a vital responding capability is mainly facilitated by fast changing customer needs that force financial services providers to provide highly customized financial products on-demand. Due to the importance of the risk management and new product development process for financial institutions, an effective and flexible IT infrastructure is essential to enhance the agility of a financial institution at an operational level, which is referred to as operational agility (Sambamurthy et al. 2003). In general, operational agility defines the ability of a firm to operate profitably in a rapidly changing and continuously fragmenting global market environment, which encompasses the capability of a firm to sense environmental changes and to respond to them in an efficient, effective and timely manner (Dove 2001, Overby et al. 2006). Since risk management can be seen as a means to sense changes in the market environment, whereas the development of new financial products can be regarded as a way to respond to these changes, we focus on the assimilation of Grid technology that is expected to effectively and efficiently facilitate both business processes and thereby to improve operational agility.

So far, the organizational assimilation of different technologies has been extensively analyzed in the extant literature (e.g., Iacovou et al. 1995, Zhu et al. 2006) and some studies already attempted to investigate the impact of IT capabilities on the operational agility (Lee et al. 2009, van Oosterhout et al. 2009). However, little empirical research has been conducted to understand the interplay of technology assimilation and the operational agility of business processes in conjunction with environmental turbulence (Overby et al. 2006, Sambamurthy et al.

2003). Hence, we provide and discuss the results of a survey conducted in the financial services industry in the U.S. to analyze the value-adding effects of Grid technology assimilation on the operational agility of two specific business processes, as well as the role of environmental turbulence as an important moderator in organizational science (Eisenhardt and Martin 2000). In particular, we address the knowledge gaps by answering the following two research questions: *1) How does Grid assimilation influence the operational agility of business processes? 2) How do turbulent environmental conditions affect the operational agility of business processes that are facilitated by Grid technology?*

This article is organized as follows: First, we provide a review of relevant research streams and develop the theoretical foundation for our research model. We then propose a methodology to test the hypotheses and discuss the results of our empirical analysis. Finally, we conclude this article by illustrating contributions of our analysis and highlighting further research opportunities.

2   Theoretical Background

The foundation of our theoretical framework comprises some theoretical elements that are presented in more detail in the following subsections.

2.1   IT Assimilation

The term "assimilation" is commonly used in IS literature and represents a comprehensive and complete process of implementation of IT innovations in organizations. Since widespread adoption of IT is not necessarily followed by widespread IT acceptance and experienced routinized use, Fichman (2001) conceptualized the degree of assimilation as the extent to which a firm has progressed through the following major stages of innovation deployment: initiation, adoption, and routinization. In the *initiation* (pre-adoption) stage, firms evaluate whether a new IT innovation can add value to the organization (Rogers 1995), such as cost reduction and enhancing business processes, which vastly impacts the final adoption decision (Dong et al. 2009). The subsequent *adoption* stage encompasses the active decision to acquire the IT innovation and to allocate the required physical resources, whereas in the *routinization* (post-adoption) stage, the innovation is institutionalized and becomes an integral part of the value chain activities (Zhu et al. 2006). Hence, if the focus is on only one stage of the assimilation life cycle, such as the decision to adopt a specific innovation, researchers overlook the fact that technology assimilation is an ongoing process (Rai et al. 2009). Therefore, we deemed the more holistic conceptualization of assimilation in contrast to pure adoption analyses as appropriate to study the enhancement of operational agility through Grid technology.

For the unit of analysis for measuring the assimilation progress and the potential enhancement of operational agility, we chose a business process perspective due to the fact that IT investments are supposed to first affect the performance of specific business processes (Davamanirajan et al. 2006). In general, a firm encompasses approximately 18 key processes being vital for the overall firm performance (Davenport 1993). To identify the key business process being primarily influenced by Grid assimilation in the financial services industry, we conducted several expert interviews with IS executives. Since the risk management process as well as the new product development process turned out to be especially appropriate and vital for the financial services industry, we analyzed the Grid assimilation stages for these two processes.

2.2   Operational Agility of Business Processes

The extant literature offers several definitions of agility at various levels, such as at the enterprise level, business function level, and business process level (Ganguly et al. 2009). Overby et al. (2006) define agility as an organization's ability to sense environmental changes (opportunities, threats, or a combination of both) in its business environment and thus to provide rapid responses to customers and stakeholders by reconfiguring its resources, processes, and strategies. In this study, we focus on agility at the operational level (Sambamurthy et al. 2003), or operational agility, that entails the ability to operate profitably in a rapidly changing, fragmented market environment by flexibly producing and offering high-quality, high-performance, customer-configured goods and services in a timely, cost-efficient manner (e.g., Dove 2001, Ren et al. 2003, Yusuf et al. 1999). In a dynamic market context, the capability to explore, exploit, and capture market opportunities and engage in relentless innovations in a timely and cost-efficient manner is imperative for organizational success (Goldman et al. 1995). Therefore, flexible and scalable capacity adjustments as well as ad-hoc access to resources and capabilities are of central importance to gain and sustain competitive advantage in highly dynamic and competitive market environments, such as in the financial services industry. As already outlined, we focus on the operational agility of the risk management and the new product development processes and argue that these business-critical processes can be facilitated by Grid technology, which enables a firm to seize opportunities and threats, respond to internal and external changes, and sustain its operational performance.

2.3   Environmental Turbulence

Previous research has revealed that environmental characteristics considerably impact on corporate strategy and outcomes (Eisenhardt and Martin 2000). For example, the concept of environmental turbulence, which encompasses uncertainty and unpredictability due to massive and rapid changes in technological developments and market preferences (Jaworski and Kohli 1993), can characterize an environment on the basis of both its market and its technological turbulence. Market turbulence refers to heterogeneity and variability in preferences and demands in the market (Helfat et al. 2007), whereas technological turbulence refers to the rate of technological change (Lichtenthaler and Ernst 2007). Environmental turbulence also demands greater organizational sense-making and responsiveness to safeguard organizational outcomes. Thus, companies might be conceived of as sense-making units, stimulated by environmental turbulence and constantly challenged to identify contextually appropriate responses (McGill et al. 1994). Moreover, organizations often acquire external resources and the related knowledge to respond to their turbulent environments (Cassiman and Veugelers 2006). The assimilation of Grid technology can be a means for dealing with the dynamic circumstances of a turbulent environment by capacity and capability adjustments. Therefore, environmental turbulence was included in our research model to capture differences across turbulent versus relatively stable market environments.

3   Hypotheses and Research Model

To validate the impact of Grid assimilation at the organizational level, we developed the research model shown in Figure 1 and analyze the impact of Grid assimilation on the operational agility of two business processes. Moreover, the role of environmental turbulence in the context of Grid-induced changes in operational agility is analyzed.

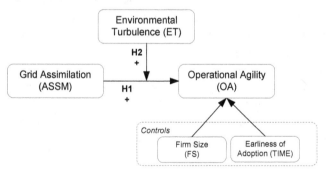

Figure 1:   Research model

Prior literature has suggested that technology adoption must support companies' value-chain activities and business processes before they will have any significant business value at the operational level (e.g., Santhanam and Hartono 2003). With regard to Grid technology, Grid infrastructures offer ad-hoc access to a large number of IT resources, which provides the potential for enhanced performance of (compute-intensive) business processes and is essential for companies to gain and sustain competitive advantage in highly dynamic and competitive market environments (Pavlou and El Sawy 2006). Moreover, Grid technology allows flexible and scalable capacity adjustments, meaning that IT resources can be rapidly provisioned (scaling up) and released (scaling down) in accordance with the resource demand, which is of crucial importance to respond more rapidly to changing business demands (Liu et al. 2008). Hence, because Grid technology is suggested to provide benefits for firms with regard to their operational agility, we anticipate a positive relationship between Grid assimilation and the operational agility of specific business processes. Hence, we propose:

Hypothesis 1:   *Later stages of Grid assimilation lead to greater*
                    operational agility.

Risk is manifested most strongly in volatile environmental conditions (e.g., Jaworski and Kohli 1993). In view of this, we argue that the extent to which Grid-enabled capabilities affect operational agility depends on the level of turbulence in the business environment. The capability to assess and respond appropriately to risk is especially vital in turbulent environments, as the variety of threats and uncertainties that can be present is enormous. Organizations need to lean upon their IT-enabled capabilities in environments where survival hinges on the ability to anticipate the unexpected and react accordingly in uncertain conditions (Sambamurthy et al. 2003). Hence, it is likely that an organization will manifest superior agility since it enjoys advantages arising from its strategic alignment with its environment. More precisely, a company needs to focus on the development and alignment of its resources and apply them to the changing environmental conditions to be able to produce innovations and respond to environmental changes cost-efficiently and promptly (Kohli and Jaworski 1990). The building of IT-enabled capabilities can be seen as the increase of options for response to uncertainties to match the range of possible risks and threats. This expands the repertoire of responses available and therefore increases the likelihood of the organization to perform better when faced with challenges posed by the volatility of the environment. Since Grid assimilation might support such adaptations through capacity and capability adjustments, we propose:

Hypothesis 2:   *In turbulent markets, compared with stable market environ-*
                    ments, Grid assimilation leads to greater operational agility.

To account for differences among the investigated companies, we included the control variables "firm size" (Rogers 1995) and "earliness of adoption" (Fichman 2001) in the model. Rogers (1995) suggests that firm size may be positively related to innovation adoption since large firms are more likely to exhibit slack resources. In contrast to this, smaller firms are assumed to be more flexible with regard to innovative technologies (Zhu et al. 2006) due to less communication and coordination requirements. The second control variable reflects the years elapsed since the first Grid adoption and captures the fact that firms having initiated Grid implementation activities earlier than others had more time to reach later stages of assimilation, leading to different magnitudes of operational agility.

4   Study Design and Data Collection

Although there are a number of valid research approaches, we deemed a quantitative, survey-based methodology appropriate since it allows minimizing the subjectivity in the analysis of the data by employing statistical tests to examine the validity of the research hypotheses (Kealey and Protheroe 1996). Moreover, by using a survey, we can investigate the perceptions and intentions of a large number of subjects (i.e., organizations), which may not be practicable with qualitative methods. Lastly, quantitative methods allow high levels of reliability and repeatability, which facilitates replication of the research (Balsley 1970). Hence, we operationalized the proposed research model as a structural equation model and used the partial least squares (PLS) method for the validation due to several reasons. First, PLS handles measurement errors in exogenous variables better than other methods, such as multiple regression analysis and, second, PLS requires fewer distributional assumptions about the data (Chin 1998). Especially in areas of newly applied research and in the early stages of measurement instrument development, little is known about the distributional characteristics of observed variables. Third, even though PLS is often used for theory confirmation, it can also suggest where relationships might exist and suggest propositions for later testing (Chin et al. 2003). Thus, the PLS approach is prediction-oriented (Chin 1998), which is regarded as an advantage since theory construction is as important as theory verification.

4.1   Measures

Whenever possible, we adapted existing measures from prior empirical studies to our research context. To ensure the content validity of these measures, we conducted several expert interviews and asked a panel of practitioners and academic judges to review the survey instrument and suggest any refinements to the wording of the indicators (measurement items). The survey items are depicted in Table A1 in the Appendix. For both constructs "Environmental Turbulence" (ET) and

"Operational Agility" (OA), reflective indictors were used and measured on a fully anchored 7-point Likert scale. Whereas the measures of the ET construct are based on the operationalization used by Pavlou and El Sawy (2006) and Jaworski and Kohli (1993), we operationalized the OA construct with regard to different characteristics of an agile enterprise. Because the extant literature offers several competing definitions of agility, we reviewed various literature resources from industry and academia and discovered the major characteristics of operational agility, as we summarize in Table A2 in the Appendix. Most definitions of agility cover time and the ability to respond at the operational level (responsiveness), though Yusuf et al. (1999), Ren et al. (2003), and Dove (2001) suggest several other essential characteristics of operational agility. Following Dove (2001), we define operational agility as the *effective response ability for rapidly, efficiently, and accurately adapting to unexpected (or unpredictable) changes in both proactive and reactive business/customer needs and opportunities, without compromising the cost or the quality of the product/process.* With this definition and the results from Table A2, we decided to operationalize the OA construct as a dependent variable that could capture the agility creation momentum of Grid assimilation, attributed mainly to the operational level. Since the risk management and the new product development processes were identified as being especially appropriate and vital for the financial services industry, we analyzed these two processes in regard to changes in (1) cost-efficiency, (2) speed, (3) effectiveness, (4) quality, (5) responsiveness, and (6) flexibility.

For the "Grid assimilation" (ASSM) construct, a 7-item Guttman scale was used to capture the current Grid assimilation stage of an enterprise. This scale was grounded on prior research on the assimilation of software process innovations (Fichman 2001) and on the assimilation of electronic procurement innovations (Rai et al. 2009). The respondents were requested to identify the current stage of Grid assimilation for their risk management and new product development processes. As already outlined, these two processes were identified as being especially appropriate and vital for the financial services industry, wherefore the measurement items of the assimilation construct focused on Grid-related activities in these processes.

4.2   Data Collection and Sample Profile

To validate the research model presented in Figure 1 and the associated hypotheses proposed above, we finally conducted a questionnaire-based field study, featuring IT decision makers from financial institutions in the U.S. In general, a Grid infrastructure requires at least a certain firm size to be implemented in a reasonable manner since there have to be at least a number of IT resources (e.g., servers) which can then be interconnected and virtualized. Therefore, we administered our study among financial institutions with more than 1,000 employees. Moreover, the financial institution had to be a Grid adopter to ask the study participants for their experience with Grid technology. As already outlined in the introduction section, we deemed the financial services industry an appropriate testing field for the research model. From an empirical perspective, our focus on a single industry and a single country enabled us to control for extraneous industry- or country-specific factors that could confound the analysis, which enhances internal validity (Zhu et al. 2004).

In August 2009, we invited 2,034 potential participants of a U.S. IT business panel to respond to the survey by completing an online questionnaire and received 459 responses (response rate of 22.6%). Since the study aimed at Grid adopters, the study participants were asked at the beginning of the questionnaire to indicate whether they have already adopted Grid technology for at least one of the analyzed processes or not. In the latter case, the non-Grid adopters were directly excluded from taking part in the survey. In total, 281 responses from non-Grid adopters or responses which exhibited missing values, that can cause bias due to systematic differences between observed and unobserved data, were removed. Consequently, this led to a final sample of 178 valid responses (from 31 CTO|COO|CIOs, 10 chief systems architects, 137 other IT decision makers), 150 of which utilize Grid technology for their risk management process and 155 of which use Grid technology for their new product development process.

5 Data Analysis and Results

As a structural equation modeling technique, PLS analyzes the measurement models and the structural model. These two models are estimated simultaneously to combine the advantages of regression analysis and multivariate measurements approaches. In our study, we obtained the results for the PLS estimation from SmartPLS (Version 2.0 M3) and a bootstrapping procedure to test the statistical significance of the estimates.

5.1 Validation of the Measurement Models

Our evaluation of both the reflective and formative models entails assessments of content validity, construct reliability, and construct validity. Because we already determined the content validity in section 4.1, we, in the following, focus on construct reliability and construct validity. Table 1 shows the validation results for the risk management and the new product development process.

Construct reliability refers to the internal consistency of the measurement model and measures the degree to which items are free from random error and yield consistent results. The reliability of the reflective constructs was assessed by using the average variance extracted (AVE), the composite reliability (CR), and the Cronbach's alpha scores. As we indicate in Table 1, the AVE of each construct is above the recommended threshold of 0.5 (Fornell and Larcker 1981), so at least 50% of measurement variance is captured by a construct. Moreover, the CR score of each construct is above the recommended threshold of 0.7 (Hair et al. 1998), which is evidence of sufficient reliability, and all Cronbach's alpha values exceed the critical value of 0.7 (Nunnally 1978), providing further support of the internal consistency among the measurement items.

Construct validity instead refers to the wider validation of measures and reveals whether indicators of the construct measure what they intend to, from the perspective of the relationships between constructs and between the constructs and their indicators. This validity can be assessed in terms of (1) convergent validity and (2) discriminant validity (Campbell and Fiske 1959). The test for *convergent validity* determines if the indicators of latent constructs that theoretically should be related are observed to be related in actuality. In general, the existence of significant inter-indicator and indicator-to-construct correlations is evidence of convergent validity of the construct. Our results clearly show that all loadings of the reflective constructs are greater than the recommended threshold of 0.707 (Chin 1998), such that there exists more shared variance between the construct and its indicators than error variance, and the measurement items used are adequate for measuring each construct.

	Risk Management Process (n=150)									
	Mean	SD	AVE	CR	Alpha	ASSM[++]	ET	OA	TIME[+]	FS[+]
ASSM[+]	5.82	1.08	n/a	n/a	n/a	**n/a**				
ET	5.58	0.93	0.52	0.88	0.85	0.16*	**0.72**			
OA	5.16	1.18	0.77	0.95	0.94	0.31*	0.49*	**0.87**		
TIME[+]	4.06	2.98	n/a	n/a	n/a	0.19*	0.03	0.01	**n/a**	
FS[+]	2.88	1.11	n/a	n/a	n/a	0.04	0.08	0.06	0.09	**n/a**

	New Product Development Process (n=155)								
	Mean	SD	AVE	CR	Alpha	ASSM⁺	ET	OA	TIME⁺	FS⁺
ASSM⁺	5.59	1.07	n/a	n/a	n/a	n/a				
ET	5.62	0.93	0.51	0.88	0.85	0.15	0.71			
OA	4.97	1.13	0.75	0.95	0.93	0.27*	0.40*	0.87		
TIME⁺	4.04	3.02	n/a	n/a	n/a	0.24*	-0.05	-0.02	n/a	
FS⁺	2.93	1.09	n/a	n/a	n/a	-0.20*	0.08	-0.05	0.09	n/a

Table 1:   Reliability scores, square root of AVE (diagonal elements), and correlations among constructs (off-diagonal elements), * $p < 0.05$ (two-tailed), +=1-item measure

For *discriminant validity*, we tested whether indicators of latent constructs that theoretically should not be related to each other are actually observed unrelated. MacKenzie et al. (2005) propose an approach appropriate for evaluating the discriminant validity of both formative and reflective measures, which analyzes whether the inter-construct correlations are relatively low. The discriminant validity for the reflective constructs can also be assessed by analyzing the cross-loadings and the Fornell-Larcker criterion. The cross-loadings reveal that each indicator loading is much higher on its assigned construct than on any other construct, in support of sufficient discriminant validity on the indicator level (Chin 1998).

The results of Table 1 show that the square roots of the AVE scores (diagonal elements) are greater than the correlations between the construct and any other construct (off-diagonal elements), which indicates that the constructs share more variance with their assigned indicators than with any other construct (Fornell and Larcker 1981). Since all constructs exhibit convergent and discriminant validity and all indicators satisfy various reliability and validity criteria, we used them to test the structural model.

5.2   Validation of the Structural

To estimate the moderating effect of environmental turbulence (ET), we followed Chin et al. (2003). First, to reduce multicollinearity, we standardized all indicators reflecting the predictor and moderator constructs to a mean of 0 and variance of 1. This step supports an easier interpretation of the resulting regression beta for the predictor variable. The path coefficient represents the effect expected at the mean value of the moderator variable, which is set to 0. Second, using the standardized indicators of the predictor and moderator variables, we generated product indicators to reflect the latent interaction variables. Third, we applied the PLS procedure to estimate the dependent variable OA.

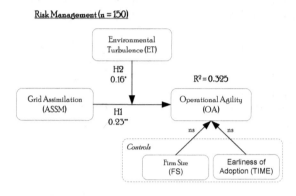

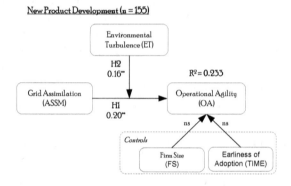

Figure 2:   Empirical results; ** p < 0.01, * p < 0.05 (two-tailed)

In Figure 2, we depict the validation results for both analyzed processes, which reveal mostly significant path coefficients above the 0.1 threshold (Sellin and Keeves 1994). Hence, for both models, the hypotheses H1 and H2 are supported by the survey data. To measure the explanatory power of the structural model, we use the squared multiple correlations (R^2) of the dependent variable OA. The R^2 values of 32.5% and 23.3%, respectively, indicate that, according to Chin (1998), the model explains a moderate amount of variance for the dependent variable. With regard to the control variables, firm size and the earliness of adoption both relate insignificantly to the OA construct.

6   Discussion of the Results

Since the hypotheses H1 and H2 are supported by the survey data for both investigated business processes, our research model provides a good illustration of how organizational assimilation of Grid technology eventually leads to greater operational agility. Moreover, the survey data suggest that this relation is positively moderated (strengthened) by environmental turbulence. Accordingly, this study discovered that the assimilation of Grid technology has a significant and positive impact on the agility of business processes, resulting in greater cost-efficiency, speed, effectiveness, quality, responsiveness, and flexibility.

Exploring the relations more closely, the empirical results indicate that later stages of Grid assimilation for the risk management and the new product development process lead to strong operational agility improvements. Enhancements in the speed, effectiveness, and quality of optimization and risk calculations can be achieved through Grid technology due to the availability and exploitation of a large network of computing and storage resources which are crucial for an accurate and comprehensive risk management. Improvements in cost-efficiency in the use of IT resources as well as enhancements with regard to the flexibility and responsiveness to changing market conditions can be achieved due to the scalable nature of a Grid-based IT landscape that is beneficial for the increasing demand for new financial products. For these products, the risk/return ratio has to be evaluated by complex and compute-intensive calculations that have to be adjusted with regard to the entire risk/return structure of the financial services provider. Once the ratio is evaluated, adjusted, and approved by the senior management, the product is market-ready. Therefore, a fast, accurate, and comprehensive risk valuation to meet the new capital requirements by laws and regulations is becoming a key driver for reducing time-to-market. Moreover, due to the capability of a scalable and, hence, a "breathing" IT infrastructure, Grid technology allows for the flexible and cost-efficient provision of large computing and storage capacities to dynamically sense changing business needs and to respond to them by developing new financial products.

Besides these findings, the study results indicate that companies operating in highly innovative and turbulent markets, compared to stable market environments, significantly benefit from the assimilation of Grid technology. These interaction effects are illustrated in Figure 3. High and low lines in the interaction plots represent $\pm$ 1 standard deviation from the mean value (middle line) of ET. The interpretation of interaction effects plots relies on comparing the slope (rather than absolute values) of the relationship between the predictor (ASSM) and the dependent variable (OA) for varying levels of the moderator (ET) (Edwards and Lambert 2007). The steeper slope of the solid black line, compared to the dotted black line, illustrates that an increase in ASSM is associated with a larger (smaller) increase in OA when ET is high (low). These findings clearly demonstrate that firms in turbulent markets can leverage from Grid technology and thereby enhance their agility. In contrast, due to the dotted line that exhibits a lower slope, it seems that for firms operating in stable markets, the additional costs and effort associated with the implementation of the Grid infrastructure appear to outweigh the positive effects, such as speed, responsiveness, and flexibility.

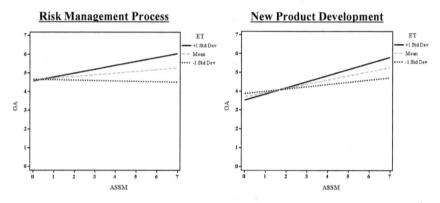

Figure 3:   Interaction plots for high (+1 SD) and low (-1 SD) environmental turbulence

7   Conclusion and Further Research

Grounded on the extensive research on business agility, we developed and tested a research model that examines the impact of Grid technology assimilation on operational agility. We perceive the findings as extremely valuable, considering the limited empirical research on the interplay between technology assimilation, operational agility, and environmental turbulence. Our results provide a better understanding of the business value (i.e., operational agility) of Grid assimilation since the data analysis reveals that an increased level of Grid assimilation leads to greater operational agility of the risk management and the new product development process. Moreover, this positive effect of Grid assimilation on the operational agility of Grid-enabled business processes is even greater in turbulent markets that are characterized by massive and rapid changes in technological developments and market preferences. These results are of importance for theory as well as for practice. Since our study is one of the first that empirically analyzes to what extent turbulent environmental conditions affect the agility of business processes, our results significantly contribute to the existing literature. From a theoretical point of view, we sharpen our understanding of the relation between IT capabilities and operational agility, strengthened by environmental turbulences. Thereby, we refer to the request of, e.g., Sambamurthy et al. (2003) and Overby et al. (2006) who encouraged further research in the field of digital option generation and the realization of agility capabilities resulting from IT investments. Besides the theoretical contribution, the implications for practitioners are also extremely valuable. Our study results clearly demonstrate that Grid technology is not only capable of accelerating resource-demanding computations and data mining operations, but can also be used as an effective and efficient strategic response to unpredictable and rapid changes in the market. Especially for the risk management and the new product development process, the timely assessment of risk exposure and complex financial products becomes feasible with the move to a Grid-based IT infrastructure.

As there are only a few empirical studies (e.g., Lee et al. 2009, van Oosterhout et al. 2009) that attempted to measure operational agility in an empirical setting, our research contributes to the existing body of knowledge on operational agility. The validation of our measurement model indicates that our operationalization of the OA construct, which is based on a thorough literature review, is suitable for measuring operational agility in an empirical setting. Despite these rich implications, the depicted work is limited with regard to the specific country, technology, industry, and the specific business processes, thus restricting the generalizability of the supported hypotheses. In addition, longitudinal instead of cross-sectional data might be better suited since it provides information that cannot be obtained from cross-sectional data and, hence, permits more sophisticated and nuanced analyses and increased precision in estimation. Furthermore, a more comprehensive operationalization of business agility according to the conceptualization of Sambamurthy et al. (2003) and Overby et al. (2006) might extend the theoretical and practical implications regarding the different dimensions of business agility, like market, network, and operational agility. Finally, objective primary or secondary performance data on the process level could be integrated to assess the impact of Grid assimilation.

Appendix

Measurement Items

Grid Assimilation (ASSM) *(formative measure)* 7-item Guttman scale		*Sources:* Rai et al. (2009), Fichman (2001)	
ASSM1	Are you aware of initial or prior Grid-related activities at site?	**ASSM5**	Are more than 5% but less than 25% of the business applications for the *PROCESS* running on a Grid?
ASSM2	Are you aware of plans to use a Grid environment for the *PROCESS* within the next 12 months?	**ASSM6**	Are more than 25% but less than 50% of the business applications for the *PROCESS* running on a Grid?
ASSM3	Is any Grid environment for the *PROCESS* currently being evaluated or trialed?	**ASSM7**	Are more than 50% of the business applications for the *PROCESS* running on a Grid?
ASSM4	Are any Grid application development projects for the *PROCESS* planned, in progress, implemented, or cancelled?		
Environmental Turbulence (ET) *(reflective measures)* 7-point Likert scale (1=strongly disagree; 7=strongly agree)		*Sources:* Pavlou and El Sawy (2006), Jaworski and Kohli (1993)	
ET1	The environment in our industry is continuously changing	**ET5**	In our kind of business, customers' product preferences change a lot over time
ET2	Environmental changes in our industry are very difficult to forecast	**ET6**	Marketing practices in our product area are constantly changing
ET3	The technology in our industry is changing rapidly	**ET7**	New product introductions are very frequent in our market
ET4	Technological breakthroughs provide big opportunities in our industry	**ET8**	There are many competitors in our market
Operational Agility (OA) *(reflective measures)* 7-point Likert scale (1=strongly disagree; 7=strongly agree)		*Sources:* see Table A2	
Grid implementation has…			
OA1	… lowered our costs in the *PROCESS*	**OA4**	… improved the quality of our *PROCESS*
OA2	… decreased the time-to-market of new financial products due to an improved *PROCESS*	**OA5**	… made us more adaptive to a changing business environment due to an improved *PROCESS*
OA3	… improved the effectiveness of our *PROCESS*	**OA6**	… improved the flexibility of our *PROCESS*
Controls *(1-item measures)* Open questions		*Sources:* Fichman (2001), Rogers (1995)	
FS	Number of employees (worldwide)	**TIME**	Years elapsed since the first Grid adoption

Table A1:   Measurement items; PROCESS = risk management process / new product development process

Conceptualization of Operational Agilty

Literature Sources	Characteristics of Operational Agility					
	(1)	(2)	(3)	(4)	(5)	(6)
Dove (2001), Ren et al. (2003), Yusuf et al. (1999)	x	x	x	x	x	x
Tsourveloudis and Valavanis (2002)	x	x	x	x	x	
Lin et al. (2006), Yang and Li (2002)	x	x	x		x	x
Jain et al. (2008)	x	x		x	x	x
Fliedner and Vokurka (1997)	x	x	x	x		
Overby et al. (2006)	x	x	x		x	
Vázquez-Bustelo et al. (2007)	x	x		x		x
Menor et al. (2001)	x			x	x	x
Goldman et al. (1995), Goranson (1999), Raschke and David (2005), Sambamurthy et al. (2003), van Hoek et al. (2001)		x	x		x	x
Ganguly et al. (2009)	x	x			x	
Total = 17	12	16	13	8	15	13

Table A2: Results of the literature research on the characteristics of operational agility; (1) cost-efficiency, (2) speed, (3) effectiveness, (4) quality, (5) responsiveness, (6) flexibility

References

Ang, S. and Cummings, L.L. "Strategic Response to Institutional Influences on Information Systems Outsourcing," *Organization Science* (8:3), 1997, pp. 235-256.

Balsley, H.L. *Quantitative Research Methods for Business and Economics*. Random House, New York, NY, 1970.

Campbell, D.T. and Fiske, D.W. "Convergent and Discriminant Validation by the Multitrait-Multimethod Matrix," *Psychological Bulletin* (56:2), 1959, pp. 81-105.

Cassiman, B. and Veugelers, R. "In Search of Complementarity in Innovation Strategy: Internal R&D and External Knowledge Acquisition," *Management Science* (52:1), 2006, pp. 68-82.

Chin, W.W. "The Partial Least Squares Approach to Structural Equation Modeling." In: *Modern Methods for Business Research* (Marcoulides, G.A.; Ed.), Lawrence Erlbaum Associates, Mahwah, NJ, 1998, pp. 295-336.

Chin, W.W., Marcolin, B.L., and Newsted, P.R. "A Partial Least Squares Latent Variable Modeling Approach for Interaction Effects," *Information Systems Research* (14:2), 2003, pp. 189-217.

Davamanirajan, P., Kauffman, R.J., Kriebel, C.H., and Mukhopadhyay, T. "Systems Design, Process Performance, and Economic Outcomes in International Banking," *Journal of Management Information Systems* (23:2), 2006, pp. 65-90.

Davenport, T. *Process Innovation: Reengineering Work through IT*. Harvard Business School Press, Boston, MA, 1993.

Dong, S., Xu, S.X., and Zhu, K.X. "Information Technology in Supply Chains: The Value of IT-enabled Resources under Competition," *Information Systems Research* (20:1), 2009, pp. 18-32.

Dove, R. *Response Ability: The Language, Structure and Culture of the Agile Enterprise*. Wiley, Hoboken, NJ, 2001.

Edwards, J. and Lambert, L.S. "Methods for Integrating Moderation and Mediation: A General Analytical Framework Using Moderated Path Analysis," *Psychological Methods* (12:1), 2007, pp. 1-22.

Eisenhardt, K.M. and Martin, J.A. "Dynamic Capabilities: What Are They?," *Strategic Management Journal* (21:10), 2000, pp. 1105-1122.

Fichman, R.G. "The Role of Aggregation in the Measurement of IT-related Organizational Innovation," *MIS Quarterly* (25:4), 2001, pp. 427-455.

Fliedner, G. and Vokurka, R. "Agility: Competitive Weapon of the 1990s and Beyond?," *Production and Inventory Management Journal* (38:3), 1997, pp. 19-24.

Fornell, C. and Larcker, D.F. "Evaluating Structural Equation Models with Unobservable Variables and Measurement Error," *Journal of Marketing Research* (18:1), 1981, pp. 39-50.

Foster, I. and Kesselman, C. *The Grid: Blueprint for a New Computing Infrastructure*. Morgan Kaufmann, San Francisco, CA, 1999.

Ganguly, A., Nilchiani R., and Farr, J.V. "Evaluating Agility in Corporate Enterprises," *International Journal of Production Economics* (118:2), 2009, pp. 410-423.

Goldman, S.L., Nagel, R.N., and Preiss, K. *Agile Competitors and Virtual Organizations: Strategies for Enriching the Customer*. Van Nostrand Reinhold, New York, NY, 1995.

Goranson, H.T. *The Agile Virtual Enterprise: Cases, Metrics, Tools*. Quorum Books, Westport, CT, 1999.

Hair, J.F., Anderson, R.E., Tatham, R.L., and Black, W.C. *Multivariate Data Analysis*. 5th Edition. Pearson Prentice-Hall, Upper Saddle River, NJ, 1998.

Helfat, C.E., Finkelstein, S., Mitchell, W., Peteraf, M.A., Singh, H., Teece, D.J., and Winter, S.G. *Dynamic Capabilities: Understanding Strategic Chance in Organizations*. Blackwell Publishing, Oxford, UK, 2007.

Iacovou, C.L., Benbasat, I., and Dexter, A.S. "Electronic Data Interchange and Small Organizations: Adoption and Impact of Technology," *MIS Quarterly* (19:4), 1995, pp. 465-485.

Jain, V., Benyoucef, L., and Deshmukh, S.G. "What's the Buzz About Moving From "Lean" To "Agile" Integrated Supply Chains? A Fuzzy Intelligent Agent-Based Approach," *International Journal of Production Research* (46:23), 2008, pp. 6649-6677.

Jaworski, B.J. and Kohli, A.K. "Market Orientation: Antecedents and Consequences," *Journal of Marketing* (57:3), 1993, pp. 53-70.

Jorion, P. *Value at Risk.* 3rd. Edition. Richard D. Irwin, Inc., Burr Ridge, IL, 2006.

Kealey, D.J. and Protheroe, D.R. "The Effectiveness of Cross-Cultural Training for Expatriates: An Assessment of the Literature on the Issue," *International Journal of Intercultural Relations* (20:2), 1996, pp. 141-165.

Kohli, A.K. and Jaworski, B.J. "Market Orientation: The Construct, Research, Propositions, and Managerial Implications," *Journal of Marketing* (54:2), 1990, pp. 1-18.

Lee, O.-K.D., Xu, P., Kuilboer, J.-P., and Ashrafi, N. "IT Impacts on Operation-Level Agility in Service Industries," *In the Proceedings of the 17th European Conference on Information Systems*, Verona, Italy, 2009.

Lichtenthaler, U. and Ernst, H. "Developing Reputation to Overcome the Imperfections in the Markets for Knowledge," *Research Policy* (36:1), 2007, pp. 37-55.

Lin, C., Chiu, H., and Cho, P. "Agility Index in the Supply Chain," *International Journal of Production Economics* (100:2), 2006, pp. 285-299.

Liu, C., Sia, C.-L., and Wei, K.-K. "Adopting Organizational Virtualization in B2B Firms: An Empirical Study in Singapore," *Information and Management* (45:7), 2008, pp. 429-437.

MacKenzie, S.B., Podsakoff, P.M., and Jarvis, C.B. "The Problem of Measurement Model Misspecification in Behavioral and Organizational Research and Some Recommended Solutions," *Journal of Applied Psychology* (90:4), 2005, pp. 710-730.

McGill, A.R., Johnson, M.D., and Bantel, K.A. "Cognitive Complexity and Conformity: Effects on Performance in a Turbulent Environment," *Psychological Reports* (75:3), 1994, pp. 1451-1472.

Menor, L.J., Roth, A.V., and Mason, C.H. "Agility in Retail Banking: A Numerical Taxonomy of Strategic Service Groups," *Manufacturing & Service Operations Management* (3:4), 2001, pp. 272-292.

Nunnally, J.C. *Psychometric Theory.* 2nd Edition. McGraw-Hill, New York, NY, 1978.

Overby, E., Bharadwaj, A., and Sambamurthy, V. "Enterprise Agility and the Enabling Role of Information Technology," *European Journal of Information Systems* (15:2), 2006, pp. 120-131.

Pavlou, P.A. and El Sawy, O.A. "The Case of New Product Development," *Information Systems Research* (17:3), 2006, pp. 198-227.

Rai, A., Brown, P., and Tang, X. "Organizational Assimilation of Electronic Procurement Innovations," *Journal of Management Information Systems* (26:1), 2009, pp. 257-296.

Raschke, R. and David, J.S. (2005). Business Process Agility. *In the Proceedings of the 11th Americas Conference on Information Systems*, Omaha, NE, 2005.

Ren, J., Yusuf, Y.Y., and Burns, N.D. "The Effects of Agile Attributes on Competitive Priorities: A Neural Network Approach," *Integrated Manufacturing Systems* (14:6), 2003, pp. 489-497.

Rogers, E.M. *Diffusion of Innovations*. 4th Edition. The Free Press, New York, NY, 1995.

Sambamurthy, V., Bharadwaj, A., and Grover, V. "Shaping Agility through Digital Options: Reconceptualizing the Role of Information Technology in Contemporary Firms," *MIS Quarterly* (27:2), 2003, pp. 237-263.

Santhanam, R. and Hartono, E. "Issues in Linking Information Technology Capability to Firm Performance," *MIS Quarterly* (27:1), 2003. pp. 125-153.

Sellin, N. and Keeves, J.P. "Path Analysis with Latent Variables." In: *International Encyclopedia of Education* (Husen, T. and Postlethwaite, T.N.; Eds.), Elsevier Publishers, London, UK, 1994, pp. 4352-4359.

Teubner, R.A. "Strategic Information Systems Planning: A Case Study from the Financial Services Industry," *Journal of Strategic Information Systems* (16:1), 2007, pp. 105-125.

Tsourveloudis, N.C. and Valavanis, K.P. "On the Measurement of Enterprise Agility," *Journal of Intelligent & Robotic Systems* (33:3), 2002, pp. 329-342.

van Hoek, R.I., Harrison, A., and Christopher, M. "Measuring Agile Capabilities in the Supply Chain," *International Journal of Operations & Production Management* (21:1), 2001, pp. 126-147.

van Oosterhout, M.P.A., Koenen, E., and van Heck, E. "The Adoption of Grid Technology and Its Perceived Impact on Agility." In: *The Network Experience. New Value from Smart Business Networks* (Vervest, P.H., Liere, D.W., and Zheng, L.; Eds.), Springer, Berlin, Germany, 2009, pp. 285-300.

Vázquez-Bustelo, D., Avella, L., and Fernández, E. "Agility Drivers, Enablers and Outcomes: Empirical Test of an Integrated Agile Manufacturing Model," *International Journal of Operations & Production Management* (27:12), 2007, pp. 1303-1332.

Yang, S.L. and Li, T.F. "Agility Evaluation of Mass Customization Product Manufacturing," *Journal of Materials Processing Technology* (129:1), 2002, pp. 640-644.

Yusuf, Y.Y., Sarhadi, M., and Gunasekaran, A. "Agile Manufacturing: The Drivers, Concepts and Attributes," *International Journal of Production Economics* (62:1), 1999, pp. 33-43.

Zhu, K., Kraemer, K.L., and Xu, S. "The Process of Innovation Assimilation by Firms in Different Countries: A Technology Diffusion Perspective on E-Business," *Management Science* (52:10), 2006, pp. 1557-1576.

Zhu, K., Kraemer, K.L., Xu, S., and Dedrick, J. "Information Technology Payoff in E-Business Environments: An International Perspective on Value Creation of E-Business in the Financial Services Industry," *Journal of Management Information Systems* (21:1), 2004, pp. 17-54.

Contractual and Relational Governance as Substitutes and Complements – Explaining the Development of Different Relationships[1]

Thomas A. Fischer

Institute of Information Systems, University of Bern, Engehaldenstrasse 8, CH-3012 Bern, Switzerland, Thomas.Fischer@iwi.unibe.ch

Thomas L. Huber

Institute of Information Systems, University of Bern, Engehaldenstrasse 8, CH-3012 Bern, Switzerland, Thomas.Huber@iwi.unibe.ch

Prof. Dr. Jens Dibbern

Institute of Information Systems, University of Bern, Engehaldenstrasse 8, CH-3012 Bern, Switzerland, Jens.Dibbern@iwi.unibe.ch

Abstract

For a long time research on the management of IS outsourcing projects viewed relational and contractual governance as substitutes. However, subsequent studies provided empirical evidence for the complementary view. Recently, some authors supported the notion that relational and contractual governance mechanisms can simultaneously be complements and substitutes.

Given these inconsistencies the question arises how contractual and relational governance become substitutes or complements. We investigate whether the relationship between governance mechanisms is the outcome of distinct

---

[1] Another version of this paper appeared as: Thomas Fischer, Thomas Huber and Jens Dibbern, "Contractual and Relational Governance as Substitutes and Complements – Explaining the Development of Different Relationships," *Proceedings of the 19th European Conference on Information Systems,* ECIS, Helsinki, Finland, June 9-11, 2011.

A. Heinzl et al. (eds.), *Theory-Guided Modeling and Empiricism in Information Systems Research*, DOI 10.1007/978-3-7908-2781-1_4, © Springer-Verlag Berlin Heidelberg 2011

processes of interaction between contractual and relational governance. For that purpose, we conduct an exploratory multiple-case study of five IS outsourcing projects at a leading global bank.

We identify three archetypical processes illustrating how the interaction between relational and contractual governance can result in a complementary relationship. In addition, we discover one process explaining their substitution.

The results of our study propose a shift in perspective. While former studies focused on explaining whether contractual and relational governance are complements or substitutes, we answer the question how and why they become complements and substitutes. Based on our findings, we give implications for further research.

1   Introduction

Despite a long lasting information systems (IS) outsourcing history, many global outsourcing projects fail to achieve estimated goals (e. g. cost reduction). Especially, the choice of control and governance mechanisms is supposed to be decisive, as governance and control costs are often higher than initially estimated (Dibbern, Winkler et al. 2008). Contractual and relational governance have been identified as the two main determinants for IS outsourcing success (Lacity, Khan et al. 2009).

From a managerial point of view the question arises how different types of governance mechanisms - such as contractual and relational governance - should be combined. To answer this question it is, first of all, important to understand how contractual and relational governance relate to each other. In recent years scholars have discussed the relationship of contractual and relational governance in IS outsourcing. For a long time the substitutional view of governance mechanisms was dominant, predicting that complex contracts are an opposing alternative to unwritten agreements based on trust (MaCaulay 1963). Empirical results, however, challenged this view and rather supported the competing perspective, implicating that relational and contractual governance are complements (Poppo and Zenger 2002; Goo, Kishore et al. 2009). However, results of novel investigations (Klein Woolthuis, Hillebrand et al. 2005; Mellewigt, Madhok et al. 2007; Tiwana 2010) favour another argument: relational and contractual governance mechanisms can simultaneously be complements *and* substitutes. Given these inconsistencies the following research question arises: *Is the relationship between gover-*

nance mechanisms (substitutes or complements) the outcome of distinct processes of interaction between contractual and relational governance?

In answering this question we close a current research gap and create a basic understanding on *how* contractual and relational governance become complements or substitutes. For that purpose, we analyzed interactions of governance mechanisms in a multiple case-study and summarized typical patterns of interaction in archetypes.

2   Literature Analysis

2.1   Contractual and Relational Governance

An outsourcing contract is a central component of each outsourcing engagement to manage the relationship between client and vendor. Usually this kind of contract contains overall objectives of the partnership as well as certain obligations for both client and vendor. Several contractual elements which are likely to appear in a contract are service levels or other performance indicators as well as corresponding measurement methodologies (Goo et al. 2009). These written obligations build the formal contract. The management based on this formal contract can be understood as contractual governance. In other words, *contractual governance* is "the use of a formalized, legally-binding agreement or a contract to govern the interfirm partnership" (Lee and Cavusgil 2006, p. 898).

In contrast to contractual governance the mechanisms underlying *relational governance* are usually unwritten (Lacity, Khan et al. 2009). It builds on the ability of social processes to enforce obligations, promises and expectations (Poppo and Zenger 2002). Relational norms on the one hand form the basis for relational governance and are on the other hand reinforced by its application. In this context former research has identified trust and commitment as the two most important relational norms (Goo, Kishore et al. 2009). Therefore a well-attuned relational governance is *indicated through* high levels of trust and commitment and *manifests in* informal adjustments between client and vendor employees (e.g. in meetings or phone calls), informal information sharing and open communication (Poppo and Zenger 2002; Goo, Kishore et al. 2009; Lacity, Khan et al. 2009). In the following, we refer to contractual governance in the sense of formal mechanisms and equate relational governance with informal mechanisms.

2.2 Complementarity versus Substitution between Contractual and Relational Governance

From a theoretical viewpoint there are two major perspectives on the relationship of contractual and relational governance: the complementary and the substitutional view. Referring to the concepts of dualism and duality[2], this chapter points out their major differences and traces them back to the agency-structure problem.

The substitutional view characterizes contractual and relational governance as dualism, meaning that contractual and relational mechanisms are separate concepts that differ in terms of their base (power vs. shared values) as well as in their mechanism to align conflicting goals (suppression vs. consensus) (Reed 2001). Characterization of contractual and relational governance as dualism also manifests in their differential modes of affecting human action. Contractual governance is part of an impersonal social *structure* determining human behavior, while elements of relational governance, such as trustful behavior, are the product of human *agency*, i.e. of free will (Möllering 2005). This conceptualization of contractual and relational governance as dualism radiates on their relationship: *contractual and relational are seen as substitutes implying that contractual governance is detrimental for relational governance, while relational governance reduces the need for contractual regulations* (Bachmann 2001). As an example the substitutional view argues that in situations of weak relational norms complex contracts are needed to mitigate opportunism, while in situations of a good relationship opportunism is less likely to occur and thus contracts are seen as unnecessary or at worst counter-productive (Poppo and Zenger 2002).

The complementary view characterizes contractual and relational governance as duality, hence it rejects their conceptual separation and therefore rather points to their similarities and mutual dependency. Consequently, the former separation of contractual and relational governance is removed in favour of an emphasis on their functional equivalence, as they are seen as "equivalent functional alternatives which simultaneously and in parallel to each other absorb uncertainty and reduce complexity" (Reed 2001, p. 204). This is not a marginal issue, because it implies that anticipation of an actor's behaviour is not based on either structure (contractual) or agency (relational), but on both at the same time. The consequence of this dualistic conceptualization is the complementary relationship between contractual and relational governance. It purports that contractual and relational elements enable each other and that the level of control exercised through contractual

---

[2]   Although subtle, the difference between dualism and duality is important (Möllering, 2005). While dualism refers to "the division of an object under study into separate and opposed paired elements", duality refers to their interdependence without discarding their conceptual distinction (Jackson, 1999, p. 545).

agreements positively affects relational norms and vice versa (Möllering 2005). As an example, the complementary view argues that precise contractual stipulations might foster trust by creating reliable mutual expectations.

Given these conflicting views, the question arises which of the views has experienced stronger empirical support. While Poppo and Zenger (2002) found evidence for a complementary relationship, other studies substantiate the substitutional view (Larson 1992; Ring and Van de Ven 1994). Moreover, recent studies found out that relational and contractual governance are both substitutes *and* complements (Woolthuis, Hillebrand et al. 2005; Tiwana 2010).

Hence, theoretical as well as empirical findings draw a contradictory picture on the relationship between contractual and relational governance. On the one hand theory suggests either a *purely* substitutional or complementary view. On the other hand empirical findings do not clearly support one of the competing views and recent evidence rather supports the more complex view that governance mechanisms can simultaneously be complements and substitutes. However, if governance mechanisms can be both substitutes and complements, we are in need for a still missing basic understanding on *how* governance mechanisms become complements or substitutes. To address this research gap, we formulate our research question as follows: *Is the relationship between governance mechanisms (substitutes or complements) the outcome of distinct processes of interaction between contractual and relational governance?*

3 Research Design

3.1 Methodology

This research takes an exploratory multiple-case study approach. This approach seemed to be particularly appropriate, as our study strives for answering a "how" question (Miles and Huberman 1994), and it deals with "operational links needing to be traced over time" (Yin 2003, p. 6). Furthermore, the events that need to be linked defy control of the researcher and they are rather contemporary than part of the "dead" past (Yin 2003). Since this study is concerned with the exploration of interaction processes between contractual and relational governance in IS outsourcing arrangements, the unit of analysis is the relationship between client and vendor. In order to allow for generalization we followed replication logic and conducted five case studies in the German financial services industry. The explorative nature of this study implies that the processes and relationships would have been difficult to access in a quantitative manner, therefore we rely on qualitative data to gain an in-depth understanding of the interaction processes described above. This data was mainly gathered in semi-structured interviews but in order to improve validity of our findings (Benbasat, Goldstein et al. 1987) we complemented them with a content analysis of contracts.

3.2   Data Collection and Analysis

To stay in line with the research objectives and the multiple case study design we pursued a purposeful sampling strategy (Eisenhardt 1989; Patton 2002). Striving for literal replication we chose similar cases, hence each case was expected to show similar results (Yin 2003). Therefore each case was required to fulfil the following criteria: 1) only projects with approximately the same size that are delivered by vendors of approximately the same size and 2) only outsourcing projects with a minimum duration of six months. The first criterion was chosen in order to improve comparability of the findings, because it was found to be an important antecedent for the choice of governance mechanisms (Van de Ven, Delbecq et al. 1976; Kirsch 1997). A minimum duration was chosen because literature suggests that substitutional and complementary effects of governance mechanisms unfold over a specific period of time (Inkpen and Currall 2004) - the value of six months was decided on because Larson (1992) reckons this as the minimum amount of time until partners in inter-organizational relationships perceive each other as trustworthy, which is seen as a major prerequisite for relational governance. In order to control for potential bias of organizational (Hofstede 1991) as well as departmental culture (Wilkins and Ouchi 1983), we chose the same department of a single client organization for all outsourcing relationships - the HR department of a German-based financial services provider (GLOBAL BANK).

A total number of 21 interviews was conducted. To reflect the unit of analysis in data collection each analyzed relationship consisted of at least two expert interviews: A client employee involved in managing the partnership with the vendor and a respective counterpart from the vendor. On client side experts from senior and operational level were interviewed, enabling us to capture interactions between relational and contractual governance, as responsibilities those mechanisms are typically situated on different levels of the hierarchy. The interviews were held either face-to-face or by telephone. All interviews were tape-recorded and transcribed. In sum, the interview protocols resulted in more than 91500 words of qualitative data.

The data was analyzed in the following way: Each piece of data - be it document or interview fragment - was carefully interpreted by the first and second author in order to explore how contractual and relational governance mechanisms interact.

This interpretation of the data consisted of three steps: First, data was scanned in order to identify interaction processes between relational and contractual governance. Second, the identified fragment was coded according to the two potential outcomes of the interaction process, that is either as "complementarity process" or "substitutional process". Subsequently, the two coders re-examined potentially ambiguous fragments and reached a consensus on their interpretation. In a third step we analyzed every single "complementarity" and "substitutional" process looking for similarities and differences in practices, cognitive processes and perceptions of the actors. The outcome of this third step were *four archetypical processes, which explain how contractual and relational governance interact to become either complements or substitutes*. In the next section we develop these archetypes from analysis of case data.

Case Name	Project Description	Interview Partner
TALENT	ALPHA delivers an online application for managing employee's talent and performance.	Client: C14, C15 Vendor: V6
GRAD-RECRUIT	BETA delivers an online application for managing the graduate recruiting process.	Client: C6, C7, C8 Vendor: V2
RECRUIT	GAMMA delivers an online workflow management application for the entire recruitment process.	Client: C11, C12, C13, Vendor: V5
PAYROLL	DELTA processes the payroll for GLOBAL BANK's Indian operations.	Client: C1, C2, C3, C4, C5, Vendor: V1
HR-OPS	EPSILON delivers HR back-office processes for GLOBAL BANK's Indian operations	Client: C9, C10 Vendor: V3, V4

Table 1:   The Analyzed IS Outsourcing Cases

3.3   Results

3.3.1   Archetype 1 - Contractual Governance as Enabler for Relational Governance

The first pattern of interaction between contractual and relational governance is characterized by contract-based mechanisms provoking relational governance by prescribing social interaction. Therefore this pattern describes a complementary relationship. To illustrate this archetype the PAYROLL case is well-suited. After taking over the services from a former vendor in 2009, currently DELTA is the provider in this business process outsourcing (BPO) relationship. After a relatively short time of collaboration, GLOBAL BANK and DELTA were satisfied with the relationship and arrived at a well attuned relational governance. This manifested itself in an open information exchange and a lot of informal ad-hoc communication via telephone and email. Interestingly, many hints point into the direction, that the *contract has built the basis for this open and trustful communication* as it contains schedules, which specify regular meetings. These formal meetings seem to have advanced the formation of the above described relational elements. Interviewee C5 supports this conclusion, when he describes, that as a result of the "formal governance" meetings an additional "continuous communication flow" has developed. Apparently the contractually prescribed social interaction (in the formal "governance meeting") has laid the foundation to utilize relational governance subsequently.

The other cases show similar interrelations between contractual and relational governance: contractually prescribed meetings enforce social interaction, which in turn promotes the evolution of informal governance mechanisms. C7 in the GRAD RECRUIT case explains, that they started with "weekly calls" in the beginning of the relationship, which were specified within the contract. Advanced by these weekly calls additional calls on a voluntary basis developed. A similar effect was reported on vendor-side. V2 describes that based on the scheduled weekly call, they coordinate further calls and meetings if necessary:

> "During the weekly call we might decide that we need to have a meeting so we schedule that during the call. There is nothing kind of systematically [for these additional meetings] in place".

Obviously, contractually specified meetings may build the basis for social exchange between client and vendor. Within this social interaction, mutual trust and shared norms among the employees can evolve. As a consequence, informal calls and meetings are agreed what reflects relational governance. Hence, contractual governance strongly supports the evolution of relational governance, but at the end both governance mechanisms seem to be equally important.

V3 in the HR OPS case explains how a transition manager who was involved in contract preparation went onshore to train the vendor team. The transition manager focused on the adherence of contractually defined meetings as well as on the formation of a shared understanding regarding relational norms and expectations. Hence, this training stirred up social interaction and as a consequence informal day-to-day interactions evolved to a confirmed habit. Apparently, contractually prescribed training, stimulated the development of relational governance.

In the GRAD RECRUIT case another effect is visible. There were some problems during the roll out in the Asia-Pacific region. An "efficient communication structure" (V5) was not in place, what was referred to as the main problem, leading to a situation which was mainly characterized by "act and react" (V5) and not by an open and trustful communication. Hence, the missing communication structure reflects a lack of contractual governance. As a consequence, social exchange was not promoted and this resulted in a poor relational governance. Subsequently, a tight communication structure was established. The impact of bringing structure into the communication process was significant:

> "Since we sort of got the governance process in place it [the relation-ship] definitely improved substantially to the point we are right now and in my twelve months working with (...) [GLOBAL BANK], I would now find it, what I would consider to be a pretty good spot." (V5)

Hence, contractual governance mechanisms like regular meetings and calls, are an important driver to form relational governance, as they route people to social interaction. In turn, this social exchange leads to shared norms and expectations as well as mutual trust, what again promotes continuous informal communication and information exchange. Having these facts in mind, we conclude that there is a regular pattern of interaction between contractual and relational governance, and which can be described as the archetype: *"contractual governance as enabler for relational governance"*.

3.3.2   Archetype 2 - Relational Governance as Enabler for Contractual Completeness

We discovered another pattern, in which a well attuned relational governance is prerequisite to refine an existing contract. Hence, this archetype describes how relational governance complements contractual governance.

In the GRAD-RECRUIT case the vendor BETA is bound by a contract to provide defined software functionalities as a web application, supporting GLOBAL BANK's graduate recruiting processes. Nevertheless, from time to time GLOBAL BANK's recruiters expect the vendor to deliver software functionalities that are "not part of the contract" (C7). In this case a requirements analysis procedure is initiated, that is: requirements are elicited, negotiated and specified *by means of relational governance*. As an example, in order to determine "what they [the re-cruiters] want" (V2) vendor's software developers and client's recruiters are "dis-cussing" (V2) these issues informally "on the phone" (V2). Interestingly, this drawing on relational mechanisms does not happen accidentally, but rather to expressly bypass a contractually defined change request process. The reason for this is that the formally specified change request process is not considered to be adequate for the complex task of establishing a shared understanding concerning the requirements. Vital for the demonstration of the interplay between contractual and relational governance is the outcome of this relational coordination process: a mutually agreed upon proposal describing the extended software functionalities. This proposal subsequently became an "addendum to the contract" (C7).

This pattern of interaction between relational and contractual governance is replicated in the PAYROLL case. The contracting parties have agreed upon an elaborate contract, defining among other things, which services the vendor is obliged to perform and what goals he is expected to achieve. However, in the beginning of the relationship the contract was *indeterminate on how to fulfil contractual obligations*. In order to bridge this gap the vendor and GLOBAL BANK started a process of intense mutual adjustments leading to a so called "Note of Understanding", expressing how the payroll services should be performed. In the process of mutual adjustments *the parties made extensive use of relational mechanisms*, such as informal "phone calls" (C5) and close personal interaction. Again, vital for the demonstration of the interplay between contractual and relational governance is what happened subsequently: the "Note of Understanding" gets "signed off" (C5) and therefore becomes part of the contract and hence refines it.

While the preceding examples pointed out how well attuned relational governance enables the parties to refine the contract we also observed the reverse effect: in the RECRUIT case the client complains about the quality of the contract, specifically that "the SLAs were not as good as they ... should have been" (C11), because there was an insufficient "understanding [of] the technology and what really could be in [a] SLA related to it" (C11). Interestingly, the cause for this undesired incompleteness of the contract is explicitly traced back to deficits in relational governance:

> "We never really got to the stage that the relationship was such that
> we ... could be consulted of about that issues." (V5).

Thus, in this case a bad relational governance was the cause for an undesired incompleteness of the contract.

Summing up, a good relational governance complements contractual governance by means of laying the foundation for a refinement of the contract. It seems that relational governance and the strong social ties associated with it give access to knowledge which would otherwise be hard to access (Nonaka and von Krogh 2009) and which is subsequently used to refine contractual clauses. This observation differs from the widely accepted view that relational aspects, such as mutual trust, facilitate initial contract negotiations because trusting parties are more willing to compromise (e.g. Kale, Singh et al. 2000). Our observations show that relational governance is not merely a remedy for a deficient willingness, but for a deficient (initial) capability to contract sufficiently complete. Therefore, we call this archetype *"relational governance as enabler for contractual completeness"*.

3.3.3   Archetype 3 - Contractual Governance as Safety Net

While in the first two archetypes presented in this paper one type of governance mechanisms *directly* stimulated the occurrence of the other, another more *indirect* constellation came apparent. The awareness of a contract mitigates the perceived relational risk. As a consequence, relational governance can develop freely. Hence, contractual governance complements relational governance. To illustrate this archetype, we first point to an apparently paradoxical situation: on the one hand the majority of interviewees emphasized the high importance of the contract. On the other hand even the very same interviewees noted that they would be aware of the *existence* of the contract, but that they *do not know its content*. The following case examples will point out how this seemingly paradoxical situation is resolved by means of the mentioned indirect interaction.

In the GRAD RECRUIT case a so called operational level agreement (OLA) was attached to the outsourcing contract. Comparable to service level agreements (SLAs), OLAs describe procedural matters, which are important for the day-to-day business within various technical domains. Although put in place to structure day-to-day interaction, as an attachment to the contract the OLA by definition represents contractual governance. Now interesting is the role and relevance the OLA takes on in the day-to-day management, as expressed by C6:

> "before acting, I *won't* have a look into the OLA, this would be too time-consuming. Knowing the basic conditions of the OLA is enough to deal with everyday occurrences"

This quote shows that the OLA does *not* structure everyday business in detail. In fact quite the opposite is true, relational governance comes to the fore and the OLA backs out. As an example, interviewees describe everyday interaction as driven by behaviour, based on a general understanding of the contract, common sense, shared norms and expectations. However, the relationship between contractual and relational governance can not be described as a substitution, because the contract is obviously not replaced by relational governance. Instead, it still seems to play an important role. This role is neither prescribing guidelines for day-to-day business nor is it directly fertilizing relational governance (like described in A1). The important fact is the *awareness, that there is a contract to appeal to in case of necessity* and this awareness gives employees a sense of security, as it mitigates the perceived risk of misconduct. This role of the contract is characterized by C6 as follows:

"[the OLA] finally defines the day-to-day business, respectively the collaboration on this level. It's a guidance. Exactly for that purpose we have an OLA. ... As long as a collaboration based on partnership via phone and email works, it is a nice thing and if it does not work that well, it is something what acts supporting, as something to rely on".

In this quote, the need for a contract (OLA) in cases of trouble becomes obvious. Each employee can "rely on" the OLA if something "does not work that well".

Furthermore, this indirect interaction between contractual and relational governance also manifests in the reverse direction: disbelief in the protecting role of the contract and distrust within the relationship are intertwined. In the RECRUIT case, the application owner on client-side (C13) delivers evidence for this interaction. She explains that she is not aware of whether the vendor has received and acknowledged distinct security policies and whether they are part of the contract. As a consequence, she is not able to rely on the contract. Interestingly, the relationship between client and vendor in this case is characterized by distrust - indicating a bad relational governance.

The interaction between contractual and relational governance described in this section can be illustrated with a metaphor - the one of a tightrope artist. As long as everything is fine, the safety net is not needed, otherwise the artist always knows that he is protected from falling if he makes a mistake. Transferred to the context of contractual and relational governance it seems that a contract may take the role of a safety net. That is, individuals know that there is something to rely on, when the other contracting party is not acting like agreed and expected. *The contract complements relational governance by enabling it to develop freely, as the perceived relational risk is reduced.* This is very similar to the safety net of the tightrope artist that enables him to dare extraordinary artistic feats. Hence, the contract complements relational governance.

The safeguarding role of the contract also explains how the above mentioned paradox is resolved: The content of the contract does not have to be known to unfold a high importance in day-to-day interaction, because a rather general awareness of the existence of relevant contractual stipulations often seems to be sufficient for the contract to take a safeguarding role. Therefore, we call this archetype "*contractual governance as safety net*".

3.3.4   Archetype 4 - Relational Governance Amplifier for Contractual Openness

Contrary to the archetypes described above, we also identified one archetype, which describes how contractual and relational governance become substitutes. Relational governance reduces the need for a complete contract.

The HR-OPS case covers two consecutive projects (Project1 and Project2) of a captive business process outsourcing between GLOBAL BANK and the vendor EPSILON. A comparison of these two projects demonstrates a further pattern of interaction resulting in the *substitution of contractual governance in favour of relational governance.*

Project1 was the first outsourcing project between GLOBAL BANK and EPSI-LON comprising HR back office services, such as benefits administration and overtime management. In order to uncover the substitution effect between contractual and relational governance an analysis of the contract crafting is necessary: the contract crafting had to adhere to a methodology called *Captive Offshoring Methodology* (COM). This methodology encompasses five successive phases, whereas the *completion of each phase can be seen as a movement towards a higher degree of contractual completeness.* In Project1 all phases were passed ranging from the filling out of "a lot of documentation" (C9), specification of preliminary requirements to the passage of detailed KPIs. Some months after the project went live, several interviewees expressed a high level of overall satisfaction with the project itself and notably explicitly emphasized their satisfaction on a relational level: [3]

> "I am satisfied with the project. Actually, very satisfied. I think it was very successful" (C10)

> "The relationship is pretty good .... They [EPSILON] are highly committed to us." (C10)

Given this in all respects successful relationship GLOBAL BANK decided to extend the scope of services and therefore initiated Project2 to hand over additional HR back office services. Comparing process of contract crafting for Project2 with Project1, a remarkable difference can be diagnosed: instead of passing all five phases of the COM completely, some of the prescribed steps were omitted.

> "In the case of Project2 ... we didn't need to do it [one of the prescribed steps]" (V4).

---

[3]   Up to this point this case example very well illustrates Archetype 1. Therefore we want to explicitly emphasize that the pattern of interaction we discovered becomes visible when *comparing* Project1 and Project2.

But as each step of the COM aims at a higher level of contractual completeness, skipping a step implies a lower degree of contractual completeness. As demonstrated above, Project1 has laid the foundation for relational governance and therefore this *lower degree of contractual completeness can be interpreted as the outcome of a substitution of contractual governance in favour of relational governance.* In other words: the relational norms and the commitment which have formed during the precursor project allow a higher degree of relational governance, which in turn allows less strict contractual stipulations for the subsequent project. Surprising is the assessment of this lower degree of contractual completeness. Instead of complaining about a higher danger of opportunism, a GLOBAL BANK manager praises the higher level of *flexibility* received through the open contract:

> "now it is much quicker to produce [an addendum to the contract] and if in future we wanted to add something slightly different or slightly a scope creep ... it would probably fit in these two paragraphs and you wouldn't have to change the [complete] contract." (C9)

In summary, a well attuned relational governance reduces the need for detailed and strict contractual stipulations. In this sense, relational governance substitutes for contractual governance. Moreover, our findings point to an underlying trade-off that explains occurrence of this substitutional effect. This is the trade-off between the need for flexibility (satisfied with a high degree of contractual openness) on the one hand and the need to safeguard against opportunism (satisfied with a high degree of contractual completeness) on the other hand (Maitland, Bryson et al. 1985). A deep relationship seems to devalue the importance of safeguarding and revalue the importance of flexibility and vice versa. Viewed in this light a high degree of relational governance amplifies contractual openness. Therefore, we call this archetype *relational governance as amplifier for contractual openness.*

3.4   Discussion

This study was motivated by the question whether the relationship between contractual and relational governance is the outcome of distinct processes. Our analysis yielded four archetypical processes, which explain *how* the interplay between contractual and relational governance result in their complementarity or substitution (see table 2 for an overview of archetypical processes). Three of the identified processes explain a complementary, while the fourth explains a substitutional relationship.

Archetype		Explained Relationship
A1	Contractual Governance as Enabler for Relational Governance	complementarity
A2	Relational Governance as Enabler for Contractual Completeness	complementarity
A3	Contractual Governance as Safety Net	complementarity
A4	Relational Governance as Amplifier for Contractual Openness	substitution

Table 2:   Overview of Archetypes

Archetypes A1, A2 and A3 share the characteristic that one type of governance mechanism is not simply the precursor for the oppositional mechanism. Rather, practicing one governance mechanism establishes the basis for additionally exercising the other governance mechanism (complementarity). While sharing this characteristic the three archetypes differ in their mode of operation: A1 explains how contractual clauses stipulate social interaction fertilizing relational governance. A2 shows how strong social ties give access to knowledge which would otherwise be hard to access and which is utilized to refine contractual clauses. The third archetype (A3) demonstrates how one mechanism (contractual governance) is protecting the application of the other one by reducing perceived relational risk. This is contrary to the fourth archetype (A4), where relational governance is not taking on a protecting role regarding the use of contractual governance. Instead, relational governance reduces the need for a strong contract.

Though there are slight overlaps, the archetypes demonstrate the essential differences that exist in the interaction between contractual and relational governance. As an example both A2 and A4 deal with the impact of relational governance on contractual completeness. However, both archetypes differ in the impact on contractual governance: While in A2 a well attuned relational governance enables a contract with a higher degree of contractual completeness (complementarity), in A4 quite the opposite is observable: a well attuned relational governance reduces the desire for a complete contract. A1 and A3 also exhibit refined but important distinctions. Both archetypes explain how contractual governance enables relational governance (complementarity), but they differ in their mode of operation. That is, *contractual stipulation of social interaction and as a consequence evolution of relational norms* on the hand (A1) and *a contractual governance assuming the role of safety net reducing perceived relational risk and enabling relational governance to develop freely* (A3) on the other hand.

3.4.1   Theoretical Implications

Our study offers a number of theoretical contributions. First of all, our study enables a shift in perspective. While former research characterized relational and contractual governance as either complements or substitutes, our findings explain the development of their relationship as the outcome of distinct processes. While our results indicate that the relationship between contractual and relational governance can still be classified as complementary or substitutional at a particular time, we argue that this relationship is far more complex than depicted in previous research. For one thing, this relationship does usually not last forever. Instead the relationship between contractual and relational governance is subject to change in course of time. This extends previous findings insofar, as not only the degree of contractual, respectively relational governance, may change over time (Inkpen and Currall 2004) but also their relationship.

This contribution is encouraged by a finding not explicitly outlined in the previous chapters, namely that the archetypical processes may emerge in a sequence. As an example, initially contractual clauses might stipulate social interaction that fertilize relational governance (A1), afterwards contractual clauses might be refined by virtue of the sticky information gained by means of strong relational ties (A2) and again after a while a follow-up project may be based on a more open contract precisely because the relationship has proven to be reliable (A4). Thus, contractual and relational governance may complement each other at an early date (A1, A2), but substitute each other at a later (A4) date and vice versa.

While the limited number of cases in our study urges us to be careful in drawing conclusions, our study does support and in other cases contradict earlier findings and, most importantly, provides insights, that challenge common beliefs on the relationship between contractual and relational governance and its causes. Our study contradicts both substitutional and complementary view as they advocate an exclusive relationship, meaning that contractual and relational governance are depicted as *either* substitutes *or* complements, while we observed complementarity *as well as* substitution in the course of time. Besides this obvious implication our study also questions and extends the underlying assumptions concerning the interplay of contractual and relational governance: so far, the substitutional view depicts contractual governance as being solely part of an impersonal social structure. However, A1 reveals that contractual governance can very well stimulate *interpersonal* interaction. Hence, the separation of contractual and relational governance in the sense of a dualism seems to be inappropriate.

The complementary view argues that contractual and relational governance are complements because they are two separate routes to do the same thing, i.e. they simultaneously but *parallel to* each other reduce complexity and absorb uncertainty (Reed 2001). While the interplay between contractual and relational governance specified in A3 confirms this rationale, A1 und A2 extend the complementary view by providing two additional rationales. First, contractual governance possesses the capability that enables relational governance by triggering that kind of social interaction required for relational norms to evolve. Second, relational governance possesses the capability to access sticky knowledge needed to refine contracts. Hence, both findings signify that relational and contractual governance are complements not only because they simultaneously *but parallel to each other* reduce complexity, but because their differential capabilities interact with each other and hence they reduce complexity *in conjunction.*

Finally, our findings might have the explanatory power to unify contradictory empirical results: While some researchers found evidence for a complementary relationship (e.g. Poppo and Zenger 2002) and others for a substitutional relationship (e.g. Ring and Van de Ven 1994) this study highlights the importance of a dynamic perspective, as the very same types of governance mechanisms could be both complements and substitutes - at different points of time. Therefore, former contradictory empirical findings could be the result of neglecting the role of time.

3.4.2   Limitations and Implications for future research

There are several limitations to take into account. First, the study's findings are based on a single-site multiple case study. This may influence the results, as there is a potential bias in the answers of the interview partners, e.g. based on the culture of the bank. Although a single-site case study enables comparability between the analyzed cases, we are aware that generalization of our findings or the transferability to other outsourcing relationships should be empirically substantiated by future research. Hence, we call for replication studies that use multiple sites in different industries in order to test or extend the archetypes presented in this study. A second limitation which should be subject to subsequent research efforts are missing quantitative measures. These should be developed to further investigate related effects caused by or in regard of different archetypes. Finally, our research focused on the identification of distinctive archetypes which lead to complementary or substitutional relationships. Moreover, first indications point into the direction, that some archetypes emerge in a certain sequence. Hence we suggest further research to investigate patterns of interdependence between distinct archetypes. Furthermore, this study could be the starting point for a new approach to investigate the interplay of different governance mechanisms by analyzing occurrence and changes of these relationships over time. This encompasses the exploration of contingencies, which may trigger the four archetypical processes or sequences of archetypes.

References

Bachmann, R. (2001). "Trust, power and control in trans-organizational relations." Organization Studies 22(2): 337-365.

Benbasat, I., D. K. Goldstein, et al. (1987). "The Case Research Strategy in Studies of Information Systems." Management Information Systems Quarterly 11(3): 369.

Dibbern, J., J. Winkler, et al. (2008). "Explaining Variations in Client Extra Costs Between Software Projects Offshored to India." Mis Quarterly 32(2): 333-366.

Eisenhardt, K. M. (1989). "Building theories from case study research." Academy of Management Review 14(4): 532.

Goo, J., R. Kishore, et al. (2009). "The Role of Service Level Agreement in relational Management of Information Technology Outsourcing: An Empirical Study." Mis Quarterly 33(1): 119-145.

Hofstede, G. (1991). Cultures and Organizations. Software of the mind. London, McGraw-Hill.

Inkpen, A. C. and S. C. Currall (2004). "The Coevolution of Trust, Control, and Learning in Joint Ventures." Organization Science 15(5): 586-599.

Kale, P., H. Singh, et al. (2000). "Learning and Protection of Proprietary Assets in Strategic Alliances: Building Relational Capital." Strategic Management Journal 21(o. Nr.): 217.

Kirsch, L. (1997). "Portfolios of control modes and IS project management." Information Systems Research 8(3): 215.

Klein Woolthuis, R., B. Hillebrand, et al. (2005). "Trust, contract and relationship development." Organization Studies 26(6): 813.

Lacity, M., S. Khan, et al. (2009). "A review of the IT outsourcing literature: Insights for practice." Journal of Strategic Information Systems 18(3): 130-146.

Larson, A. (1992). "Network Dyads in Entrepreneurial Settings: A Study of the Governance of Exchange Relationships." Administrative Science Quarterly 37(1): 76-104.

Lee, Y. and S. Cavusgil (2006). "Enhancing alliance performance: The effects of contractual-based versus relational-based governance." Journal of Business Research 59(8): 896-905.

MaCaulay, S. (1963). "Non-Contractural Relations in Business: A Prelimnary Study." American Sociological Review 28(1): 55-67.

Maitland, I., J. Bryson, et al. (1985). "Sociologists, Economists, and Opportunism." The Academy of Management Review 10(1): 59.

Mellewigt, T., A. Madhok, et al. (2007). "Trust and formal contracts in interorganizational relationships—substitutes and complements." Managerial and Decision Economics 28(8): 833-847.

Miles, M. and A. Huberman (1994). Qualitative data analysis: An expanded sourcebook, SAGE publications, Inc.

Möllering, G. (2005). "The trust/control duality." International sociology 20(3): 283.

Nonaka, I. and G. von Krogh (2009). "Perspective---Tacit Knowledge and Knowledge Conversion: Controversy and Advancement in Organizational Knowledge Creation Theory." Organization Science 20(3): 635-652.

Patton, M. Q. (2002). Qualitative Research and Evaluation Methods. Thousand Oaks, Sage Publications.

Poppo, L. and T. Zenger (2002). "Do formal contracts and relational governance function as substitutes or complements?" Strategic Management Journal 23: 707-725.

Reed, M. I. (2001). "Organization, Trust and Control: A Realist Analysis." Organization Studies (Walter de Gruyter GmbH & Co. KG.) 22(2): 201.

Ring, P. S. and A. H. Van de Ven (1994). "Developmental processes of cooperative interorganizational relationships." Academy of Management Review 19(1): 90.

Tiwana, A. (2010). "Systems Development Ambidexterity: Explaining the Complementary and Substitutive Roles of Formal and Informal Controls." Journal of Management Information Systems 27(2): 87-126.

Van de Ven, A. H., A. L. Delbecq, et al. (1976). "Determinants of Coordination Modes within Organizations." American Sociological Review 41(2): 322.

Wilkins, A. and W. Ouchi (1983). "Efficient cultures: Exploring the relationship between culture and organizational performance." Administrative Science Quarterly 28(3): 468-481.

Woolthuis, R. K., B. Hillebrand, et al. (2005). "Trust, Contract and Relationship Development." Organization Studies (01708406) 26(6): 813-840.

Yin, R. (2003). Case study research. California, Thousand Oaks.

Technology Adoption by Elderly People – An Empirical Analysis of Adopters and Non-Adopters of Social Networking Sites[1]

Christian Maier

Centre of Human Resources Information Systems, Otto-Friedrich University Bamberg, Feldkirchenstr. 21, 96052 Bamberg, Germany
christian.maier@uni-bamberg.de

Sven Laumer

Centre of Human Resources Information Systems, Otto-Friedrich University Bamberg, Feldkirchenstr. 21, 96052 Bamberg, Germany
sven.laumer@uni-bamberg.de

Dr. Andreas Eckhardt

Centre of Human Resources Information Systems, Goethe University Frankfurt am Main, Grueneburgplatz 1, 60323 Frankfurt am Main, Germany
eckhardt@wiwi.uni-frankfurt.de

1 Introduction

Due to new information and communication technologies, organizations can simplify the work of their employees, which is the largely overlooked perspective in IS research (Choudrie and Dwivedi 2006). In addition, households could integrate these technological innovations within their daily routine to handle ordinary or uncommon tasks within short periods of time. One essential innovation of the last years was the introduction of Social Network Sites (SNS), which can be defined as "online shared interactive spaces, in which a group of people use a repertoire of technological features (forums, newsgroups, messaging) to carry out a wide range of social interaction" (Khan and Jarvenpaa 2010; Jones et al 2004). Nowadays, a lot of different SNS compete to be the market leader, however, at the moment

---

[1] Another version of this paper appeared as: Maier, Christian et al., "Technology Adoption by Elderly People – An Empirical Analysis of Adopters and Non-Adopters of Social Networking Sites," *Proceedings of the 10th International Conference on Wirtschaftsinformatik 2011*, pp. 901-911.

A. Heinzl et al. (eds.), *Theory-Guided Modeling and Empiricism in Information Systems Research*, DOI 10.1007/978-3-7908-2781-1_5, © Springer-Verlag Berlin Heidelberg 2011

Facebook (Facebook 2010), with more than 400 million active users, is the most used SNS around the world. On the other side, certain countries as Germany (studiVZ 2010) have other online communities with more than 8 Million users. In Germany, over 30 Million people are members of social communities on the internet (BitKom 2010).

These users can inform all their friends and acquaintances with just one message, communicate or chat to maintain social relationships. Apart from that, many people use SNS to share private information like photos or videos or try to enlarge their circle of friends. Others just pursue the aim to collaborate or to have fun while playing online games and compete with friends (Correa et al.2010; Raacke and Bonds-Raacke 2008; Ross et al. 2009; Walther et al. 2008; Lewis et al. 2008; Subrahmanyam et al. 2008). Additionally, further SNS (such as Xing or LinkedIn) support the application process of job seekers by providing the possibility to upload CVs, connect with their job network or communicate with recruiters and headhunters for job offers (Weitzel et al. 2009). In Germany, the three most important reasons to participate in a SNS are to stay in contact with family and friends, to exchange information about common interests and to search for new friends (BitKom 2010). Nonetheless, these potentials of SNS can only be realized if people participate within the same social network.

Although, modern information technology offers various advantages and is used by many people – often daily (Joos 2008; Ross et al. 2009; Walther et al. 2008) – the amount of people that are not willing to use and adopt to SNS is surprisingly high (Johansen and Swigart 1996; Moore 1999; Norman 1999; Wiener 1993). In Germany, there are around 50 Million people who do not have a profile in a SNS. This accounts for almost two thirds of the people living in Germany1. Such a non-adoption behavior of IT in general has been recognized within IS research and potential reasons were raised and identified concerning different applications. Different reasons have been identified in previous research such as fear and threats as concern for privacy (Bhattacherjee and Hikmet 2007; Bhattacherjee and Hikmet 2007), psychological issues like resistance (Laumer et al. 2010); or simply social issues as age, education or income (Azari and Pick 2005; Dewan and Riggins 2005). In addition, Peter Mertens analyzed why IT implementation projects fail (Mertens 2008).

Nonetheless, if people reject using new technologies or applications as social network platforms non-adoption will entail various problems. From a societal point of view, the most important one is the advancing spread of society in one group of people adopting new technologies and another one rejecting it. This phenomenon is actually discussed and known as Digital Divide or Digital Inequality (Dewan and Riggins 2005). It describes the amount of people, who have limited access to the internet or do not have the ability to use computers effectively and efficiently. Major reasons for the Digital Divide in Germany are the lacking availability of broadband internet access points (Holznagel 2008) and especially demographic factors such as level of education, gender and age (Kubicek and Welling 2000).

Concerning the factor age for use and acceptance of the internet, there are distinct differences in the German population. More than 90 per cent of the young people between 14-and 29 years are internet users. In contrast, only 48.5 per cent of people between 60-69 years and just 19 per cent of the people 70+ years of age are internet users (TNS Infratest 2009). A large proportion of these people do not adopt the internet and its applications. Reasons for this non-adoption lie in the rapid development of the internet in the past 20 years and the related dissemination of information and communication technology. For example, people who retired around the millennium did mostly not come in contact with new media during their working career (Wege ins Netz 2010).

In order to counter the phenomenon of Digital Divide, the German Federal Government introduced several initiatives to reduce resistance and foster internet use of elderly people. SNS exist that target specifically the elderly population. In Germany feierabend.de is one example of a platform designed to support the social interaction of people aged 50 and older. This specific platform was awarded in 2008 as the "Best Community" in Germany by the German Federal Department of Economics and Technology as the platform supports especially the generation 50+ to find their way into and through the World Wide Web. The platform is designed to support the exchange of information and experiences as well as interactions of people with similar interests. For example feierabend.de established over 100 regional groups to enable meetings of their members within their city or region. These regional groups enabled feierabend.de to connect the online and offline lifes of elderly people. However, with only 600,000 visitors each month this particular SNS as well as other similar platforms only reach a small part of the potential user group of people at the age of 50 and older.

Based on the previous analysis, this paper focuses on people with at least 50 years of age and leaves out the "wired from birth" (Brown 2008) generation. By using the Model of Adoption of Technology in Households (MATH; Venkatesh and Brown 2001; Brown and Venkatesh 2005) this paper will analyze factors leading to adoption or non-adoption behavior of SNS by elderly persons. This research is in line with Brown who argued that adoption research in the household context should focus on SNS (Brown 2008) and with Pak et al. (2009) who identified age-sensitive design of online services as an important aspect of IS research (Pak et al. 2009).

Therefore, this paper analyzes which factors of MATH have an influence on the decision to adopt a modern technology such as SNS. Apart from that it is investigated, which MATH construct has the strongest predictive value and if there are differences for adopters and non-adopters in relation to the observed antecedents of the intention to use SNS.

For this purpose, this paper provides an overview of the research background and relevant literature in section 2 dealing with the Digital Divide in general, SNS as well as IT adoption and non-adoption in the household context. Based on this, section 3 contains the central hypotheses and explains the used research design. Section 4 comprises the research results which are then discussed in section 5.

2   Research Background

Within in this section the Digital Divide in general, SNS and IT adoption and non-adoption in the household context are discussed in order to provide the relevant background information for the developed research model.

2.1 IT Adoption and Non-Adoption in Households

IT adoption in general is a highly studied research area within the IS discipline. According to Williams et al. (2009), since 1985 345 paper on technology adoption were published in the top 19 peer-reviewed journals of the IS community. Nonetheless, most of these articles analyzed IT adoption in organizations. In principle, IT-adoption and non-adoption can be investigated within organizational (Venkatesh et al. 2003) and private contexts (Brown and Venkatesh 2005; Brown 2008). In order to analyze the private domain, Venkatesh and Brown processed the Model of Adoption of Technology in Households (MATH; Venkatesh and Brown 2001; Brown and Venkatesh 2005), which is based on the Theory of Planned Behavior (Ajzen 1991) and explains the Behavioral Intention using Attitudinal Beliefs, Normative Beliefs and Control Beliefs. Attitudinal Beliefs subsume Utilitarian Outcomes (degree of effectiveness and utility of using PC within households), Hedonic Outcomes (degree of pleasure or fun) and Social Outcomes (degree of status, power or knowledge resulting from PC household adoption). Normative Beliefs consider the impact of friends, family members and acquaintances and Control Beliefs regard possible inhibitors as cost, difficulty of use or Fear of Technology, which can end in rejecting a new technology. The resulting model was enlarged in 2005 as Brown and Venkatesh (2005) identified Age, Income and Marital Status as moderator effects.

In terms of age Brown and Venkatesh showed that in general age is a moderator for Utilitarian, Hedonic and Social Outcomes as well as for Normative and Control Beliefs. The relationship between Utilitarian Outcomes and Behavioral Intention is moderated in such way that it is increasingly significant with age and even more for those who are married. The relationship between Hedonic Outcomes and Intention is moderated by age such that with increasing age Hedonic Outcomes are less important. In terms of Social Outcomes the impact of status gains on Intention to Use increase with age. Also Normative Beliefs are moderated by age such that friends and family as well as secondary sources are more important for elderly people. In terms of Control Beliefs (Fear of Technology and Perceived Behavioral Control or Perceived Ease of Use) a moderation effect by age were identified. Consequently, these antecedents are more important for older people.

Another distinguishing criterion within IT adoption research is the motivation why people use IT. Generally, people can use it because of a voluntary incentive or due to mandatory settings. Social network sites, which are the underlying technology within this paper, are a good research domain to analyze adoption behavior in households (Brown 2008). Within such a setting many people – especially elderly people – reject using new technologies because they are not in a position to handle technologies and are not willing to ask for help if something did not work as planned (Blackwell 2004). This could be one reason, why the diffusion of broadband in households moves slower than expected (Choudrie and Lee 2004; Dwivedi et al. 2006). Based on this observation, Choudrie and Dwivedi [1] investigated the adoption of broadband in households with the help of MATH. According to Venkatesh and Brown (2001) they identified several barriers as high costs, ease or difficulty of PC and internet use, lack of skill and lack of needs, which could result in a rejection of new technologies. For non-users only the lack of knowledge played a subordinated role in order to understand non-adoption behavior. On the other side, it was possible to show that each attitudinal factor was important to predict the usage behavior.

The complex theme "non-adoption" has not yet been researched as extensive as the actual adoption decision (Lapointe and Rivard and 2005). Nonetheless, several IS researchers started to investigate this behavior (Hirschheim and Newman 1988; Markus 1983) and tried to motivate for further research endeavor. A recent publication within MISQ identified perceived values, switching costs or support as factors which can tip the balance and lead to non-adoption (Kim and Kankanhalli 2009). Such factors differ depending on the underlying context, so that other authors identified loss of status or power, uncertainty(Jiang et al. 2000), pressure, exchange (Enns et al. 2003) or perceived threat (Bhattacherjee and Hikmet 2007; Bhattacherjee and Sanford 2006) as significant influence factors which increase the probability to reject technologies. Eckhardt et al.(2009) focused on the other side of social influence and investigated what groups exert an influence on the decision of people to refuse adopting a technology. A research model which explicitly should explain why people do not adopt social network platforms with the help of the Theory of Reasoned Action (TRA; Fishbein and Ajzen 1975; Ajzen and Fishbein 1980) was conducted by Laumer et al. (2010). In doing this, the authors disclosed negative significant correlations between an individual's personality trait resistance and each TRA construct.

2.2 Social Network Sites

Internet usage and cognition changed due to new opportunities within information and communication technologies. One of the most influential alteration emerged through Social Network Sites (SNS) as Facebook or the VZ-network (meinVZ, StudiVZ, SchülerVZ), which are popular SNS for German students and pupils.

Nowadays, about 11.44 per cent of the total population of the world is registered within Facebook (Hutter 2010). Focusing more sophisticated countries as USA, Sweden, Canada or UK, this percentage rate rises up to 40 per cent. Such a high number of users could be explained by the variety of SNS possibilities. Each SNS user can communicate with friends or strangers, maintain relationships, enlarge their circle of friends, share private information, collaborate or just have fun (Correa et al. 2010; Raacke and Bonds-Raacke 2008; Ross et al. 2009 ;Walther et al. 2008; Lewis et al. 2008 ;Subrahmanyam et al. 2008). Due to this, many people integrated social network sites in their daily routine (Joos 2008; Ross et al. 2009; Walther et al. 2008) and spend there between 10 minutes and 3 hours every day (Ellison et al. 2007; Valenzuela et al. 2009; Raacke and Bonds-Raacke 2008).

Contrary to internet flirtation pages, in which people search new friends and try to meet them afterwards in real life, social network sites are used in most instances to keep in touch with friends and acquaintances, which are known from the real offline world. Only afterwards, these known people will be added in the online friends list. This behavior is called Offline-to-Online phenomenon and is a distinctive characteristic of Facebook and comparable platforms (Ellison et al. 2007; Lewis et al. 2008; Mayer and Puller 2008; Khan and Jarvenpaa 2010).

Regarding different platforms Facebook with around 13 million users in January 2010 is the number one in Germany in terms of total users considering the VZ platforms as different ones. The VZ community has 14.4 million users in total. Also important are wer-kennt-wen.de, stayfriends.de and myspace.com. Feierabend.de has around 600.000 regular visitors as illustrated by Figure 1.

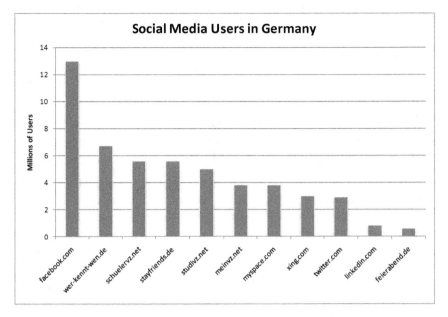

Figure 1:   General SNS users in Germany (COMPASS HEADING 2010)

In Germany, Facebook users are mainly students or young professionals between the age of16 and 28. On the other side, Figure 2 shows that with an increasing age, the user percentage decreases continuously. Consequently, only 5.12 per cent of all German Facebook users are at least 50 years old. Considering the whole German age distribution, which illustrates that the majority of people are older than 40, it is obvious that the percentage rate for elderly Facebook users is very small.

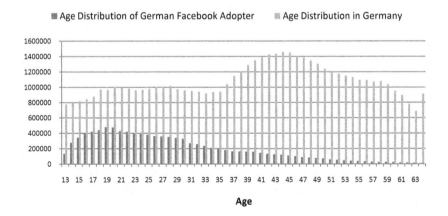

Figure 2:   Age distribution of Facebook users

These figures indicate that SNS in general are mostly used by people younger than 30 and that platforms aimed at elderly are used only by few people in relation to the posible number of users.

2.3 Digital Divide

Contrariwise to persons using SNS, people refusing such technologies, can get social problems through losing social contacts. This is one problematic consequence of the often discussed issue named Digital Divide.

The underlying question of the phenomenon Digital Divide is, whether people have access to internet or not. Afterwards, the scientific focus changed and age, income, rural residence, education, gender or race were studied together with their influence on non-usage of people. Along with it, researchers investigated not only non-adoption reasons but also differences in people's online skills and thus the ability to find effectively and efficiently information on the web (Hargittai). The latter is often called Second-Level Digital Divide or Digital Inequality and distinguishes self from Digital Divide by focusing not only on the question whether people have access to internet or not. Moreover, it focuses on skills and knowledge of people using several technologies such as computers, internet or SNS (Venkatesh 2008).

Lots of problems, which were discussed through the rise of ICT, as privacy issues, interface issues, a lack of incentives or too complex technologies for most of the households (e.g. Venkatesh 2008) bias elderly in a more serious manner than younger persons. It is not self-evident that each person had contact with modern ICT within their workplace or has friends, acquaintances or family members who can explain them how to handle each new application. Another important facet for elderly persons is their preference to sustain their habitual daily routine and their reluctance to change their way of life. If people had no contact with ICT like computers or social network sites, such a technology or application can change one's life in dramatically way. Because of this, especially the elderly people try to maintain their status quo (Lewin 1947) and burke new innovations. In this context, the extent of an inherit attitude towards changing the status quo has to be regarded as well (Bhattacherjee and Hikmet 2007; Bhattacherjee and Hikmet 2007; Laumer et al. 2010; Oreg 2003).

To overcome this problem in Germany, the Federal Government identified this issue and started initiatives to introduce elderly or inexperienced people to internet possibilities. Next to this, the program of the Federal Government also focuses on population groups with different backgrounds, women in rural areas or internet-interested people and thus takes account of the phenomenon Digital Inequality. Apart from the Federal Government, many other initiatives try to give elderly or unprivileged people an understanding of new and modern ICT. For example, the social network site Feierabend.de tries to address exactly this group of elderly people (50 years or older) and provides them a platform to stay in contact with friends, to enlarge their circle of friends or just to discuss topics which are important and interesting for elderly persons as acoustic hearing apparatus. Apart from that, this SNS throws light on privacy problems and alerts for tricksters and other potential traps.

Based on this general research background of digital inequality and SNS as well as the theoretical background of IT adoption in households, the following sections describes the used research model and design to investigate adoption of SNS by elderly people.

3 Research Model and Design

Within this section, our research model will be developed. Based on the *Model of Adoption of Technology in Households* (MATH); Venkatesh and Brown 2001; Brown and Venkatesh 2005), the influence of different constructs will be analyzed for adopters and non-adopters of SNS. Finally, the used data sample is provided and the research design will be explained.

3.1 Research Model

The general theoretical foundation for the presented research model is the MATH, which investigates the influence of Attitudinal, Control and Normative Beliefs on Behavioral Intention. With the help of this model, both adopters and non-adopters behavioral intention will be analyzed separately.

For both groups, the six hypotheses as arranged by Brown and Venkatesh (2001; 2005) will be adapted and analyzed for elderly people. Thereby, the hypotheses are:

> *H1: Utilitarian Outcomes (Attitudinal Beliefs) have a direct positive influence on Intention of elderly people.*

> *H2: Hedonic Outcomes (Attitudinal Beliefs) have a direct positive influence on Intention of elderly people.*

H3: Social Outcomes (Attitudinal Beliefs) have a direct positive influence on Intention of elderly people.

H4: Subjective Norm (Normative Belief) has a direct positive influence on Intention of elderly people.

H5: Perceived Ease of Use (Control Beliefs) has a direct positive influence on Intention of elderly people.

H6: Fear of Technology (Control Beliefs) has a direct negative influence on Intention of elderly people.

The research model is illustrated by Figure 3.

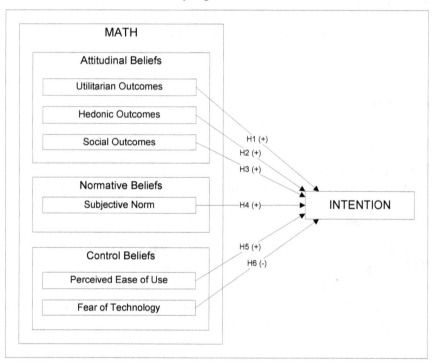

Figure 3:   Research Model

3.2 Research Design and Participants

For the evaluation of the research model data of SNS (non)-adoption was collected within a general study of IT usage. The aim of this study was to explain why people do (not) use particular online services even if they have access to the internet. Therefore, an online survey was conducted to collect empirical data. In order to reach people who are used to the internet in general and with different social background, demographics and knowledge background, this method seemed to be the most appropriate. Using this methodology and focusing on SNS as well as on elderly people within the study who are used to the internet and have a profile in an SNS or not could be researched.

Based on this data, SPSS Statistics 17.0 and Smart PLS (Ringle et al. 2005) were utilized to analyze the influence of the six MATH constructs on intention to use SNS. The evaluation did not include incomplete data samples. As the focus within this paper is to analyze the adoption and non-adoption behavior of elderly people data of 53 SNS non-adopters and 115 SNS adopters, older than 50 years, is the underlying for this research endeavor.

The demographic information, separated by the actual adoption behavior could be seen in Table 1. In both groups are more men than women additionally more participants are between 50 and 54 years old as people older than 55. Nonetheless, the annual income and the whole demographics of both groups are comparable.

Demographics of ...		115 Adopters	53 Non-Adopters
Gender	Men	72.2%	75.5%
	Women	27.8%	24.5%
Age	50 - 54	55.5%	54.5%
	55 - 59	32.3%	34.0%
	60 - 64	12.2%	11.5%
Annual Income	< 20 K	25.2%	34.0%
	20 - 25 K	7.8%	11.3%
	25 - 35 K	16.5%	11.3%
	35 - 45 K	16.5%	11.3%
	45 - 55 K	7.8%	9.4%
	55 - 65 K	7.0%	3.8%
	65 - 80 K	4.4%	5.7%
	>= 80 K	14.8%	13.2%

Table 1:   Research participants

4   Research Results

This section validates the research model for SNS adopters and non-adopters. Therefore, a measurement model and a structural model will be provided within the following two sections as we transferred our research model into a structural equation model and used Partial Least Squares for data analysis.

4.1 Measurement Model

Each of the seven constructs used – Social Outcomes, Hedonic Outcomes, Utilitarian Outcomes, Subjective Norm, Perceived Ease of Use, Fear of Technology and Intention – are measured with reflective indicators as in previous publications. Consequently, content validity, indicator reliability, construct reliability and discriminant validity have to be validated for each construct (Bagozzi 1979).

4.1.1   Content validity

While setting up the questionnaire, the aim was to refer to questions within the questionnaire, which were already used in empirical research by other researchers. However, following a recent discussion in IS research about the use of Fast Forms for empirical data collection (Chin et al. 2008) the item identified in prior research were converted to fast forms using semantic differentials and some of these questions had to be modified in order to fit the SNS context. The items used are illustrated at Table 2. These items have been pretested within the general study of IT usage (*anonymous*).

	Item	Question	Semantic Differentials		
Intention	INT-1	I plan ... use social network sites in the future.	not to use	...	to use
	INT-2	I intend ... social network sites this year.	not to use	...	to use
	INT-3	I will ... social network sites anymore.	not use		still use
	INT-4	I intend ... social network sites w for application processes	not to use		to use
SO	SO-1	The usage of social network sites ... my image.	decline	...	increase
	SO-2	People, who use social network sites, seem to be ... intelligent.	less	...	more
	SO-3	People of my social envirnment, who use social network sites, have a ... standing	bad	...	good
HO	HO-1	The usage of a social network site is ...	objectionable		entertaining
	HO-2	The usage of a social network site is ...	waste	...	exciting
	HO-3	The usage of a social network site is ...	unpleasant	...	enjoyable
	HO-4	The usage of a social network site is ...	boring	...	interesting
UO	UO-1	The usage of social network sites ... to achieve my objectives	complicates		faciliates
	UO-2	The usage of social network sites makes it ... ro achieve my objectives	more difficult	...	easier
	UO-3	All in all, the usage of a social network site is	useless	...	usefull
SN	SN-1	People, who have an influence on my behavior think that I should use social network sites.	totally disagree	...	totally agree
	SN-2	People, who are important for me think, that I should use social network sites.	totally disagree	...	totally agree
PEOU	PEOU-1	It seems to be ... to use social network sites.	very difficult	...	very easy
	PEOU-2	For me, it is ... to learn how to handle social network sites.	very difficult	...	very easy
	PEOU-3	All in all, it is ... to use social network sites.	very difficult	...	very easy
FOT	FOT-1	In my opinion, technologies change	very slow		very fast
	FOT-2	For me, it is ... to acclimaatize to new technologies and standards.	very difficult	...	very easy

Table 2:   Measurement items

4.1.2   Indicator reliability

The proportion of the variance of an indicator, which derives from the relevant latent variables, will be shown by the indicator reliability. Each item should have at least a greater loading than 0.4, so that item SO-2 has to be removed within the non-adopter case (Hulland 1999). For the rest, each value is greater than 0.7, whereby 50 per cent of the variance of a latent variable is explained by the used indicators (Carmines and Zeller 2008). All loadings have a significance level of p < 0.001 and are highly significant. This was calculated by using a bootstrap method with 5000 samples (Henseler et al. 2009).

	Item	Loading	Mean	AVE	CR	Latent Variable Correlation						
Intention	INT-1	0.971										
	INT-2	0.934										
	INT-3	0.970										
	INT-4	0.843	3.316	0,8666	0.9628	0,93091						
SO	SO-1	0.878										
	SO-2	0.901										
	SO-3	0.844	3.152	0,7645	0.9068	0,87436	0.5225					
HO	HO-1	0.828										
	HO-2	0.810										
	HO-3	0.981										
	HO-4	0.908	4.308	0,7587	0.9261	0,87103	0.5549	0.5711				
UO	UO-1	0.896										
	UO-2	0.893										
	UO-3	0.939	3.243	0,8268	0.9347	0,90929	0.6437	0.5892	0.6637			
SN	SN-1	0.975										
	SN-2	0.973	3.720	0,9485	0.9736	0,97391	0.5847	0.4234	0.5257	0.5753		
PEOU	PEOU-1	0.956										
	PEOU-2	0.945										
	PEOU-3	0.955	3.488	0,9061	0.9666	0,95189	0.4627	0.4953	0.5531	0.4455	0.4142	
FOT	FOT-1	0.887										
	FOT-2	0.845	3.605	0,7499	0.8570	0,86597	-0,0605	-0,1048	0.1563	0.078	-0,0046	0.2040
Note: All loadings are significant at p<0.001; Square Root of AVE is listed on diagonal by LVC												
Adopter												

Table 3:   Indicator reliability, construct reliability and discriminant validity for adopter

4.1.3   Construct reliability

Composite Reliability (CR) and Average Variance Extracted (AVE) were used to assess the quality at the construct level (Fornell and Larcker 1981). Therefore, each CR value should be over 0.7 and AVE should be higher than 0.5 (Bagozzi 1998). Both conditions are fulfilled for users and non-users as illustrated in Table 3 and Table 4

4.1.4 Discriminant validity

Discriminant validity describes the extent, to which measurement items differ from each other (Campell and Fiske 1959). In order to show this, the construct correlations should be smaller than the root of the corresponding AVE (Hulland 1999; Fornell and Larcker 1981). As Table 3 and Table 4 show, this criterion is fulfilled by the data collected for this study.

	Item	Loading	Mean	AVE	CR	Latent Variable Correlation						
Intention	INT-1	0.956										
	INT-2	0.958										
	INT-3	0.944										
	INT-4	0.895	2.176	0,8809	0,9673	0,93856						
SO	SO-1	0.808										
	SO-2											
	SO-3	0.874	2.984	0,7079	0,8288	0,84137	0.4551					
HO	HO-1	0.802										
	HO-2	0.952										
	HO-3	0.823										
	HO-4	0.934	3.651	0,7748	0,9319	0,88023	0.2223	0.5848				
UO	UO-1	0.907										
	UO-2	0.937										
	UO-3	0.942	2.591	0,8626	0,9496	0,92876	0.5380	0.7681	0.6659			
SN	SN-1	0.975										
	SN-2	0.957	2.818	0,9327	0,9652	0,96576	0.2977	0.4949	0.6786	0.5871		
PEOU	PEOU-1	0.946										
	PEOU-2	0.952										
	PEOU-3	0.977	2.737	0,9182	0.9712	0,95823	0.1994	0.6105	0.3312	0.5257	0.1884	
FOT	FOT-1	0.752										
	FOT-2	0.927	3.433	0,7123	0.0500	0,84398	-0,425	-0,2267	-0,217	-0,347	-0,4069	0.0759
Note: All loadings are significant at p<0.001; Square Root of AVE is listed on diagonal by LVC												
Non-Adopter												

Table 4:   Indicator reliability, construct reliability and discriminant validity
             for non-adopter

As a consequence, it is possible to conclude that the measurement model has a high validity.

4.2 Structural model

After validating the measurement model, the structural model will be evaluated. In order to do this, the coefficient of determination (R^2) and the significance levels of the path coefficients (Chin 1998) need to be observed.

Figure 4 shows that in the adopter case, 52.9 per cent of the variance of Intention can be explained by the six used constructs. Within the non-adopter case, 40.3 per cent of the variance is clarified. According to Chin (1998) both models provide an acceptable goodness of fit. For non-adopters, two significant relationships can be confirmed. The first one is the negative influence of Fear of Technology on Intention and a positive impact of Utilitarian Outcomes on the dependent variable.

On the other side, these two relationships were also significant for the group of adopters. Apart from this, two more impacts were identified. These are the influence of Subjective Norm and Perceived Ease of Use on Intention. Only Social and Hedonic Outcomes seem to have no effect on Intention for both elderly adopters and non-adopters of SNS.

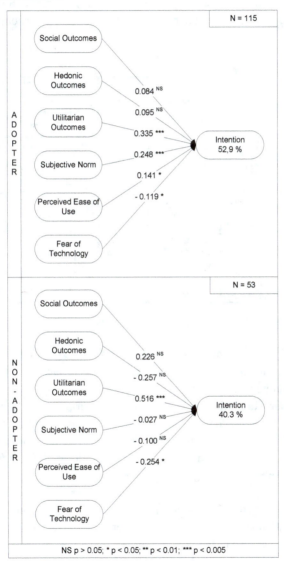

Figure 4:   Structural Model

4.3 Group Comparison

Next to the previous results like the correlation between intention and each construct, figure 4 represents the strength of effect for each construct and both groups. For adopters and non-adopters, the construct Utilitarian Outcomes has the highest impact on intention. Apart from that Fear of Technology plays an important role for non-adopters, whereas for adopters, this aspect is only of little importance.

Whether comparisons of means are investigated, only the aspect Social Outcomes is not significantly different for both adopter groups. The responsiveness of all other constructs is significantly different.

Inputfactor	Group	Correlation with Intention	Strength of Effect	Mean	Comparison of means		
					Levene-Test & Homogeneity of Variance	T	Sig.
Intention	Adopter	-	-	3.316	Yes (0.520)	5.635	0.000
	Non-Adopter	-	-	2.176			
Social Outcomes	Adopter	Not significant	1.6%	3.152	Yes (0.124)	1.529	0.133
	Non-Adopter	Not significant	2.9%	2.984			
Hedonic Outcomes	Adopter	Not significant	1.6%	4.308	Yes (0.322)	2.561	0.013
	Non-Adopter	Not significant	2.7%	3.651			
Utilitarian Outcomes	Adopter	Significant	14.1%	3.243	Yes (0.532)	3.622	0.001
	Non-Adopter	Significant	13.1%	2.591			
Subjective Norm	Adopter	Significant	7.9%	3.720	Yes (0.302)	2.683	0.010
	Non-Adopter	Not significant	0.0%	2.818			
Perceived Ease of Use	Adopter	Significant	0.4%	3.488	Yes (0.420)	3.596	0.001
	Non-Adopter	Not significant	3.1%	2.737			
Fear of Technology	Adopter	Significant	2.3%	3.605	Yes (0.150)	2.064	0.042
	Non-Adopter	Significant	11.4%	3.433			

Table 5:   Strength of Effect & Comparison of means

Finally, the significance of the path coefficients was compared for adopters and non-adopters using the proposed procedure by Chin and Dibbern [69]. While doing so, it can be identified, that all paths are highly different for both adopters and non-adopters. In particular, for non-adopters Fear of Technology has an higher mean value for non-adopters and the mean of the generated bootstrapped samples is significantly different from adopters. Moreover, for Utilitarian Outcomes the mean value is higher for non-adopters and significant different from adopters. For adopters, Subjective Norm and Perceived Ease of Use has a higher mean for adopters and is significant different from non-adopters. In terms of the two insignificant paths in both samples Social Outcomes has a higher mean for non-adopters and Hedonic Outcomes for adopters. Both are significantly different between the two groups tested. The comparison of path coefficient is illustrated by Table 6.

Path	Group	Mean Value	Standard Deviation	Comparison of Path Coefficient		
				Levene-Test	T	Sig.
SO --> INT	Adopter	0.103	0.068	No (0.000)	17.088	0.000
	Non-Adopter	0.223	0.142			
HO --> INT	Adopter	0.112	0.078	No (0.000)	-43.454	0.000
	Non-Adopter	-0.281	0.182			
UO --> INT	Adopter	0.349	0.098	No (0.000)	17.866	0.000
	Non-Adopter	0.534	0.210			
SN --> INT	Adopter	0.244	0.090	No (0.000)	-57.252	0.000
	Non-Adopter	-0.164	0.131			
PEOU --> INT	Adopter	0.148	0.079	No (0.000)	-48.119	0.000
	Non-Adopter	-0.130	0.102			
FOT --> INT	Adopter	-0.118	0.065	No (0.000)	-27.812	0.000
	Non-Adopter	-0.280	0.079			

Table 6:   Comparison of Path Coefficient

4.4 Limitations

This paper is a first try to analyze the intention of adopters and – separately – non-adopters within the MATH for elderly persons. Consequently, the results cannot be generalized limitless. First of all, the presented results derive from one online survey, so that only persons with internet access could participate. It is conceivable that the elderly people without internet access cannot participate and might show other reasons and therefore, other correlations which lead to a non-adoption of SNS. On the other hand, it was important to ensure that each SNS non-adopter knows SNS and the involved advantages and disadvantages. This issue was addressed with different questions such as "I know the possibility to engage in social network sites like Facebook", "Advantages of social network sites are (participants could chose between different items or 'I don't know')" or "The first time I heard about social network sites was in (date)". Consequently, each non-adopter analyzed within this paper knows about SNS but does not use it. By collecting data in another way, it could be more problematic to separate between adopters, non-adopters and non-adopters which do not know about the existence of SNS.

Another crucial aspect within this publication is that only one technology was analyzed. Although Brown (2008) advised using SNS when household adaption should be investigated, the model has to be confirmed by other researchers observing other technologies. The same will be true for the underlying culture. Dependent on the cultural background, the model could offer different correlations (Gallivan and Srite 2005).

The last restriction is the relative small number of SNS non-adopters (N = 53) which participated. Considering, that the impact of six constructs on Intention was investigated, 60 data samples should have been the underlying basis (Chin and Newsted 2000). By increasing the data sample up to the crucial threshold (by adding non-users which do not know SNS or by not eliminating incomplete samples), the results were still the same.

5   Discussion and Future Research

In general, the findings of this paper show, that elderly people's adoption of SNS is determined by other perceptions and constructs than their non-adoption of SNS. For adopters a significant impact of Normative Beliefs measured as Subjective Norm, Perceived Ease of Use as a part of Control Beliefs on Intention to use SNS could be observed. Contrary, for non-adopters these perceptions have no significant influence on their intention. Nonetheless, these results do not implicate that non-adopters regard new IS as simple to use. By regarding the comparison of means, non-adopters consider the handling of SNS more cumbersome to use than people adopting SNS. The same could be monitored for Subjective Norm. Elderly non-adopters sense that the perceived pressure to adopt social network sites applied by their circle of friends and acquaintances is less than by the social environment of adopters. Future research could consider whether elderly SNS non-adopters have a smaller circle of friends or analyze whether their friends are also SNS non-adopters. Taking into account the Utilitarian Outcomes, which is the most important factor influencing the Intention, reveal that elderly non-adopters face SNS and their possibilities as less useful than elderly adopters.

Most of the people using such modern ways to communicate just use it to stay in contact with friends, they know from the offline world, and do not try to enlarge their circle of friends by finding new contacts with equal interests. This phenomenon is called Offline-to-Online paradigm (Ross et al. 2009) and reveals that SNS users first know people from school, job, leisure activities or other activities based in the offline world and afterwards add these people in online communities to their friend lists. As the example of feierabend.de illustrates, SNS for elderly people are designed to enable social exchange between their users in both cases, known form the offline world or not. Therefore, another opportunity for future research is to analyze whether the discussed offline-to-online paradigm also holds for elderly people.

Moreover, other research activities identified enjoyment as the major predictor for using social networks whereas Usefulness is just less relevant (Rosen and Sherman 2006). The findings of this research cannot confirm this totally for elderly people. Our research indicates that people, which are older than 50 years, emphasize utilitarian facets of social networks and regard hedonic outcomes as less relevant. Nonetheless, elderly SNS adopters report having significantly more fun in using SNS than non-adopters, but in both cases, no significant influence on the usage decision could be observed. This could be explained by Phang et al. (2009) who investigated the individual behavior in online communities depending on the distinct usage causes. They differentiated between knowledge seeking and knowledge contribution and support that usefulness is essential for people searching knowledge. Since, it is likelier that younger persons use the internet and social network sites to play games or funny quizzes, elderly people will utilize platforms as Facebook or feierabend.de as a source of information (for example about friends or acquaintances) whereby the usefulness is a more crucial issue.

Another important difference between adopters and non-adopters of SNS is the perceived Fear of Technology. In both cases, an influence on Intention could be monitored as well as significant unequal means. Thereby especially non-adopters have problems to engage with new technologies as computers, internet or social networks. For this reason, Fear of Technology has a strong impact on the decision for non-adopters. For these anxiously elderly people, new initiatives should be initiated to make SNS and other technologies accessible to them. The Digital Divide can be addressed, if these persons could be prepared for using new technologies. Nonetheless, this is not only a challenge for the Federal Government, to ensure that people can use modern ICT at home, it is also essential to handle these technologies within organizational contexts. If this group of people, who reject to adopt new technologies, is not able to deal with them or if they fear them, they will hinder the operating schedule. This is clearly reflected by Luftman and Kempaiah (2009), which ranked the management of change as the sixth most critical issue for Chief Information Officers. This also comprises IS modifications, but these can only be successful if employees are able to engage in new situations (Laumer et al. 2010) and are not afraid of IS. The latter could diminished by offering regular IS courses and IT trainings by the organization and thus, organizations could create competitive advantages. Feierabend.de has implemented an extended support for elderly people (e.g. offering services to scan pictures, hotline activities, extended explanation of services, etc.) Summing up, it is essential to give people an understanding of IT and IS because of both, to maintain a balanced economy – or sustainability at the corporate level – and from a sociological point of view to reduce the Digital Divide and Digital Inequality.

In general, regarding the MATH the results of this research have some implications for the understanding of technology adoption in a private environment. By focusing on people older than 50 and by distinguishing between adopters and non-adopters the results indicate that within the group of people older than 50 the importance of each factor within the MATH is different for adopters and non-adopters. Elderly adopters are mainly driven by Utilitarian Outcomes, Subjective Norm, Perceived Ease of Use and Fear of Technology. In contrast elderly non-adopters are mainly influenced by Utilitarian Outcomes, and Fear of Technology. Moreover, regarding significant difference in the mean of each construct the results indicate that Social Outcomes, Hedonic Outcomes, Utilitarian Outcomes, Subjective Norm and Perceived Ease of Use have a higher acceptance by adopters than by non-adopters. In contrast non-adopters are more afraid in terms of Fear of Technology. In addition, regarding the strength of effect the results show that for adopters and non-adopters the strongest effect can be observed for Utilitarian Outcomes as well as for Fear of Technology. In general, these results point out that the relevance of each antecedent is different for adopters and non-adopters.

Apart from that by considering the R^2 of both adopters and non-adopters it is obvious that the explanatory power is higher for adopters than for non-adopters. Consequently it would be quite conceivable to develop a model which explains – in particular – the non-adoption behavior. Therefore, first attempts which discussed such an approach could be found in the literature (Laumer et al. 2009). Nonetheless, it would be necessary to identify different reasons leading to non-adoption, as a status quo bias (Kim and Kankanhalli 2009), resistance (Laumer et al. 2010; Bhattacherjee and Hikmet 2007; Bhattacherjee and Hikmet 2007) or other inhibitors (Cenfetelli 2004) as fear or threats.

Nonetheless this research shows that the MATH model is also valid for elderly people. Although, lots of future research will be necessary to understand the behavior of the elderly people altogether. This research was just a first attempt to enlighten factors influencing adoption and non-adoption of the elderly people.

In terms of the methodology used it could be evaluated that the proposed Fast Form approach (Chin et al. 2008) is applicable to the MATH and empirical studies using MATH as all items are statistically useable for the model evaluation.

By analyzing the domain social network sites it is interesting that Hedonic Outcomes as fun provided by the platform have no impact on the intention. Given that fun is no significant impact factor for elderly people it is probable that these people for example do not play online social games in SNS. Thereby researchers could analyze which SNS services and applications (e.g. enlarge circle of friends, stay in contact with friends, communicate, exchange pictures or videos, have fun by playing online games) are utilized by which SNS users. In doing so it could be investigated which reasons or perceptions are responsible for such a SNS behavior. Furthermore, the usefulness of social network sites is essential for people to register in such communities. Consequently it would be interesting to know which services are explicitly most important for elderly people. Apart from that, the correlation between Perceived Ease of Use and Intention discloses a certain level of PC and internet skills.

In terms of practical implications, this research shows that adopters and non-adopters are different regarding their motivation to adopt or not to adopt SNS. Given that it is important to motivate elderly people to participate in those networks one should focus on describing the Utilitarian Outcomes and by allaying the fear of technologies. As these two aspects are the most important perceptions for those who do not want to use SNS in the future. In contrast those who have experience with SNS point out that they perceive positive Utilitarian Outcomes, that the platforms are easy to use and do not perceive as much as non-adopters a fear due to the technology. In addition, their normative beliefs encourage them to continue using SNS. Therefore, it is important for SNS providers for elderly people to point out the usefulness of their platforms as feierabend.de does by establishing regional groups and supporting offline activities of the users. Moreover, the Fear of Technology can be addressed as feierabend.de does by explicitly focusing on explaining and supporting the usage of the platform. This is a first step towards an age-sensitive design of online services as demanded by Pak et al. (2009), which reveals that online services for elderly people should be connected with offline activities in order to support the use and usefulness of these platforms.

6   Conclusion

Why do elderly people adopt or not adopt SNS, is the main research question of this research. By using MATH the results indicate that adopters are mainly driven by Utilitarian Outcomes, Normative Beliefs, Perceived Ease of Use and Fear of Technology and non-adopters by Utilitarian Outcomes and Fear of Technology. As a consequence the research provides evidence that beside the moderator age within the math it is important to consider the difference between adopters and non-adopters within the group of elderly persons as well.

References

Ajzen, I. "The theory of planned behavior," *Organizational Behavior and Human Decision Processes* (50:2), 1991, pp. 179–211.

Ajzen, I., and Fishbein, M.. *"Understanding attitudes and predicting social behavior"*, Englewood Cliffs, NJ: Prentice-Hall, 1980.

Azari, R., and Pick, J. B.. "Technology and society: socioeconomic influences on technological sectors for United States counties," *International Journal of Information Management* (25:1), 2005, pp. 21–37.

Bagozzi, R. P. "The Role of Measurement in Theory Construction and Hypothesis Testing: Toward a Holistic Model," in *Conceptual and theoretical developments in marketing*, Ferrell et al. (ed.), Chicago, Ill, 1979.

Bagozzi, R. P., and Yi, Y. "On the Evaluation of Structural Equation Models," *Journal of the Academy of Marketing Science* (16:1), 1998, pp. 74–94.

Bhattacherjee, A., and Hikmet, N. "Physicians' resistance toward healthcare information technology: a theoretical model an empirical test," *European Journal of Information Systems* (16:6), 2007, pp. 725–737.

Bhattacherjee, A., and Hikmet, N. "Physicians' Resistance toward Healthcare Information Technologies: A Dual-Factor Model," *Hawaii International Conference on System Sciences*, 2007.

Bhattacherjee, A., and Sanford, C. "Influence Processes for Information Technology Acceptance: An Elaboration Likelihood Model," *MIS Quarterly* (30:4), 2006, pp. 805–825.

BitKom. *30 Millionen Deutsche sind Mitglieder in Communitys*. http://www.bitkom.org/de/themen/36444_62772.aspx. Accessed 21 August 2010.

Blackwell, A. F. "End-user Developers at Home," *Communications of the ACM* (47:9), 2004, pp. 65–66.

Brown, S. A. "Household Technology Adoption, Use, and Impacts: Past, Present, and Future," *Information Systems Frontiers* (10:4), 2008, pp. 397–402.

Brown, S. A., and Venkatesh, V. "Model of Adoption of Technology in Households: A Baseline Model Test and Extension Incorporating Household Life Cycle," *MIS Quarterly* (29:3), 2005, pp. 399–426.

Campell, D. T., and Fiske, D. W. "Convergent and discriminant validation by the multitrait-multimethod matrix," *Psychological Bulletin* (56:2), 1959, pp. 81–105.

Carmines, E. G., and Zeller, R. A. *Reliability and validity assessment*, Newbury Park, Calif.: Sage Publ., 2008.

Cenfetelli, R. T. "Inhibitors and Enablers as Dual Factor Concepts in Technology Usage," *Journal of the Association for Information Systems* (5:11-12), 2004, pp. 472–492.

Chin, W. W. "The Partial Least Squares Approach to Structural Equation Modeling," in *Modern methods for business research*, G. A. Marcoulides (ed.), Mahwah, N.J., London: Lawrence Erlbaum, 1998.

Chin, W. W., and Dibbern, J. "An Introduction to a Permutation Based Procedure for Multi-Group PLS Analysis: Results of Tests of Differences on Simulated Data and a Cross Cultural Analysis of the Sourcing of Information System Services Between Germany and the USA," in *Handbook of Partial Least Squares. Springer Handbooks of Computational Statistics. Concepts, Methods and Applications*, Vinzi et al. (ed.), s.l.: Springer-Verlag, 2010.

Chin, W. W., and Newsted, P. R. "Structural Equation Modeling analysis with Small Samples Using Partial Least Squares," in *Statistical strategies for small sample research*, R. H. Hoyle (ed.), Thousand Oaks, Calif.: Sage Publ, 2000.

Chin W. W., Johnson, N.; Schwarz, A. "A fast form approach to measuring technology acceptance and other constructs," *MIS Quarterly* (32:4), 2008, pp. 687–703.

Choudrie, J., and Dwivedi, Y. K. "Investigating Factors Influencing Adoption of Broadband in the household," *Journal of Computer Information Systems* (46:4), 2006, pp. 25–34.

Choudrie, J., and Lee, H. J. "Broadband development in South Korea: institutional and cultural factors," *European Journal of Information Systems* (13:2), 2004, pp. 103–114.

COMPASS HEADING. *Nutzerzahlen Sozialer Netzwerke Januar 2010*. http://www.compass-heading.de/cms/nutzerzahlen-sozialer-netzwerke-januar-2010/. Accessed 21 August 2010.

Correa, T.; Hinsley, A. W.; de Zúniga, H. G. "Who interacts on the Web?: The intersection of users' personality and social media use," *Computers in Human Behavior* (26), 2010, pp. 247–253.

Dewan, S., and Riggins, F. J. "The Digital Divide: Current and Future Research Directions," *Journal of the Association for Information Systems* (6:13), 2005.

Dwivedi, Y. K.; Choudrie, J.; Brinkman, W.-P. "Development of a survey instrument to examine consumer adoption of broadband," *Industrial Management & Data Systems* (106:5), 2006, pp. 700–718.

Eckhardt, A., Laumer S., Weitzel, T. "Who influences whom? Analyzing workplace referents' social influence on IT adoption and non-adoption," *Journal of Information Technology* (24:1), 2009, pp. 11–24.

Ellison, N.; Steinfield, C.; Lampe, C. A. "The Benefits of Facebook "Friends:" Social Capital and College Students' Use of Online Social Network Sites," *Journal of Computer-Mediated Communication* (12:4), 2007, pp. 1143–1168.

Enns, H. G., Huff, S. L., Higgins, C. A. "CIO Lateral Influence Behaviors: Gaining Peers' Commitment to Strategic Information Systems," *MIS Quarterly* (27:1), 2003, pp. 155–176.

Facebook. *Statistics*. http://www.facebook.com/press/info.php?statistics. Accessed 1 July 2010.

Ferrell, O. C., Brown, S. W., Lamb, C. W. (ed.). *Conceptual and theoretical developments in marketing*, Chicago, Ill, 1979.

Fishbein, M., and Ajzen, I. "Belief, attitude, intention and behavior. An introduction to theory and research," *Reading, Mass,* 1975.

Fornell, C., and Larcker, D. F. "Evaluating Structural equation models with unobservable variables and measurement error," *Journal of Marketing Research* (18:1), 1981, pp. 39–50.

Gallivan M.J., and Srite, M. "Information Technology and Culture: Identifying Fragmented and Holistic Perspectives of Culture," *Information & Organization* (15:2), 2005, pp. 295–338.

Hargittai, E. *Second-Level Digital Divide: Differences in People's Online Skills.* http://www.firstmonday.dk/issues/issue7_4/hargittai. Accessed 1 July 2010.

Henseler, J., Ringle, C. M., Sinkovics Rudolf R. "The use of partial least squares path modeling in international marketing," *Advances in International Marketing* (20), 2009, pp. 277–319.

Hirschheim, R., and Newman, M. "Information Systems and User Resistance: Theory and Practice," *The Computer Journal* (31:5), 1988, pp. 398–408.

Holznagel, B. "Frequenzeffizienz und Rundfunkspektrum," *MMR* (4), 2008, pp. 207–215.

Hoyle, R. H. (ed.) *Statistical strategies for small sample research*, Thousand Oaks, Calif.: Sage Publ., 2000.

Hulland, J. S. "Use of partial least squares (PLS) in strategic management research: A review of four recent studies," *Strategic Management Journal* (20:2), 1999, pp. 195–204.

Hutter, T. *Facebook Demographische Zahlen der Länder > 1 Mio.* www.thomashutter.com, 2010.

Jiang, J. J., Muhanna, W. A., Klein, G. "User resistance and strategies for promoting acceptance across system types," *Information and Management* (37:3), 2000, pp. 25–36.

Johansen, R., and Swigart, R. "Upsizing the individual in the downsized organization. Managing in the wake of reengineering, globalization, and overwhelming technological change," *Reading, Mass,* 1996.

Jones, Q., Ravid, G., Rafaeli, S. "Information Overload and the Message Dynamics of Online Interaction Spaces: A theoretical model and empirical exploration," *Information Systems Research* (15:2), 2004, pp. 194–210.

Joos, J. G. "Social media: New frontiers in hiring and recruiting," *Employment Relations Today* (35:1), 2008, pp. 51–59.

Khan, Z., and Jarvenpaa, S. L. "Exploring temporal coordination of events with Facebook.com.," *Journal of Information Technology* (25:2), 2010, pp. 137–151.

Kim, H. W., and Kankanhalli, A. "Investigating User Resistance to Information Systems Implementation: A Status Quo Bias Perspective," *MIS Quarterly* (33:3), 2009, pp. 567–582.

Kubicek, H., and Welling, S. "Vor einer digitalen Spaltung in Deutschland? Annäherung an ein verdecktes Problem von wirtschafts- und gesellschaftspolitischer Brisanz," *Medien und Kommunikationswissenschaft* (48:4), 2000, pp. 497–517.

Lapointe, L., and Rivard, S. "A Multilevel Model of Resistance to Information Technology Implementation," *MIS Quarterly* (29:3), 2005, pp. 461–491.

Laumer S., Maier C., Eckhardt E. "Towards an Understanding of an Individual's Resistance to Use an IS - Empirical Examinations and Directions for Future Research," *DIGIT 2009 PROCEEDINGS,* 2009.

Laumer S., Maier C., Eckhardt E. "Why do they resist? - An empirical analysis of an individual's personality trait resistance regarding the adoption of new information systems," *Pretoria, South Africa,* 2010.

Lewin, K. "Frontiers in Group Dynamics: Concept, Method and Reality in Social Science; Social Equilibria and Social Change," *Human Relations* (1:1), 1947, pp. 5–41.

Lewis, K., Kaufman, J., Gonzales, M., Wimmer, A., Christakis, N. "Taste, Ties, and Time: A new social network dataset using Facebook.com," *Social Networks* (30:4), 2008, pp. 330–342.

Lewis, K., Kaufman, J., Christakis, N. "The Taste for Privacy: An Analysis of College Student Privacy Settings in an Online Social Network," *Journal of Computer-Mediated Communication* (14:1), 2008, pp. 79–100.

Luftman, J., Kempaiah, R., Rigoni E. H. "Key Issues for IT Executives 2008," *MIS Quarterly Executive* (8:3), 2009, pp. 151–159.

Marcoulides, G. A. (ed.) *Modern methods for business research,* Mahwah, N.J. , London: Lawrence Erlbaum, 1998.

Markus, M. L. "Power, Politics, and MIS Implementation," *Communications of the ACM* (26:6), 1983, pp. 430–444.

Mayer, A., and Puller, S. "The Old Boy (and Girl) Network: Social network formation on university campuses," *Journal of Public Economics* (92:1-2), 2008, pp. 329–347.

Mertens, P. "Fehlschläge bei IT-Großprojekten der öffentlichen Verwaltung - ein Beitrag zur Misserfolgsforschung in der Wirtschaftsinformatik," *Working Paper,* 2008.

Moore, G. A. *Crossing the chasm. Marketing and selling high-tech products to mainstream customers,* New York: HarperBusiness, 1999.

Norman, D. A. "Things that make us smart. Defending human attributes in the age of the machine," *Reading, Mass,* 1999.

Oreg, S. "Resistance to Change: Developing an Individual Differences Measure," *Journal of Applied Psychology* (88:4), 2003, pp. 680–693.

Pak, R., Price, M., Thatcher, J. B.. "Age-Sensitive Design of Online Health Information: Comparative Usability Study," *Journal of Medical Internet Research* (11:4), 2009.

Phang, C. W., Kankanhalli, A., Sabherwal, R.. "Usability and Sociability in Online Communities," *Journal of the Association for Information Systems* (10:10), 2009, pp. 721–747.

Raacke, J., and Bonds-Raacke, J. "MySpace and Facebook: Applying the Uses and Gratifications Theory to Exploring Friend-Networking Sites," *CyperPsychology & Behavior* (11:2), 2008, pp. 169–174.

Ringle et al. "SmartPLS, 2.0 (beta)," 2005.

Rosen, P., and Sherman, P. "Hedonic Information Systems: Acceptance of Social Networking Websites," *AMCIS 2006 Proceedings,* 2006.

Ross, C., Orr, E. S., Sisic, M., Arseneault, J. M., Simmering, M. G., Orr, R. R. "Personality and motivations associated with Facebook use," *Computers in Human Behavior* (25:2), 2009, pp. 578–586.

studiVZ. *Data and Facts*. http://www.studivz.net/l/about_us/1/. Accessed 14 July 2010.

Subrahmanyam, K., Reich, S. M., Waechter, N., Espinoza, G. "Online and offline social networks: Use of social networking sites by emerging adults," *Journal of Applied Developmental Psychology* (29:6), 2008, pp. 420–433.

TNS Infratest. "(N)Onliner Atlas: Eine Topographie des digitalen Grabens durch Deutschland: Nutzung und Nichtnutzung des Internets, Strukturen und regionale Verteilung," *TNS Infratest Juni,* 2009.

Valenzuela, S., Park, N., Kee. K. F. "Is there social capital in a social network site? Facebook use, and college students' life satisfaction, trust, and participation," *Journal of Computer-Mediated Communication* (14:4), 2009, pp. 875–901.

Venkatesh, A. "Digital home technologies and transformation of households," *Information Systems Frontiers* (10:4), 2008, pp. 391–395.

Venkatesh, V., and Brown, S. A. "A Longitudinal Investigation of Personal Computers in Homes: Adoption Determinants and Emerging Challenges," *MIS Quarterly* (25:1), 2001, pp. 71–102.

Venkatesh, V., Morris, M. G., Davis, G. B., Davis, F. D. "User Acceptance of Information Technology: Toward a unified View," *MIS Quarterly* (27:3), 2003, pp. 425–478.

Vinzi, V., Chin, W. W., Henseler, J., Wang, H. (ed.). *Handbook of Partial Least Squares. Springer Handbooks of Computational Statistics. Concepts, Methods and Applications*, s.l.: Springer-Verlag, 2010.

Walther, J. B., Van der Heide, B., Kim, S.-Y., Westerman, D., Tong, S. T. "The Role of Friends' Appearance and Behavior on Evaluations of Individuals on Facebook: Are We Known by the Company We Keep?," *Human Communication Research* (34:1), 2008, pp. 28–49.

Wege ins Netz. *Der Wettbewerb für mehr digitale Kompetenz.* http://www.bmwi.de/BMWi/Navigation/Technologie-und-Innovation/Informationsgesellschaft/internet-erfahren,did=339642.html. Accessed 21 August 2010.

Weitzel T., Eckhardt, A., Laumer S. "A Framework for Recruiting IT Talent: Lessons from Siemens," *MIS Quarterly Executive* (8:4), 2009, pp. 175–189.

Wiener, L. R. "Digital woes. Why we should not depend on software," *Reading, Mass,* 1993 .

Williams, M. D., Dwivedi, Y. K., Lal, B., Schwarz, A. "Contemporary trends and issues in IT adoption and diffusion research," *Journal of Information Technology* (24:1), 1990, pp. 1–10.

Design Science Research and the Grounded Theory Method: Characteristics, Differences, and Complementary Uses[1]

Dr. Robert Wayne Gregory

Chair of Electronic Finance and Digital Markets | University of Göttingen |
Platz der Göttinger Sieben 5 | 37073 Göttingen, Germany
gregory@wiwi.uni-goettingen.de

1 Introduction

The information systems (IS) research community is characterized by a large diversity of research approaches and topics. Although empirical quantitative research approaches dominate (Orlikowski et al. 1991), new research strategies are on the rise. Two research strategies that have received increasing scholarly attention recently are design science research (DSR) and the grounded theory method (GTM). For example, the European Journal of Information Systems (EJIS) recently published a special issue on DSR edited by Baskerville (2008). In addition, there is a call for papers by the same journal for a special issue on the GTM which will appear in the near future. Leading scholars that are very familiar with either one of these research strategies are in the editorial board of some of the leading journals (e.g., Alan Hevner and Juhani Iivari are senior editors at MIS Quarterly and Richard Baskerville is editor-in-chief at EJIS) and new special interest groups are emerging (e.g., the Association of IS special interest group on grounded theory). Despite the fact that both research strategies are not new, they have something in common: They both have become popular in IS research only recently while originating from related fields (GTM from sociology and DSR from engineering and architecture). Hence, there is a need for IS scholars to deal with these research strategies to enhance our understanding how they can yield new findings in the study of IS phenomena.

---

[1] Another version of this paper appeared as: Robert W. Gregory, "Design Science Research and the Grounded Theory Method: Characteristics, Differences, and Complementary Uses", *Proceedings of the 18th European Conference on Information System,* ECIS; Pretoria, South Africa, Category: Proceedings Reference No. 2010-15.

A. Heinzl et al. (eds.), *Theory-Guided Modeling and Empiricism in Information Systems Research*, DOI 10.1007/978-3-7908-2781-1_6, © Springer-Verlag Berlin Heidelberg 2011

Comparing different research strategies can help us to better understand and differentiate them and hence, might provide new ideas how they can be combined with
each other in a complementary way within one single research project. IS researchers have called for a more pluralist research tradition in IS (Mingers 2001).
There are some IS studies that critically compare DSR with other research approaches, for example with action research (AR). Some studies find similarities
between the two strategies (e.g., Järvinen 2007), while others find differences
(e.g., Baskerville et al. 2009, Iivari et al. 2009). DSR has also been compared
directly with the GTM. For example, Goldkuhl (2004) offers an approach how to
use techniques of the GTM in a DSR project. He presents three different types of
grounding, internal, empirical, and theoretical grounding, that can enhance a DSR
project to generate grounded practical knowledge. However, the author does not
link his ideas explicitly to the GTM and bases his arguments upon myths such as
the one that the GTM involves purely inductive reasoning from empirical data and
does not permit the inclusion of other knowledge sources (e.g., extant literature) in
the theory building process (see Urquhart & Fernandez (2006) for a discussion of
myths about the GTM). Another study that compares these two research strategies
finds that both research strategies complement each other well (Holmström et al.
2009). In particular, they develop a framework how DSR as an exploratory research approach can be complemented by a second research cycle including the
development of substantive and formal theory (which is the focus of GTM) to
make a contribution to the knowledge base besides focusing entirely on the problem solution and the information technology (IT) artifact. While the paper must be
acknowledged as the first major contribution towards a pluralistic research design
that integrates design science with behavioral science, one limitation of this paper
is that the GTM is classified as an explanatory research method while in fact it is
an exploratory theory-generating research method (Glaser 1978, Stebbins 2001).

In summary, while some IS scholars have made attempts to compare DSR with
GTM and even explore complementary uses, there is a lack of understanding and
consensus concerning the exact characteristics of both research strategies and how
they are similar or different from one another. Developing a more precise understanding thereof provides us with the identification of complementary uses and
serves as a guide for IS researchers pursuing a more pluralistic research approach.
Hence, the focus of this paper is the comparison of DSR with the GTM to lay the
foundation for a more intensive scholarly debate in IS about possible complementary uses in pluralist research projects and possible pitfalls or risks.

The remainder of this paper is structured as follows. The following two sections
present the main characteristics of DSR and the GTM. Thereby, it is important to
notice that the characteristics are derived inductively from reviewing existing
design science and grounded theory works and that they do not represent the au-

thor's view of the most appropriate characteristics that either research approach should have. We discuss the differences between the two approaches in the fourth section. Finally, I conclude with a discussion of the implications for IS research and possible complementary uses.

2   Characteristics of Design Science Research (DSR)

The focal research attention in DSR is given to the 'design' of artificial artifacts (i.e., IT artifacts) and creating something new that does not yet exist. Hence, design is both a process (set of activities) of 'creating something new' and a product (i.e., the artifact that results out of this process) (Walls et al. 1992). In other words, design is both a verb and a noun. Hence, we must consider different types of design processes and design outcomes or artifacts. Besides distinguishing between build and evaluate in the design process, which we will discuss in the next section, different types of design outputs (i.e., artifacts) have been identified in the literature. The relevant artifacts are either constructs, models, methods, instantiations, or a combination thereof (March et al. 1995). Concerning the evaluation of design artifacts, this categorization can serve as a guideline with the goal to assess the utility or overall quality of the designed artifact (i.e., construct, model, method, instantiation) to solve the problem that was formulated in the outset of the research process. The following table provides the reader with an overview over the four different types of design artifacts and their definitions (March, et al. 1995).

Design Artifact	Definition based on March & Smith (1995)
Constructs	...or concepts form the vocabulary of a domain. They constitute a conceptualization used to describe problems within the domain and to specify their solutions.
Model	...is a set of propositions or statements expressing relationships among constructs. In design activities, models represent situations as problem and solution statements.
Method	...is a set of steps (an algorithm or guideline) used to perform a task. Methods are based on a set of underlying constructs (language) and a representation (model) of the solution space.
Instantiation	...is the realization of an artifact in its environment. IS research instantiates both specific IS and tools that address various aspect of designing information systems.

Table 1:   Four different types of design artifacts

Elaborating on the above mentioned design 'process' more in detail, it may be distinguished between design research, which deals with the IT artifact creation, and design science, which is more about generating new scholarly insights. Prior DSR has been criticized for failing short regarding the latter (Hevner et al. 2004). In summary, I derive the following characteristic of DSR:

> DSR-1: The primary focus in a DSR project is mostly given to the design research part (i.e., the creation of an IT artifact), as opposed to the design science part (i.e., generating new knowledge).

The DSR activity itself can be described as "the proper study of those who are concerned with the artificial is the way in which that adaptation of means to environments is brought about--and central to that is the process of design itself" (Simon 1996). Simon himself labelled this the 'science of design' which is used interchangeably in the literature with the term 'design science'.

Mainly two different types of design processes have been distinguished that are deeply intertwined with each other. The first important design process is the sequence of activities to produce 'something new', an innovative product. In this process, the design artifact is built. The second important design process involves the evaluation of the created artifact to provide feedback and generate new knowledge about the problem at hand. The newly generated insights serve to improve both the quality of the artifact and the design process (Hevner, et al. 2004). The build and evaluate processes are deeply intertwined with each other. Moreover, they are not only conducted once in the overall DSR process. Rather, they are iterated multiple times until the design artifact is fully generated to the satisfaction of the researchers and practitioners that later make use of it (Markus et al. 2002).

Whereas prior DSR has viewed the research process as episodic, recently it has been acknowledged that it is rather an iterative research process (Baskerville, et al. 2009). The following figure summarizes the DSR process.

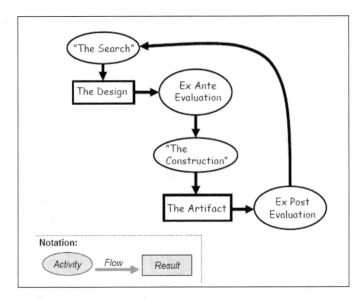

Figure 1:   Iterative DSR process (Baskerville, et al. 2009)

Accordingly, the first step involves the search for a relevant problem to be solved. This leads the researcher to the design of a possible solution. Afterwards, the design (e.g., set of guidelines) has to be evaluated before moving to the next stage of construction or implementation. The final outcome is the design artifact which then has to be evaluated. The outcomes of this process trigger the redefinition of the problem or trigger the development of new problems to be solved in a separate study. The DSR process as presented by Baskerville et al. (2009) is one perspective, besides others, that we build upon in this paper. In summary, I derive the following characteristic of DSR:

> DSR-2: The DSR process involves the search for a relevant problem, the design and construction of an IT artifact, and its ex ante and ex post evaluation.

As mentioned in the description of the DSR process above, the first step is the identification and search for a relevant practical problem. The focus of DSR to solve a practical problem originates from its historical development. DSR has its historical origins in architecture and engineering (Au 2001, McKay et al. 2005). In the engineering field, scientists are concerned with the design of a broad range of artifacts, including machines, devices, and systems. These artifacts are only designed and implemented if there is a practical need and a real-world problem to be solved. Similarly, architects design and construct something new, i.e., buildings and other physical structures. Again, the main purpose is to deliver a solution to a practical need. DSR originates from these two fields and is characterized by the same basic notion of building, constructing, or creating something new that solves a real-world problem. This is also the reason why many scholars in IS have come to believe that DSR conducted by researchers is not science but consulting. This is the reason why we distinguish between design science, which has its focus on the artifact construction and evaluation, and DSR, which lays additional emphasis on the study of design artifacts and the involving processes to generate new insights and make a contribution to knowledge (Winter 2008). However, even in DSR, an integral part of the research process is the search for a solution of a relevant problem (Hevner, et al. 2004). In other words, "a design science research projects seeks a solution to a real-world problem of interest to practice" (Kuechler et al. 2008). In summary, I derive the following characteristic of DSR:

> DSR-3: An important goal in DSR is to search and solve practically relevant real-world problems (or classes of problems).

Design science researchers have been debating for quite some time whether DSR is a method or methodology, a more general research approach, or even a research paradigm. A research method or methodology involves the collection of a set of pre-defined processes or steps that have to be carried out to do some kind of research. In other words, a research method provides the researcher with a kind of 'recipe' that shows him 'how' to find answers to a specific research question or problem. Hence, a research method or methodology is usually quite structured and proposes readily applicable techniques for the researcher. The researcher is then evaluated to what extent he 'followed' the defined method or methodology before his presented research results are accepted for publication. When Hevner et al. (2004) proposed a set of guidelines and evaluative criteria for DSR, many IS researchers interpreted them to form a recipe and hence thought of DSR as a method or methodology. However, recent scholarly debate over this topic shows that DSR has its own particular facets such as "the purpose-driven creation of artifacts and the introduction of these artifacts into otherwise natural settings" (Baskerville 2008). Hence, some scholars argue that DSR is rather a paradigm than a method (e.g., Iivari 2007). We would not go so far to conclude that DSR is a paradigm (Hevner, et al. 2004) because then we would raise DSR to the same level as philosophy of science or epistemological perspectives which would not be justifiable. Rather, we suggest DSR to be a research approach, something in between a hands-on research method and a more general philosophy of science, or research paradigm. Hence, many different research methods can be used within a DSR project. Examples in the extant literature show that DSR can be combined with action research (e.g., Allen et al. 2000), ethnography (e.g., Baskerville et al. 2001), and other research methods. In summary, I derive the following characteristic of DSR:

DSR-4: DSR is a general research approach with a set of defining characteristics and can be used in combination with different research methods.

The majority of DSR publications have adopted a positivist epistemological perspective. For example, Baskerville et al. (2009) state that DSR tends to be positivistic which is also stated by McKay and Marshall (2005). The latter authors criticize this finding and call for more DSR that is carried out within an interpretive or social constructionist perspective. In a way, by combining DSR with anti-positivistic research methods such as action research or ethnography, IS scholars have already made attempts to bridge the gap between the two camps and work towards a pluralistic research tradition (Allen, et al. 2000, Baskerville, et al. 2001). However, the majority of DSR is purely positivistic. One possible explanation is that DSR focuses on the IT artifact and the term artifact implies something real which exists in reality and which is not dependent upon subjective viewpoints. This is consistent with positivistic thinking which assumes that there exists an objective reality that can be readily depicted and described. The reality in this case consists of artifacts, e.g., a piece of software that can be objectively identified in terms of its source code which is explicitly documented. In summary, I derive the following characteristic of DSR:

DSR-5: DSR is conducted most frequently within a positivistic epistemological perspective.

As mentioned above, the main goal of DSR is solving a real-world problem and creating an IT artifact. However, solving a particular problem of a particular entity in a particular context inhibits the challenge of generating generalizable solutions and findings. Design science researchers often solve a local and situation-specific problem and do not give uttermost attention to making a contribution to the knowledge base (Hevner, et al. 2004). Frequently, the problem solved by design science researchers is so specific to the situational and contextual conditions that the solution is not generalizable. Orlikowski and Iacono (2001) support this notion by stating that IT artifacts are always embedded in some time, place, discourse, and community. Hence, while the main goal of design science research is to solve a practical problem, this comes at a price, i.e., the generalizability of the solution and the findings. In summary, I derive the following characteristic of design science research:

DSR-6: The outcome of DSR (i.e., the problem solution) is mostly an individual or local solution and the results cannot be readily generalized to other settings.

3 Characteristics of the Grounded Theory Method (GTM)

The GTM originates from sociology back in the 1960s and has since been further developed and applied in a variety of disciplines, including information systems research. At the focus of scholarly attention in a grounded theory study is the 'discovery' or generation of 'grounded theory' (Glaser et al. 1967). Prior research in sociology and related fields had focused more on deductive reasoning, deriving hypotheses from a priori theory and testing these hypotheses in empirical settings. Out of this well established research tradition, the GTM was invented to achieve a shift of scholarly focus from theory testing to theory generation and discovery. The assumption was that there is a lot of experience and data 'out there' in the empirical world to be discovered and explored and that researchers needed advice in forms of a research method to exploit the existing opportunities to generate new insights from real-world observations. With this motivation, the GTM came into existence which gave exploratory researchers in the social sciences a tool to discover and generate grounded theory through a combination of inductive, deductive, and abductive reasoning (Glaser 1978). The main attention in a grounded theory study is given to the process of discovering concepts and categories, depicting the core categories and the relationships between them. The result is usually a substantive theoretical contribution to the domain of study, i.e., the grounded theory. In summary, I derive the following characteristic of GTM:

> GTM-1: The focus of GTM is the discovery of grounded theory (i.e., categories and relationships between them).

The term grounded theory is given both to the end product (as described above) and to the process itself. Doing grounded theory involves a number of techniques that are prescribed by the GTM (Glaser 1998, Glaser 1978, Glaser, et al. 1967). Two key techniques of doing grounded theory are theoretical sampling and the constant comparative method (Suddaby 2006). Theoretical sampling means that insights from initial data collection and analysis guides subsequent data collection and analysis. In other words, the grounded theory emerges over time through iterative cycles of data collection and analysis that are deeply intertwined with each other. Over time, the researchers reach 'theoretical saturation' which means that additional data collection and analysis efforts do not yield any new findings (Eisenhardt 1989) and hence, the researchers concentrate on integrating their findings and working out the theoretical contribution to the domain of study. The other important technique in applying GTM is the constant comparative method which means constantly comparing indicators from their empirical data with each other as well with the concept that is given as label to a group of indicators. Concepts are grouped into categories and over time the core categories evolve from the analysis and form the basis for the development of substantive theory. To do this, grounded theory researchers make comparisons between different 'slices of data' (e.g., primary data such as qualitative interviews and secondary data such as documentations and the extant literature) to reach higher levels of abstraction and advance with the conceptualization. Relations are identified between the categories and through theoretical integration the substantive theory is formed. The following figure gives an overview over the process of grounded theory development.

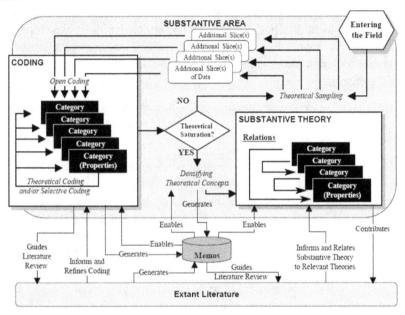

Figure 2:   Grounded theory research model (Fernandez 2004)

In summary, I derive the following characteristic of the GTM:

> GTM-2: The grounded theory research process involves theoretical sampling and constant comparisons to develop grounded theory and make a substantial theoretical contribution.

One of the main goals of grounded theory is to produce theory that has 'grab' or 'works' (Glaser 1978). In other words, the resulting theory must 'fit' or must be grounded in the empirical data to have practical relevance. This is also the reason why grounded theory usually appeals to practitioners and seems to fit well with their own real-life experiences. The process of grounded theory development, as described above, involves techniques of theoretical sampling and constant comparisons that makes this kind of outcome possible. Accordingly, by following carefully the GTM, research results may be produced that combine practical relevance with scientific rigor. Due to the fact that in a grounded theory study specific attention is given to the real-life world to produce theoretical insights that have 'grab', the myth emerged that a prior knowledge on a given subject is not included in a grounded theory study and that the emerging theory grows entirely from the empirical data. In fact, as we explain above in describing the research process itself, extant literature and prior knowledge is included as additional 'slices of data' in a grounded theory study to work out the theoretical contribution and addition to the knowledge base and also to reach higher levels of theoretical abstraction. Hence, in a way the resulting grounded theory must fit and must be grounded in both the empirical data but also in the relevant literature upon which the conceptualization is based upon. However, it remains an important issue in a grounded theory study to produce theory that 'works'. In summary, I derive the following characteristic of the GTM:

> GTM-3: An important goal in grounded theory research is to produce theory that fits with the real world and is grounded in the empirical data.

Different viewpoints exist in the literature whether doing grounded theory is a general research approach or a research method. Many scholars state in their research articles that they do grounded theory but by stating this they do not refer to the method as originally proposed by Glaser and his co-authors (Suddaby 2006). Rather, they refer to grounded theory in a general sense as a way of inductively deriving insights from empirical data instead of deductively deriving hypotheses from a priori theory and testing them. Scholars doing grounded theory in a more narrow sense in the intellectual tradition of Glaser and his co-authors often criticize such works for not following the method. Hence, another group of scholars which forms a larger research community views grounded theory as a research method with a set of guiding principles and techniques. Guidelines include the ones mentioned before, theoretical sampling and constant comparisons, but there are more. For example, Cathy Urquhart, who has published grounded theory studies in the IS discipline, outlines five guidelines: Doing a literature review for orientation, coding for theory not superficial themes, use of theoretical memos, building the emerging theory and engaging with other theories, and clarity of procedures and chain of evidence (Urquhart 2007). Due to the limitations of space, I cannot provide the reader with a full overview over the techniques and guidelines offered by the GTM. However, there is enough evidence for the fact that grounded theory has evolved to be become rather a research method than a more general research orientation or approach. One could also view grounded theory as a 'family of methods' due to the variety of ways in which grounded theory is carried out (Bryant et al. 2007). In fact, the flexibility and openness needed by scholars using the GTM is something that is stated repeatedly in the methods books on grounded theory and the research techniques provided by the grounded theory should not be misinterpreted to be applied in a too narrow sense (Glaser 1998, Glaser 1978, Glaser, et al. 1967). In summary, I derive the following characteristic of the GTM:

> GTM-4: Grounded theory is an evolving research method with sets of guidelines, principles, and techniques.

In principle, the GTM can be used within any epistemological frame of reference. For example, Madill et al. (2000) state that the method can be used with an interpretive, naive realist, or critical realist lens. Furthermore, researchers have also used the research method within a positivist lens (e.g., Kirsch 2004). However, the overwhelming amount of research applied this method has adopted an interpretive or social constructivist lens. The reason for this lies both in the nature of the research method itself, which places a larger emphasis on developing deep understanding from the empirical data than other more traditional research methods, as well as the history and origins of the research method. As mentioned before, the research method emerged in the 1960s in sociology as a response to the dominating positivistic research tradition which focused continuously on applying statistical analysis in a rigorous manner instead of producing practically relevant research results. Hence, the motivation for the GTM came from an anti-positivistic movement which stimulated the use and development of new research methods. The positivistic thinking was however still reflected in the first book on grounded theory (Glaser, et al. 1967), which stated that the objective was to 'discover' new theory as if it already existed in reality independently of subjective viewpoints. But due to the origins and its nature, GTM is most frequently used within an interpretive epistemological perspective (e.g., Orlikowski 1993). In summary, we derive the following characteristic of GTM:

> GTM-5: GTM is conducted most frequently within an interpretive epistemological perspective.

There has been much debate in qualitative research in general over the issue of generalizability. Scholars with a positivistic background and that are trained heavily in quantitative research methods and statistics often criticize qualitative case studies for producing only context-specific and situational knowledge that cannot be generalized or transferred to other settings. Qualitative researchers frequently respond to this critique that it is not the goal of qualitative research to produce (statistically) generalizable research results, but to provide a deep understanding of real-world phenomena in specific cases that may help to understand other cases in different settings. Yet other qualitative researchers respond to this critique by analyzing more cases and conducting multiple-case studies to increase the sample size. However, then the debate arises over the 'n', i.e., how many cases are sufficient to produce scientifically sound research results and make a genera-lized contribution to the knowledge base? GTM provides researchers with a very pragmatic way how to respond to this critique more efficiently by forcing re-searchers to reach high levels of theoretical saturation, abstraction, and integra-tion. Theoretical saturation is reached by grounded theorists when additional data collection and analysis does not yield any additional findings to the prior steps in the research process. Finding this 'optimal' point where to stop collecting and analyzing data is not easy and requires high levels of 'theoretical sensitivity' (Glaser 1978). Ultimately, by evaluating the theory that is presented for publica-tion, reviewers also take part in judging whether theoretical saturation has been reached. Researchers in a grounded theory study should also strive for conceptua-lizing and go beyond descriptive codes and analysis. Taking in the extant literature as additional slices of data may help researchers in this process. Finally, the theo-retical insights must be integrated and prepared carefully for presentation. Grounded theorists must work out the theoretical contribution of their work. By following these and other guidelines of GTM, a substantive theoretical contribu-tion in the domain of study becomes possible which is the main goal of grounded theory research. In addition, Glaser also provides guidelines how to develop for-mal theory based upon prior substantive theories (Glaser 1978). Both substantive theory and formal theory are considered 'middle-range' theories which fall be-tween minor working hypotheses of everyday life and so-called grand theories (Merton 1968). In summary, I derive the following characteristic of the GTM:

> GTM-6: The outcome of applying the GTM is mostly a substantive theory in the domain of study and on its basis it is possible to further develop formal theory.

4 Differences between DSR and GTM

The following table provides an overview and comparison of the characteristics of DSR and the GTM. Thereby, six categories inductively emerged from the literature analysis when identifying the main characteristics.

Identified Category	Design Science Research (DSR)	Grounded Theory Method (GTM)
Theory focus	DSR-1: The focus in a DSR project is mostly given to the design research part (i.e., the creation of an IT artifact), as opposed to the design science part (i.e., generating new knowledge).	GTM-1: The focus of the GTM is the discovery of grounded theory (i.e., categories and relationships between them).
Research process	DSR-2: The DSR process involves the search for a relevant problem, the design and construction of an IT artifact, and its ex ante and ex post evaluation.	GTM-2: The grounded theory research process involves theoretical sampling and constant comparisons to develop grounded theory and make a substantial theoretical contribution.
Research goal	DSR-3: An important goal in DSR is to search and solve practically relevant real-world problems (or classes of problems).	GTM-3: An important goal in grounded theory research is to produce theory that fits with the real world and is grounded in the empirical data.
Nature of research	DSR-4: DSR is a general research approach with a set of defining characteristics and can be used in combination with different research methods.	GTM-4: Grounded theory is an evolving research method with sets of guidelines, principles, and techniques.
Epistemology	DSR-5: DSR is conducted most frequently within a positivistic epistemological perspective.	GTM-5: GTM is conducted most frequently within an interpretive epistemological perspective.
Research outcome	DSR-6: The outcome of DSR (i.e., the problem solution) is mostly an individual or local solution and the results cannot be readily generalized to other settings.	GTM-6: The outcome of applying GTM is mostly a substantive theory in the domain of study and on its basis it is possible to further develop formal theory.

Table 2:   Comparison of Characteristics of DSR and GTM

By comparing some of the most salient characteristics of DSR and the GTM, I find some specific differences between these two research strategies. The first difference is the focus on the IT artifact (DSR-1) versus on grounded theory (GTM-1) as the main outcome and goal of the research strategy. A related difference concerns the research process where one strategy focuses on designing and constructing (DSR-2) while the other strategy focuses on discovery and theory development (GTM-2). Another difference results from the orientation towards practice. While both research strategies aim at producing practically relevant research results, the difference is that one strategy emphasizes the solution of a real-world problem (DSR-3) while the other research strategy focuses on producing theory that fits well with reality and generates an enhanced understanding of the problem at study (GTM-3). Hence, the difference is one of problem-solving versus problem understanding and explanation. The next difference is that one strategy can be characterized more as a research approach (DSR-4) while the other has grown to become a research method (GTM-4). Last but not least, one research strategy is conducted more frequently within a positivistic perspective (DSR-5) and the other within an interpretive perspective (GTM-5). Finally, one research strategy produces mostly results that solve an individual or local problem (DSR-6) while the other produces substantive theory in the domain of study (GTM-6).

5   Summary and Outlook

By comparing DSR and the GTM with each other in this paper, I stimulate a scholarly debate over the characteristics of each research strategy and possible complementary uses. Both research strategies are relatively new to IS research and are gradually receiving more attention and being developed further. In my comparison, I identified six defining characteristics of both research strategies that show that there are precise differences between them. While prior research has made valid attempts to integrate both research strategies into one research framework (Goldkuhl 2004, Holmström, et al. 2009), this paper is the first to systematically compare the two strategies which provides a guidance for future researchers who wish to combine them into one single research design.

In fact, the results from my comparison suggest that there are opportunities for future researchers to combine the two research strategies as they may complement each other well. For example, DSR is a more general research approach that has been combined in the past with research methods such as action research (e.g., Allen, et al. 2000). We suggest that DSR may also be used in combination with GTM. For example, Hevner et al. (2004) call for more DSR that makes a scholarly contribution to the knowledge base. And Peffers et al. (2007) identify the missing link to theory as one of the main problems of DSR as an IS research approach. The GTM has the goal to develop a substantive grounded theory and thereby contribute to scientific knowledge. A substantive theory in a DSR project could deal with the relationships between the IT artifact, human behaviour (i.e., people), and the organization (i.e., tasks). For example, 'how is user behaviour influenced by the IT artifact and vice versa?'. Developing grounded substantive theory about IT artifact use and its relationships with human behaviour and the organizational environment may provide the means for IT artifact evaluation (an inherent part of the DSR cycle) and leverage a DSR project to make a theoretical contribution to the knowledge base to go beyond the local solution of a problem and the implementation of an IT artifact.

Another opportunity is to use the GTM in the 'search' phase of a DSR project, where a problem is defined for which an IT artifact shall be developed in subsequent steps. So-called 'participatory' DSR approaches have made attempts in the past to use methods such as ethnography to develop a deep understanding of the problem area prior to developing an IT artifact. Using the GTM may enable design science researchers to develop a more systematic understanding of the problem area and identify the requirements for the construction of an IT artifact.

However, researchers combining DSR with the GTM have to be aware of the possible pitfalls. There is the risk of not following the guidelines offered by each research strategy rigorously, thus leading to flawed research designs. Editors have criticized past qualitative research of claiming to have done grounded theory while in fact the guidelines offered by the method have not been followed (Suddaby 2006). If the ultimate goal of our research is to get it published in top scholarly outlets, researchers pursuing a pluralistic research design must take great care in combining the different research strategies in a way that is consistent with the principles of each single strategy.

References

Allen, D. K., Colligan, D., Finnie, A. and Kern, T. "Trust, power and interorganizational information systems: the case of the electronic trading community TransLease," *Information Systems Journal* (10:1), 2000, pp. 21-40.

Au, Y. A. "Design Science I: The Role of Design Science in Electronic Commerce Research," *Communications of the Association for Information Systems* (7: 1), 2001, pp. 1-17.

Baskerville, R. "What Design Science is not, "*European Journal of Information Systems* (17:5), 2008, pp. 441-443.

Baskerville, R., Pries-Heje, J. and Venable, J. "Soft Design Science Methodology," *Design Science Research in Information Systems and Technology* DESRIST, 2009.

Baskerville, R. and Stage, J. "Accommodating emergent work practices: Ethnographic choice of method fragments". Kluwer, New York, 2001.

Bryant, A. and Charmaz, K. "The SAGE Handbook of Grounded Theory," SAGE Publications, London, 2007.

Eisenhardt, K. M. "Building Theories from Case Study Research," *Academy of Management Review* (14:4), 1989, pp. 532-550.

Fernandez, W. D. "The Grounded Theory Method and Case Study Data in IS Research: Issues and Design," *Information Systems Foundations Workshop: Constructing and Criticising*, 2004.

Glaser, B. G. "Doing Grounded Theory: Issues and Discussions," Mill Valley, USA, 1998.

Glaser, B. G. "Theoretical Sensitivity," Mill Valley, USA, 1978.

Glaser, B. G. and Strauss, A. L. "The Discovery of Grounded Theory: Strategies for Qualitative Research," Chicago, USA, 1967.

Goldkuhl, G. "Design Theories in Information Systems - A Need for Multi-Grounding," *Journal of Information Technology Theory and Application*, (6:2) 2004, pp. 59-72.

Hevner, A., March, S., Park, J. and Ram, S. "Design Science in Information Systems Research," *MIS Quarterly* (28:1), 2004, pp. 75-105.

Holmström, J. B., Ketokivi, M. and Hameri, A. P. "Bridging Practice and Theory: A Design Science Approach," *Decision Science* (40:1), 2009, pp. 65-87.

Iivari, J. "A Paradigmatic Analysis of Information Systems as a Design Science," *Scandinavian Journal of Information Systems* (19:2), 2007, pp. 39-63.

Iivari, J. and Venable, J. "Action Research and Design Science Research - Seemingly Similar But Decisively Dissimilar," *17th European Conference on Information Systems*, 2009.

Järvinen, P. "Action Research is Similar to Design Science," *Quality and Quantity* (41:1), 2007, pp. 37-54.

Kirsch, L. J. "Deploying Common Systems Globally: The Dynamics of Control," *Information Systems Research* (15:4), 2004, pp. 374-395.

Kuechler, B. and Vaishnavi, V. "On Theory Development in Design Science Research: Anatomy of a Research Project," *European Journal of Information Systems* (17:5), 2008, pp. 489-504.

Madill, A., Jordan, A. and Shirley, C. "Objectivity and reliability in qualitative analysis: Realist, contextualist and radical constructionist epistemologies," *British Journal of Psychology* (91:1), 2000, pp. 1-20.

March, S. T. and Smith, G. "Design and Natural Science Research on Information Technology," *Decision Support Systems* (15:4), 1995, pp. 251-266.

Markus, M. L., Majchrzak, A. and Gasser, L. "A Design Theory for Systems that Support Emergent Knowledge Processes," *MIS Quarterly* (26:3), 2002, pp. 179-212.

McKay, J. and Marshall, P. "A Review of Design Science in Information Systems," *16th Australasian Conference on Information Systems,* 2005.

Merton, R. K. "Social Theory and Social Structure," *The Free Press*, New York, USA, 1968.

Mingers, J. "Combining IS Research Methods: Towards a Pluralist Methodology," *Information Systems Research* (12:3), 2001, pp. 240 - 259.

Orlikowski, W. J. "CASE Tools as Organizational Change: Investigating Incremental and Radical Changes in Systems," *MIS Quarterly* (17:3), 1993, pp. 309-340.

Orlikowski, W. J. and Baroudi, J. "Stuying Information Technology in Organizations Research Approaches and Assumptions," *Information Systems Research* (2:1), 1991, pp. 1-28.

Orlikowski, W. J. and Iacono, C. S. "Research Commentary: Desperately Seeking the 'IT' in IT Research – A Call to Theorizing the IT Artifact," *Information Systems Research* (12:2), 2001, pp. 121-134.

Peffers, K., Tuunanen, T., Rothenberger, M. A. and Chatterjee, S. "A Design Science Research Methodology for Information Systems Research," *Journal of Management Information Systems* (24:3), 2007, pp. 45-78.

Simon, H. A. "The Sciences of the Artificial," (3rd ed.), *MIT Press*, Cambridge, MA, 1996.

Stebbins, R. A. "Exploratory Research in the Social Sciences," Sage Publications, Thousand Oaks, USA, 2001.

Suddaby, R. "From the Editors: What Grounded Theory is Not," *Academy of Management Journal* (49:4), 2006, pp. 633-642.

Urquhart, C. "The Evolving Nature of Grounded Theory Method: The Case of the Information Systems Discipline," SAGE Publications, London, 2007.

Urquhart, C. and Fernández, W. D. "Grounded Theory Method: The Researcher as Blank Slate and Other Myths," *Twenty-Seventh International Conference on Information Systems,* pp. 457-464, 2006.

Walls, J. G., Widmeyer, G. R. and El Sawy, O. A. "Building an Information System Design Theory for Vigilant EIS," *Information Systems Research* (3:1), 1992, pp. 36-59.

Winter, R. "Design Science Research in Europe," *European Journal of Information Systems* (17:5), 2008, pp. 470-475.

Goal Commitment and Competition as Drivers for Group Productivity in Business Process Modeling[1]

Peter Rittgen

Vlerick Leuven Gent Management School, Reep1, 9000 Gent, Belgium, & University of Borås, 501 90 Borås, Sweden, peter.rittgen@hb.se

1 Introduction

Computer support for collaborative modeling (or group modeling) has been an issue of research for two decades now. Early studies include Dean et al. (1994) and they found that a collaborative tool (basically a text editor) for the IDEF0 activity modeling language was able to reduce modeling time substantially by splitting large groups of more than 20 people into smaller teams each of which would work on a computer to elaborate a different chunk of a large model.

So far computer support of modeling groups has not gone very far. In practice it is restricted to the facilitator and modeling sessions are still mostly supported by brown paper and sticky notes. More sophisticated tools exist but they are often limited to collaborative drawing. From a theoretical perspective such tools are unsatisfactory as collaborative work is not structured in any way. The professional facilitators refrain from using them as they fear that such tools will only increase the cognitive overhead of modeling sessions.

In such a situation it seems hopeless to introduce yet another tool-based approach. But the aim of this paper is not to advocate a tool but to study the methodological features that a sophisticated tool allows for. In particular, our hypothesis is that goal commitment and competition have a positive impact on group productivity mediated by motivation, participation, and individual effort.

To leverage participation and competition we employ a computer-based tool. On the one hand, it allows group members to make direct contributions to the model,

---

[1]   Another version of this paper appeared as: Rittgen, Peter, "Goal Commitment and Competition as Drivers for Group Productivity in Business Process Modeling," Proceedings of the 15th Pacific Asia Conference on Information Systems (PACIS) 2011, Brisbane, Queensland, Australia, 7-11 July, 2011, AIS Electronic Library

thereby facilitating participation. On the other hand, it can also bring about a competitive situation, in our case the mutual scoring of models created by group members. Although such a competition is in principle also possible with brown paper and sticky notes, computer support greatly facilitates it.

The remainder of the paper is structured as follows. We first take a look at related research in the area of collaborative work. We then describe the research methodology, followed by an analysis of measuring instruments for group productivity in modeling. After that we introduce some factors that control productivity in group modeling, and also discuss measurements for them. We continue with an explanation of the set-up of the field experiments and the analysis of the data collected in these experiments.

We derive a factor model that is validated with Structured Equation Modeling (SEM) and discuss the implications and limitations of this model.

2   Related Research

Group modeling has been studied intensively in the literature concerning all major aspects such as the structure of the process itself, its organizational environment, and the supporting tools and techniques.

The basic roles and activities in modeling were studied in Bommel et al. (2006), Frederiks & Weide (2006), and Hoppenbrouwers et al. (2006) who argue for a separation of knowledge elicitation and model creation. Hoppenbrouwers et al. (2005) add that modeling is also knowledge creation and dissemination in the form of a structured conversation. We basically agree with the latter, more inclusive, view on modeling but question the separation as discussed in the next section.

(Frederiks & Weide, 2006) identify natural language as the primary instrument and calls for face-to-face meetings supported by a simple, easy-to-use medium. The computer as a medium has been studied by Fjermestad & Hiltz (2001) and Reinig & Shin (2002) for general meetings and in Dean et al. (1994, 2000) for modeling sessions. The conclusion is that tool support has a moderating impact on the group process, which in turn controls the meeting outcome. Therefore, it is necessary to look at the process itself to identify effects of different media. We do so by including parameters of the process in our study such as team factors.

In more general terms, the rich work on brainstorming methods is also relevant for us. Brainstorming is useful for structuring an unstructured problem (see e.g. Belton et al. (1997) and Conklin et al. (2003)) but it can also be used to structure existing business process knowledge in the face of different views on the process, i.e. different versions of knowledge.

Beyond the modeling process itself, Araujo & Borges (2007) and Persson (2001) look at the environment in which this process is embedded. They study situational factors with the aim of creating better support for software engineering or collaborative modeling in enterprise, respectively.

Lind & Seigerroth (2010) look at the way a whole modeling project needs to be organized in the context of a process change effort. They argue for the need of different types of process models at different stages in the project.

Success factors of process modeling have been studied thoroughly in Bandara et al. (2005). The focus of this work is on management factors that are related to the whole modeling project. In contrast, we concentrate on factors for a particular modeling session.

The present research is also closely related to our earlier work on success factors as documented in Rittgen (2010a, 2010b), which it extends and refines by considering more factors. Self-organization of modeling teams has been studied in Rittgen (2009) where we looked at the roles and team structures that evolve when a group is allowed to model on its own. In particular Rittgen (2010b) already introduced the variables competition, individual effort, degree of participation and motivation for modeling which are pivotal in this study.

Tool support and techniques for collaborative modeling are suggested in e.g. Kemsley (2010) and vom Brocke & Thomas (2006).

3   Research Methodology

We conducted 15 field experiments, three at each of five organizations. The organizations were:

ME: a large manufacturer of electronics
PH: a large psychiatric hospital
IC: a large insurance company
BL: A medium-sized bio-engineering laboratory
PA: a large public (city) administration

We used *competition* as the exogenous variable assuming two states, competition or no competition. Each experiment consisted of two business process modeling sessions, one for either state, and lasted approximately four hours. The unit of analysis was the session. *Competition* was controlled by either making use of the competition module of the group modeling tool or not (see below). The endogenous variables were *goal commitment, motivation for modeling, degree of participation, individual effort* and *group productivity*. Their measurements are explained in sections 4 and 5.

Both the competitive and non-competitive sessions were conducted in the same way, i.e. using the same method, the same tool and the same modeling assignment (a business process). The only factors that changed were the use of the competition module (yes/no), and the group that did the modeling. The latter is motivated as follows.

Using the same group twice for the same assignment makes no sense. Giving the group a different assignment for the other session introduces too much uncontrolled variation as different modeling exercises can vary substantially in complexity. Using two different groups with the same assignment also introduces some variation but it is easier to control. In both cases, we selected members with the same background and domain knowledge. The selection was performed by a senior process manager who knew all individuals thoroughly.

4   Group Productivity in Modeling

Determining group productivity in modeling is a challenging task. Conventionally, group performance is measured with respect to the level of achievement regarding a specific task. The task is often designed in such a way that productivity measurement is simple: e.g. the relation of completed steps and the maximum possible steps (Rosenbaum et al., 1980), or economic efficiency or effectiveness in terms of a monetary valuation of inputs vs. outputs or outputs vs. goals, respectively (Goodman & Leyden, 1991; Pritchard, 1995).

Most of these measures assume that the task is summative, i.e. that the group productivity is the sum of the individual productivities. This assumption is not true in modeling. Many measurements also presume that a benchmark exists against which performance can be evaluated. As there is no such thing as the "perfect model", such measures have likewise to be discarded.

Non-summative measures have been developed in the context of artificial tasks (Crown & Rosse, 1995) but they require relative comparability of one group to another. A model is an artifact that is unique and that is not only developed **by** a group but usually also for the group. Only the group itself can therefore assess its quality in their own context and in an inter-subjective manner. In other words: group performance in modeling is the extent to which group members agree with the model and with each other regarding its correctness and completeness w.r.t. to individual cognition.

Social model quality (SMQ) embodies this idea by measuring the extent to which interpretations of different users agree with each other. As both the process of arriving at a model and its use are collaborative endeavors, social quality is an important factor of overall model quality. A measure for social quality was introduced in Krogstie (1995). It is called Relative Agreement in Interpretation (RAI) and is defined as the average mutual agreement among pairs of users w.r.t. their interpretation of the model.

$$RAI = 1 - \frac{\left| \left\{ s \middle| \exists i, j, i \neq j : s \in \mathfrak{I}_i \wedge s \notin \mathfrak{I}_j \right\} \right|}{\left| M_E \right|}$$

s stands for a statement of the model. In a process model that could be "There is an activity called Enter PIN code" or "Activity B has to be carried out after activity A". This means that a statement refers to a node or an arc in the process model. $\mathfrak{I}_i$ is the interpretation that modeler i associates with the model. It is the set of all statements that the modeler considers to be true. M_E is the set of all explicit statements of the model. A statement is controversial if at least two people have a differing opinion on it. If we divide the number of controversial statements by the overall number of statements, we arrive at the relative disagreement in interpretation. Subtracting this from one yields the RAI.

To operationalize this measure we have developed a social quality questionnaire. For this, we first labeled all the nodes and arcs of the final model with numbers and gave the participants a printout of the model including these numbers. We also gave them a piece of paper with a table. The first column contained the numbers from 1 to 50 (max. expected node and arc count) in ascending order. The second column was empty. Participants were asked to put a cross in this column for each number of a node or arc that they considered to imply a wrong statement. If a node was in a wrong swim lane they put a p for position instead. They also had to put a circle around the number that represented the total number of nodes and arcs.

Putting the filled-in questionnaires of all group members side by side we counted the number of rows that only showed identical markings, i.e. eight empty fields, eight crosses or eight p's. This was then divided by the circled number to yield the RAI. The resulting RAI value is already a group value that relates to a single model. The questionnaire for the RAI is administered directly after each session to make sure that the social context is still present.

5   Factors of Productivity in Group Modeling

This section introduces measurements for the four factors that we consider to be relevant. The primary and exogenous factor is that of competition. It is a categorical variable with two values: 0 for no competition and 1 for competition. It is controlled by either using the competition module of the group modeling tool, or not. The endogenous variables are motivation for modeling, degree of participation, and individual effort.

All factors are derived from Focus Theory (Briggs, 1994) and from earlier theory development as described in Rittgen (2010b). These works also exhibit the factor interactions that can be expected and that we have taken into account when devising the experiments of the current study.

While the list of considered factors is not exhaustive, the two sources mentioned comprise, as far as we know, the most comprehensive set of cognitive factors determining collaborative work in general and in modeling in particular, respectively.

5.1   Competition

The impact of competition and cooperation on group productivity was comprehensively addressed for the first time in the Theory of Cooperation and Competition (Deutsch, 1949). Deutsch found that groups perform better when their members cooperate instead of compete. But interestingly, his so-called cooperative mode, where members are equally rewarded for group success, also bears distinct elements of competition: the group had to beat other groups to be successful.

Hammond & Goldman (1961) discovered that it is precisely the combination of intra-group cooperation and inter-group competition that leads to highest group productivity. The competition with other groups raises the group members' desire for achieving the group goal, and the cooperation with other group members helps them achieve it.

We have reproduced this condition in some of our field experiments by dividing a group into modeling teams. Each team would cooperate on the creation of a model proposal but only one team's model will eventually win and be selected for further development.

Our hypothesis is that the competitive-cooperative modeling sessions will outperform the cooperative groups in terms of group productivity as measured by social quality of the model.

In the competitive-cooperative modeling scenario, we introduce a scoring of each model proposal by the other participants. After the complete scoring round, the facilitator shows the whole group the average scores of all proposals as bars of different sizes and numbers. This is an exciting moment for the participants as they get to know their own scores and how they relate to the other groups.

Being judged by their own peers (often colleagues) is a strong incentive to put as much effort into the modeling as possible and that is precisely what we want to achieve: the best possible effort by all group members. Nobody can hide behind more active group members. Competition thereby introduces a group-centric individual goal beyond the group goal of creating the overall model, which facilitates group productivity (Crown & Rosse, 1995).

The result of the scoring round, which usually takes ten minutes, is not only a winner but also a winning model. This is the basis for all further development as the highest overall score clearly indicates that this model has the strongest support and therefore the best chance of creating consensus. It cannot be taken as the final version, though, as some details might still be missing or misrepresented, in particular views represented in the discarded models. This needs to be settled in a consolidation step.

In the non-competitive case, there was no mutual scoring. Instead the model to proceed with was selected by the facilitator. Group members were neither informed of the criteria for selection nor of the winner to avoid a competitive spirit. According to theory, competition is expected to increase motivation (see section 5.3).

5.2   Goal commitment

While competition can be assumed to increase motivation, a participant's basic motivation is driven by the desire to achieve the group goal. This desire for goal (or goal commitment) is considered highly relevant in many studies of group performance (Klein & Mulvey, 1995; O'Leary-Kelly et al., 1994; Weingart, 2006) and is also present in cognitive theories such as Focus Theory (see section 5.5). We have therefore decided to include it in our study.

Goal commitment is measured according to (Hollenbeck et al., 1989) with the 4-indicator measure. The indicators are (all items are reverse-coded):

1. It is hard to take this goal seriously.
2. It is unrealistic for me to expect to reach this goal.
3. It is quite likely that this goal may need to be revised, depending on how things go.
4. Quite frankly, I do not care if I achieve this goal or not.

All items are measured on a 7-point Likert scale ranging from *strongly disagree* to *strongly agree*.

5.3   Motivation for Modeling

Much has been said about the elusiveness of motivational gains in group work (see (Karau et al., 2000) for an overview and (Hertel et al., 2003) for a discussion on computer support) and the Collective Effort Model has often been used to explain such gains (Karau & Williams, 1993). According to the model, individual motivation will be high if group members perceive their own contribution to the group work as instrumental in reaching the group goal.

A fundamental problem with collaborative modeling is the fact that participants of such an exercise have no intrinsic motivation for the result itself. Most people are not interested in the model and do not see a need for it. But extrinsic motivation implies the risk of shirking (i.e. underperforming when not noticed). Consequently intrinsic motivation seems to be more promising. As we focus on the modeling process and not the model, motivation for modeling becomes the key factor.

The measurement of intrinsic motivation is a difficult issue. In principle there are two ways in which this can be done, behavioral and self-reported.

The behavioral measure requires actual observation of motivated behavior. The usual instrument is free-choice persistence (Deci, 1981) where the observant is instructed to perform a task while being knowingly observed. The experimenter then leaves the observant "alone", i.e. he observes him unknowingly. The time that the observant continues with the task while being "unobserved" is the behavioral measure of intrinsic motivation.

As this measure cannot be readily extended to group work it could not be applied in our study. The self-reported measure consists of a questionnaire that is administered immediately after the task has been performed. It is the most wide-spread instrument as it can be applied in all situations. It has been shown in meta-studies that self-reported measures deliver results similar to behavioral ones (Patall et al., 2008).

The self-reported measures use a combination of task enjoyment, interest and liking as a proxy for intrinsic motivation (Puca & Schmalt, 1999). They come in single and multi-item versions.

We use the interest/enjoyment sub-scale of the Intrinsic Motivation Inventory (IMI) measure that was introduced in (Deci & Ryan, 1985). It is based on Self-Determination Theory (Ryan & Deci, 2000) and has been validated in McAuley et al. (1989).

The items are scored on a 7-point Likert scale ranging from *not at all true* (1) via *somewhat true* (4) to *very true* (7) and read as follows (items 3 and 4 need to be reverse-coded):

1. I enjoyed doing this activity very much.
2. This activity was fun to do.
3. I thought this was a boring activity. (R)
4. This activity did not hold my attention at all. (R)
5. I would describe this activity as very interesting.
6. I thought this activity was quite enjoyable.
7. While I was doing this activity, I was thinking about how much I enjoyed it.

5.4   Degree of Participation

Another important factor is the degree of participation. It indicates the relative number of group members that are actually active in a session. A higher degree raises model quality by making models richer but lowers consensus by adding additional views.

The former means that a higher degree of participation yields more proposals which leads to more contributions to the group model and hence a more complete model. This makes it more likely that group members agree with it as they can find their view in the integrated model. As a result, group productivity will increase following this line of reasoning.

On the other hand, a higher degree of participation has a negative impact as group member might also introduce elements in the model that, in some individuals' opinion, do not make the model more complete but rather obfuscate it. In this case, the overall agreement decreases and with it group productivity according to that line of reasoning.

It is therefore unclear whether the overall effect of the degree of participation on group productivity is positive or negative and how significant and strong it is.

To measure the degree of participation we counted the relative number of individuals per group who provided at least one proposal, i.e. this variable can be measured by directly observing behavior which should always be preferred if possible.

5.5   Individual effort

Focus Theory by Briggs (Briggs, 1994) assumes that individual effort can be on communication, deliberation, and information access, but not at the same time. Therefore, high productivity in one area limits the effort that can be spent on the others. The overall productivity of an individual depends on high productivity in all three areas which constitutes a kind of a vicious circle.

In short, his model comprises the factors perceived difficulty of task, desired certainty of success, perceived effort required, perceived effort available, self-efficacy, desire for goal, individual effort, and group productivity. Figure 1 shows Briggs' model.

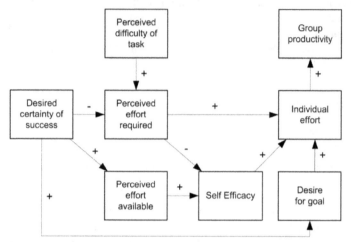

Figure 1   Briggs' model of individual and group effort in e-collaboration

We focus in our study on the direct antecedent of group productivity in Briggs' model, i.e. individual effort.

We measured individual effort in a result-oriented way, i.e. we have not tracked the cognitive efforts themselves but their traces, the number of proposals that were produced by each participant. They were recorded for each participant and averaged for the group. Again this variable can be observed directly providing a more objective measurement.

6   Set-Up of the Field Experiments

For the experiments in the field we selected the five organizations mentioned above. In each of the organizations, we carried out three experiments. An experiment consisted of two parts: a morning session with competition, and an afternoon session without. The sessions included between 5 and 9 participants and lasted 3 to 4 hours. The measurement of a session was pooled so the overall sample size was 30 (5 x 3 x 2).

Participants were domain experts without formal training in modeling. Most of them had been present in conventional chauffeured modeling sessions before but have never created models themselves. The modeled processes varied in size from 32 to 47 activities and were of medium complexity.

To keep the two parts as similar as possible we used the same method and tool for them (for the latter see www.coma.nu). For the non-competitive experiment we just did not perform the scoring and the facilitator chose the model to proceed with by his own judgment, not telling the participants about the reasons for his choice. We also used the same modeling assignment in both cases. The people for the second round were recruited from the same functional units as those of the first round and they were close colleagues of the latter.

After the competitive morning session, we handed out a questionnaire to each participant that contained the measurements for intrinsic motivation (7 indicators, IM1 – IM7). We also gave them the model printout and the table for the measurement of social quality. During the experiment we kept track of the number of proposals by each participant for the individual effort measure and the degree of participation. This data was collected with the help of the computer-based modeling tool that each participant was provided with. The same was done for the non-competitive afternoon session.

7   Data Analysis

In order to understand how the factors are related to each other we investigated the theoretical model with the help of Structured Equation Modeling (SEM). SEM is a statistical technique that allows for the confirmation of a factor model. From the theory presented in section 5 we can conclude that goal commitment and competition influence motivation, which in turn influences individual effort and the degree of participation. The latter two will then determine group productivity.

To confirm these relations we used structural equation modeling with the help of the WarpPLS 1.0 tool. The analysis was done with the help of the Warp3 PLS regression (partial least squares) and the default method of bootstrapping resampling. This particular analysis was chosen as it can also deal with non-linear relations and categorical variables (e.g. binary variables).

The result is depicted in Figure 2, which also shows the path coefficients (β values) that indicate the strength of the relations. All correlations are significant on the 1% level.

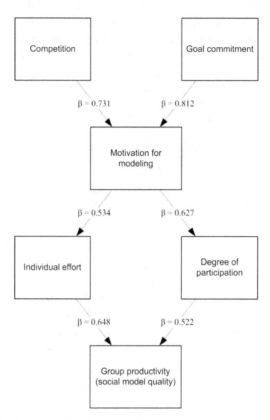

Figure 2   The factor model with SEM results

The average R^2 (coefficient of determination) is 0.824 which represents a good fit. In order to assess the structural fit of the model we have compared it against the base-line model where all variables are considered direct predictors of group productivity (no latent variables), and against another plausible model where competition, goal commitment, motivation and participation are predictors of individual effort, which in turn determines group productivity.

The average R^2 of the base-line model is 0.601; that of the model with individual effort as single latent variable is 0.717. Hence the model shown in Figure 2 represents the best fit with the data.

8   Conclusion

While the study has shown that motivation, participation and competition are important factors that control individual effort and hence the productivity of a group, it is still unclear which other factors control group productivity. The mentioned factors mostly operate on the level of the individual. But it is reasonable to assume that there are also factors that operate on group level.

Such group-level factors could for example be the organization of the group. Should all members work individually or should they work in smaller units (teams)? How should teams be composed? Should they be matched or complimentary, i.e. should team members come from the same or from different organizational units? An argument for the former is that teams with matched people can work together more effectively as they share a similar background. An argument for the latter is that complimentary teams comprise richer knowledge about the business process and can therefore produce richer proposals.

When we introduce the level of a team, which is between an individual and a group, there are again factors to be considered on this level. Examples of such factors are: the quality of the proposals submitted by a team, their formality, their richness, their understandability and so on.

All the mentioned factors might explain some of the variance that is not yet covered by the factors considered in this study. We therefore suggest to include these factors in further studies or to at least investigate their influence separately.

References

Araujo, R. M. d., & Borges, M. R. S. (2007). The Role of Collaborative Support to Promote Participation and Commitment in Software Development Teams. *Software Process Improvement and Practice, 12*(3), 229-246.

Bandara, W., Gable, G. G., & Rosemann, M. (2005). Factors and measures of business process modeling: Model building through a multiple case study. *European Journal of Information Systems, 14*(4), 347-360.

Belton, V., Ackermann, F., & Shepherd, I. (1997). Integrated support from problem structuring through to alternative evaluation using COPE and V.I.S.A. *Journal of Multi-Criteria Decision Analysis, 6*(3), 115-130.

Bommel, P. v., Hoppenbrouwers, S. J. B. A., Proper, H. A. E., & Weide, T. P. v. d. (2006). Exploring modeling strategies in a meta-modeling context. In R. Meersman, Z. Tari & P. Herrero (Eds.), *On the move to meaningful internet systems 2006: Otm 2006 workshops - otm confederated international workshops and posters, awesome, cams, cominf, is, ksinbit, mios-ciao, monet, ontocontent, orm, persys, otm academy doctoral consortium, rdds, swws, and sebgis, proceedings* (Vol. 4278, pp. 1128-1137). Berlin, Germany: Springer.

Briggs, R. O. (1994). *The Focus Theory of Group Productivity and its Application to the Design, Development, and Testing of Electronic Group Support Technology.* University of Arizona, Tucson.

Conklin, J., Selvin, A., Buckingham Shum, S., & Sierhuis, M. (2003). *Facilitated Hypertext for Collective Sensemaking: 15 Years on from gIBIS.* Paper presented at the Proceedings of the 8th International Working Conference on the Language-Action Perspective on Communication Modeling (LAP'03), Tilburg, The Netherlands.

Crown, D. F., & Rosse, J. G. (1995). Yours, Mine, and Ours: Facilitating Group Productivity through the Integration of Individual and Group Goals. *Organizational Behavior and Human Decision Processes, 64*(2), 138-150.

Dean, D. L., Orwig, R. E., Lee, J. D., & Vogel, D. R. (1994). Modeling with a group modeling tool: Group support, model quality, and validation *Information systems: Collaboration technology, organizational systems and technology, Proceedings of the 27th Hawaii International Conference on System Sciences* (Vol. 4, pp. 214-223). Los Alamitos, CA: IEEE Computer Society Press.

Dean, D. L., Orwig, R. E., & Vogel, D. R. (2000). Facilitation Methods for Collaborative Modeling Tools. *Group Decision and Negotiation, 9*(2), 109-127.

Deci, E. L. (1981). *The psychology of self-determination.* Lexington, MA: Health.

Deci, E. L., & Ryan, R. M. (1985). *Intrinsic motivation and self-determination in human behavior.* New York: Plenum.

Deutsch, M. (1949). A theory of co-operation and competition upon group process. *Human Relations, 2* (2), 129-152.

Fjermestad, J., & Hiltz, S. R. (2001). Group Support Systems: A Descriptive Evaluation of Case and Field Studies. *Journal of Management Information Systems, 17*(3), 115-159.

Frederiks, P. J. M., & Weide, T. P. v. d. (2006). Information Modeling: the process and the required competencies of its participants. *Data & Knowledge Engineering, 58*(1), 4-20.

Goodman, P. S., & Leyden, D. P. (1991). Familiarity and group productivity. *Journal of Applied Psychology, 76*(4), 578-586.

Hammond, L. K., & Goldman, M. (1961). Competition and Non-Competition and its Relationship to Individual and Group Productivity. *Sociometry, 24*(1), 46-60.

Hertel, G., Deter, C., & Konradt, U. (2003). Motivation Gains in Computer-Supported Groups. *Journal of Applied Social Psychology, 33*(10), 2080-2105.

Hollenbeck, J. R., Klein, H. J., O'Leary, A. M., & Wright, P. M. (1989). Investigation of the Construct Validity of a Self-Report Measure of Goal Commitment. *Journal of Applied Psychology, 74*(6), 951-956.

Hoppenbrouwers, S. J. B. A., Lindeman, L., & Proper, H. A. (2006). Capturing Modeling Processes - Towards the MoDial Modeling Laboratory. In R. Meersman, Z. Tari & P. Herrero (Eds.), *On the Move to Meaningful Internet Systems 2006: OTM 2006 Workshops - OTM Confederated International Workshops and Posters, AWESOMe, CAMS, COMINF, IS, KSinBIT, MIOS-CIAO, MONET, OnToContent, ORM, PerSys, OTM Academy Doctoral Consortium, RDDS, SWWS, and SebGIS, Proceedings, Part II, Montpellier, France* (Vol. 4278, pp. 1242-1252). Berlin, Germany: Springer.

Hoppenbrouwers, S. J. B. A., Proper, H. A., & Weide, T. P. v. d. (2005). Formal Modeling as a Grounded Conversation. In G. Goldkuhl, M. Lind & S. Haraldson (Eds.), *Proceedings of the 10th International Working Conference on the Language Action Perspective on Communication Modeling (LAP '05), Kiruna, Sweden* (pp. 139-155). Linköping and Borås: Linköpings Universitet and Högskolan i Borås.

Karau, S. J., Markus, M. J., & Williams, K. D. (2000). On the Elusive Search for Motivation Gains in Groups: Insights from the Collective Effort Model *Journal Zeitschrift für Sozialpsychologie, 31*(4), 179-190.

Karau, S. J., & Williams, K. D. (1993). Social loafing: A meta-analytic review and theoretical integration. *Journal of Personality and Social Psychology, 65*(4), 681-706.

Kemsley, S. (2010). Enterprise 2.0 Meets Business Process Management. In J. v. Brocke & M. Rosemann (Eds.), *Handbook on Business Process Management 1* (pp. 565-574). Berlin: Springer.

Klein, H. J., & Mulvey, P. W. (1995). Two Investigations of the Relationships among Group Goals, Goal Commitment, Cohesion, and Performance. *Organizational Behavior and Human Decision Processes, 61*(1), 44-53.

Krogstie, J. (1995). *Conceptual Modeling for Computerized Information Systems Support in Organizations* (PhD Thesis). Trondheim: Faculty of Electrical Engineering and Computer Science, The University of Trondheim.

Lind, M., & Seigerroth, U. (2010). Collaborative Process Modeling: The Intersport Case Study. In J. v. Brocke & M. Rosemann (Eds.), *Handbook on Business Process Management 1* (pp. 279-298). Berlin: Springer.

McAuley, E., Duncan, T., & Tammen, V. V. (1989). Psychometric properties of the Intrinsic Motivation Inventory in a competitive sport setting: A confirmatory factor analysis. *Research Quarterly for Exercise and Sport*(60), 48-58.

O'Leary-Kelly, A. M., Martocchio, J. J., & Frink, D. D. (1994). A Review of the Influence of Group Goals on Group Performance. *The Academy of Management Journal, 37*(5), 1285-1301.

Patall, E. A., Cooper, H., & Robinson, J. C. (2008). The Effects of Choice on Intrinsic Motivation and Related Outcomes: A Meta-Analysis of Research Findings. *Psychological Bulletin, 134*(2), 270–300.

Persson, A. (2001). Enterprise Modeling in Practice: Situational Factors and their Influence on Adopting a Participative Approach. Unpublished PhD thesis. Department of Computer and Systems Sciences, Stockholm University.

Pritchard, R. D. (Ed.). (1995). *Productivity measurement and improvement: Organizational case studies*. Westport, CT: Praeger Publishers/Greenwood Publishing Group.

Puca, R.-M., & Schmalt, H.-D. (1999). Task enjoyment: A mediator between achievement motives and performance. *Motivation and Emotion, 23*(1), 15-29.

Reinig, B. A., & Shin, B. (2002). The Dynamic Effects of Group Systems Support on Group Meetings. *Journal of Management Information Systems, 19*(2), 303-325.

Rittgen, P. (2009). Self-organization of interorganizational process design. *Electronic Markets, 19*(4), 189-199.

Rittgen, P. (2010a). *Quality and perceived usefulness of process models*. Paper presented at the Proceedings of the 2010 ACM Symposium on Applied Computing.

Rittgen, P. (2010b). Success Factors of e-Collaboration in Business Process Modeling. In B. Pernici (Ed.), *Advanced Information Systems Engineering, 22nd International Conference, CAiSE 2010, Hammamet, Tunisia, June 2010, Proceedings* (Vol. LNCS 6051, pp. 24-37). Berlin: Springer.

Rosenbaum, M. E., Moore, D. L., Cotton, J. L., Cook, M. S., Hieser, R. A., Shovar, M. N., et al. (1980). Group productivity and process: Pure and mixed reward structures and task interdependence. *Journal of Personality and Social Psychology, 39*(4), 626-642.

Ryan, R. M., & Deci, E. L. (2000). Self-determination theory and the facilitation of intrinsic motivation, social development, and well-being. *American Psychologist, 55*, 68-78.

vom Brocke, J., & Thomas, O. (2006). Reference Modeling for Organizational Change: Applying Collaborative Techniques for Business Engineering *Proceedings of the 12th Americas Conference on Information Systems: Connecting the Americas, Acapulco, México, August 4-6, 2006* (pp. 680-688). Atlanta, Georgia, USA: AIS.

Weingart, L. R. (2006). Impact of Group Goals, Task Component Complexity, Effort, and Planning on Group Performance. In J. M. Levine & R. L. Moreland (Eds.), *Small Groups* (pp. 309-326). New York: Psychology Press.

Inferring Decision Strategies from Clickstreams in Decision Support Systems: A New Process-Tracing Approach using State Machines

Dr. Jella Pfeiffer

Chair of Information Systems and Business Administration, Johannes Gutenberg-Universität Mainz, jella.pfeiffer@uni-mainz.de

Malte Probst

Chair of Information Systems and Business Administration, Johannes Gutenberg-Universität Mainz, probst@uni-mainz.de

Wolfgang Steitz

Chair of Information Systems and Business Administration, Johannes Gutenberg-Universität Mainz, steitzw@uni-mainz.de

Prof. Dr. Franz Rothlauf

Chair of Information Systems and Business Administration, Johannes Gutenberg-Universität Mainz,rothlauf@uni-mainz.de

1   Introduction

The importance of online shopping has grown remarkably over the last decade. In 2009, every West European spent on average € 483 online and this amount is expected to grow to € 601 in 2014[1]. In Germany, the number of online shoppers has almost doubled since 2000: 44% of all adults regularly buy products online

---

[1]   http://www.forrester.com/rb/Research/western_european_online_retail_forecast\ %2C_2009_to/q/id/56543/t/2

A. Heinzl et al. (eds.), *Theory-Guided Modeling and Empiricism in Information Systems Research*, DOI 10.1007/978-3-7908-2781-1_8, © Springer-Verlag Berlin Heidelberg 2011

today. In Western Europe, online sales reached € 68 billion in 2009 and Forrester research forecasts it will reach € 114 billion by 2014 with an 11% compound annual growth rate.

In contrast to traditional shopping, e-commerce allows the easy gathering of a large amount of consumer data. Webstores can easily store information on all kinds of process data that describe consumer behavior: clicks on single elements of the user interface, navigation, user profile data, search texts, etc. This kind of data is both interesting to merchandisers as well as to researchers in the field of decision-making behavior. Merchandisers can further improve their webstores and product offerings based on knowledge gained from such data. They may improve conversion rates or even influence purchase behavior. Researchers can use this data to study how people make decisions.

The goal of this work is to introduce an algorithm that infers decision behavior from clickstream data. Because of the diversity and large amount of clickstream data, we suggest focusing on very specific parts of clickstreams. We focus only on clicks related to elements of decision support systems (DSSs). We take a DSS which was programmed for online purchase decisions, also called interactive in-formation management tools (IIMTs). The algorithm works as follows. Clicks on elements of these IIMTs are used as input. These clicks can then activate different state machines, where each state machine represents a certain kind of decision strategy. By analyzing which state machines are activated, when they are activated and how long they are activated for, the algorithm is able to output a set of deci-sion strategies that best explain the observed clickstream.

The paper is structured as follows. In the second section, we define the problems people are faced with when purchasing a product online and we describe decision strategies. In section three, we point out how existing approaches study decision behavior based on process data such as the clickstreams used in our approach. In the following section, we then present the DSS which we used in our analysis and allude to the relationship between DSS and decision strategies. In subsection 4.3, we describe our newly proposed algorithm and validate it in the subsequent sec-tions five and six in two empirical studies. We finish the paper by concluding and explaining potential future work.

2   Decision Strategies and Choice Tasks

Decision-making behavior is typically modeled by various decision strategies. Decision strategies describe the process of acquiring, evaluating, and comparing choice task information elements (Hogarth 1987; Tversky 1969, 1972; Beach 1990; Russo and Dosher 1983; Payne et al. 1993). We define choice tasks as multi-attribute decision problems with a limited number of alternatives. The goal of a choice task is to select the most attractive alternative, e.g., the product the consumer likes the most.

More formally, a choice task is a multi-alternative multi-attribute problem, which consists of n alternatives $alt_j, j = 1, ..., n, n \geq 2$, which are described by a_{ij} attribute levels, one for each of the m attributes, $attr_i, i = 1, ..., m$ (Keeney and Raiffa 1993; Harte and Koele 2001). Attribute levels are concrete occurrences of the attributes. As an example, imagine a set of different cell phones (alternatives) characterized by a number of different attributes, such as price, brand and battery runtime. For example, the price of cell phone A is 100 €, its brand is Samsung and its battery runtime is 48h, whereas the price of cell phone B is 150 €, its brand is Nokia and its battery runtime is 60h. Each of these characteristics corresponds to a certain attribute level. Table 1 displays this example.

Attribute	Phone A	Phone B
price	€100	€150
brand	Samsung	Nokia
battery runtime	48h	60h

Table 1   Example of a product-comparison matrix with two alternatives and three attributes

We assume that decision makers have preferences concerning attribute levels. For some strategies, these preferences can have a simple ordinal form such as "yellow is preferred over red". Sometimes, it is further assumed that decision makers assign so-called attribute values to attribute levels (Eisenfuhr and Weber 2002). These attribute values reflect the degree of attractiveness the decision maker assigns to the attribute level. Each decision maker hence is assumed to have m value functions, v_i, that assign attribute values to all available attribute levels, $v_i(a_{ij})$. Furthermore, we assume that decision makers find some attributes more important than others and represent this kind of preference with attribute weights, w_i. Moreover, in some strategies, attribute levels are compared to aspiration levels. Aspiration levels can be interpreted as thresholds or acceptable levels. Dependent on the strategy, an alternative is either immediately excluded from further consideration once an aspiration level is not met or this attribute level is marked as negative. The maximum price one would be willing to pay for a product would be an example of an aspiration level.

In the literature, about fifteen decision strategies have been empirically observed (Riedl et al. (2008); Pfeiffer et al. (2009b)). Since it is beyond the scope of this work to introduce all fifteen strategies in detail, we focus only on a subset and list the rest in the appendix. For a more detailed overview, the reader can consult Payne et al. (1993); Riedl et al. (2008); Pfeiffer et al. (2009b).

EBA (elimination-by-aspects strategy): First, all alternatives are evaluated so as to detect whether they fulfil the aspiration level for the most important attribute. Alternatives are deleted if they do not meet the aspiration level. Then, the remaining alternatives are tested on the second most important attribute. This decision process is repeated until only one alternative is left.

CONJ (conjunctive rule): The decision maker uses an alternative-wise approach where he or she considers a complete alternative before proceeding to the next one. The alternative where the aspiration levels of all the attributes are satisfied is selected. If there is no such alternative, nothing is selected. If several alternatives satisfy all aspiration levels, one of them is selected at random.

LEX (lexicographic rule): The alternative with the best attribute level on the most important attribute is selected. If there is a tie, the best alternatives are compared according to the second most important attribute and so on.

WADD (weighted additive strategy): The utility-maximizing alternative is selected. The decision maker therefore assigns attribute values to all attribute levels and attributes weights to attributes. The overall utility of an alternative is the sum of all weighted attribute values. A weighted attribute value is defined as the product of an attribute value times the weight of its corresponding attribute. Attribute weight allows the decision maker to weigh some attributes higher than others.

FRQ (frequency of good and/or bad features rule): first of all, the aspiration levels of all attributes are determined. This allows the decision maker to decide whether the attribute level of an alternative is 'good' or 'bad'. The amount of 'good' and/or 'bad' attributes for each alternative is then counted and the highest scoring alternative is selected.

MCD (majority of confirming dimensions rule): The alternatives are compared two at a time, using all of their attributes: the alternative with a higher number of superior attributes is compared with the next alternative. Such pairwise comparisons are conducted until only one alternative is left.

Typically, it is assumed that decision makers apply one of these strategies when making a decision (Payne et al. 1993). However, several researchers have recently found that the decision process is sometimes separated into different stages (Russo and Leclerc (1994); Pfeiffer et al. (2009a)). In the first stage, decision makers try to reduce choice task complexity by eliminating alternatives. Examples for decision strategies which eliminate alternatives are EBA and LEX. EBA and LEX belong to the group of *non-compensatory* strategies, which do not take all attributes into account. A low value on an attribute removes the alternative from the choice task regardless of the values of the other attributes. In the second stage, decision makers put more effort into comparing the remaining alternatives (Payne 1976; Olshavsky 1979; Svenson 1979; Payne et al. 1988). Hence, in the first stage, they use simple heuristics and focus on only a few attributes, while in the second stage they consider the choice task holistically, using more effortful strategies such as WADD or EQW[2] (Payne 1976; Bettman and Park 1980; Luce et al. 1997; Gilbride and Allenby 2004, 2006). WADD and EQW belong to the group of *compensatory* strategies where the low value of one attribute can be compensated by a high value of another attribute (Payne 1976; Ford et al. 1989). Such strategies require all attribute levels to be considered. The decision maker is, in these cases, often required to possess high cognitive capabilities.

We can further distinguish between strategies that induce an attribute-wise or an alternative-wise comparison of attribute levels. Attribute-wise behavior characterizes a decision maker who picks one attribute, compares its attribute levels across all alternatives, and then moves to the next attribute (examples are EBA and LEX). Comparing all products first according to their color and then according to their price is an example of attribute-wise processing. Alternative-wise strategies, by contrast, define the behavior of the decision maker who sequentially evaluates alternatives according to several or all attribute levels (examples are EQW, WADD, MAJ[3]). Several studies have found that eliminating alternatives is easier if the alternatives are compared attribute-wise rather than alternative-wise and there is empirical evidence that people use strategies with attribute-wise comparison in the first stage and strategies with alternative-wise comparison in the second stage (Russo and Dosher 1983; Tversky 1969; Bettman and Park 1980; Luce et al. 1997; Pfeiffer et al. 2010a).

---

[2]   See the appendix for a definition of EQW.

[3]   See the appendix for a definition of MAJ.

3   Inferring Decision Behavior

The question remains: how can we know which kind of decision strategy is being used by the decision maker? Process-tracing techniques try to infer decision behavior from data which is gathered during the decision process. The data is typically recorded in the form of verbal protocols, eye movements or clickstreams. With verbal protocols, decision makers describe their behavior either during or after the decision process. Russo et al. (1989) criticize both simultaneous and retrospective verbal protocols. They argue that simultaneous protocols might interfere with the choice task and found that in retrospective protocols respondents either forgot what actually happened or did not report truthfully. Besides a potential lack of validity, several other disadvantages such as the amount of time necessary to transcribe and code statements have caused a decrease in the use of verbal protocols (Reisen et al. 2008). Now, due to advances in the field of information technology in recent years, much more sophisticated and automatized techniques such as eye-tracking and clickstream analyses are available. An eye tracker system is able to precisely record fixations on attribute levels or other pieces of information (Lohse and Johnson 1996; Reisen et al. 2008). It keeps track of not only the exact position and sequence of the fixations, but also of the length of fixations. Eye tracking is of high external validity as it allows researchers to capture the information acquisition happening at the level of the decision maker's visual system and creates a situation which is closer to a natural purchasing process than other techniques do (Russo 1978; Russo and Dosher 1983; Russo and Leclerc 1994). However, both eye tracking and verbal protocols can only be applied in laboratory settings and are, for instance, not suitable for anonymous online experiments and online purchase decisions.

We therefore suggest using clickstream analysis as the main technique to analyze decision behaviors on the Internet. Clickstream analysis is the predominant method used not only in real-world online webstores, but also in research, with the so-called Mouselab-technique. The mouselab keeps track of information acquisition, response time and choices by recording the mouse movements of a choice task on a computer screen (Bettman et al. 1990). At the beginning of the choice task, all attribute levels are hidden behind boxes. Only by clicking or moving the cursor on each box can the respondent retrieve the attribute level. In the original version, the box is hidden again once the cursor moves away (Payne et al. 1988). Several works which rely on the Mouselab technique and its variants have studied the time it takes to make a decision, the number and variety of different attribute levels a decision maker considers, the average number of attribute levels per alternative and the sequence in which information is acquired (Bettman et al. 1993; Böckenholt et al. 1991; Fasolo et al. 2003; Garbarino and Edell 1997; Klein and Yadav 1989). Unfortunately, the insights gained from these studies are almost always too general, describing only if the decision maker used an overall alterna-tive-wise or attribute wise strategy, rather than describing which particular deci-sion strategy was used. This is because the amount of time needed to make a deci-sion, the quantity of attribute levels and the information acquisition sequences constitute insufficient data for determining which decision strategy has been ap-plied (Bröder and Schiffer 2003).

4 Clickstream on DSS-elements as a New Process-Tracing Method

In this section, we describe the main contribution of this work. First, we describe a DSS consisting of a set of IIMTs that has recently been introduced to help con-sumers when making online purchase decisions. Then, we point to the relationship between these IIMTs and decision strategies. In the third part, we introduce our algorithm, which infers decision strategies by using clickstreams on these IIMTs.

4.1 IIMTs as DSS in Choice Tasks

IIMTs are "tools which enable buyers to sort through and/or compare available product alternatives. For example, these tools allow buyers to limit and sort choic-es on levels of various attributes and/or engage in side-by-side comparisons of products in dynamically created tables" (Gupta et al., 2009, p. 163). IIMTs are one of the most widely used forms of DSS that can be currently found on the Internet. They support both phases of the two-stage decision-making behavior which we examined in section 2. Simple filter and sort tools help consumers to screen the available products and to narrow down their search to the most promising ones. Usually in this overview, products are described by some key attributes such as price, product name, etc. (see figure 1). The user can then select several products and compare them in-depth thanks to a product-comparison matrix in another window (see figure 2).

In this work, we focus on IIMTs for product-comparison matrices, but the algo-rithm can also easily be used for both phases of the clickstream analysis. Several IIMT have been introduced by Pfeiffer et al. (2009b, 2010b). We will describe their functionality based on some prototypical implementation for a product-comparison matrix which was presented in Pfeiffer et al. (2010b).

FILTER: with a *FILTER*, one can remove all alternatives that do not meet the aspiration levels for an attribute. In the example, in Figure 3 (c), the user has set the filter to only show phones that support Bluetooth.

SORT: changes the order in which the products ($SORT_{hierarchically}$) or attributes ($SORT_{drag\&drop}$) are displayed. $SORT_{hierarchically}$ enables to sort products according to several criteria, so that all products with the same attribute level for the first criterion are sorted according to the second criterion, etc. (see Figure 3 (a)). $SORT_{drag\&drop}$ allows the decision maker to swap rows in the product-comparison matrix.

PAIRWISE COMPARISON: two alternatives are picked from the matrix and are compared with each other. The other products are hidden.

SCORE: allows the user to assign weights to attributes ($SCORE_{attribute}$) and attribute values to attribute levels ($SCORE_{attributeLevels}$) with stars (see Figure 3 (b), lower box).

MARK: with $MARK_{manually}$, one can highlight single attribute levels negatively or positively (see Figure 3 (b), upper box). With the $MARK_{diffcom}$ variant, attribute rows with either different or similar attribute levels are highlighted (see the highlight options in Figure 2).

CALCULATE: calculates the utility of different alternatives using the customer's preferences indicated by *MARK* or *SCORE*. $CALCULATE_{weighted}$ multiplies attribute weights with attribute values. $CALCULATE_{markings}$ sums up the number of positively and negatively marked attribute levels, where a negatively marked attribute level has a value of -1 and a positive level a +1 (see Figure 3 (b)).

REMOVE: removes an alternative or attribute from the matrix (see Figure 2) or all products with at least one negatively marked attribute level ($REMOVE_{markings}$).

Figure 1   Screening phase with the IIMT *FILTER* and the possibility to *SORT* and choose products, which can then be compared in-depth in a product-comparison matrix with the IIMT *PAIRWISE COMPARISON* (www.cdw.com).

You have 3 products to compare

COMPARE BY:
- ⦿ Key Attributes
- ○ Technical Specifications

HIGHLIGHT OPTIONS:
- ⦿ Off
- ○ Different Values
- ○ Similar Values

	Lenovo ThinkPad SL510 2847 - Core 2 Duo T6670 2.2 GHz - 15.6" TFT	HP EliteBook 2540p - Core i7 640LM 2.13 GHz - 12.1" TFT	HP EliteBook 8440p - Core i5 520M 2.4 GHz - 14" TFT
	☒ Remove	☒ Remove	☒ Remove
	Advertised Price $454.99	Advertised Price $1,524.99	Advertised Price $1,712.99
	Qty [ ] Add To Cart	Qty [ ] Add To Cart	Qty [ ] Add To Cart
Availability	In Stock	In Stock	Call
MFG Part #	2847CZU	XT932UT#ABA	WJ683AW#ABA
CDW Part #	2209431	2196549	1991063
Brand	LENOVO TOP-SELLER PRODUCTS	Hewlett Packard Smart Buy	Hewlett Packard Non Smart
UNSPSC	43211503	43211503	43211503
Notebook Type	Notebook	Notebook	Notebook
Platform	PC	PC	PC
Operating System	Microsoft Windows 7 Professional 64-bit Edition	Microsoft Windows 7 Professional 64-bit Edition	Microsoft Windows 7 Professional
Processor Type	Core 2 Duo	Core i7	Core i5
Processor Clock Speed	2.2 GHz	2.13 GHz	2.4 GHz
Screen Size	15.6 in	12.1 in	14 in
Memory Installed	2 GB	4 GB	2 GB

Figure 2   Product-comparison matrix (www.cdw.com) with the IIMT $REMOVE_{alternative}$ and $MARK_{diff/com}$

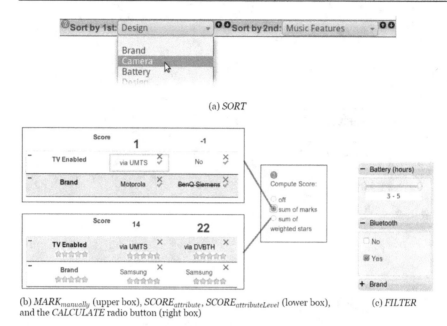

(a) *SORT*

(b) $MARK_{manually}$ (upper box), $SCORE_{attribute}$, $SCORE_{attributeLevel}$ (lower box),   (c) *FILTER*
and the *CALCULATE* radio button (right box)

Figure 3   IIMTs examples.

4.2   Relationship between IIMTs and Decision Strategies

Each IIMT is supposed to perform certain tasks which the decision makers would otherwise have to perform in their minds. For instance, the IIMT *CALCULATE* computes the decision maker's utility function and thus reduces the decision maker's cognitive burden. Furthermore, whenever decision makers apply a *CALCULATE*, we can come to the conclusion that they applied a strategy which calculates a utility function. Thus, the IIMTs are related to particular strategies. However, one IIMT does not necessarily support just one decision strategy. On the contrary, one IIMT can support several strategies, but it is important to understand that each combination of IIMTs supports exactly one strategy. For instance, in the prototype for which we tested our algorithm, the IIMT $CALCULATE_{weighted}$ must be clicked once before the user can assign attribute values with *SCORE*. Without applying the IIMT $CALCULATE_{weighted}$, the interface hides all the stars and thus does not provide the possibility to prompt in the preference information with SCORE (see Figure 3 (b)).

Pfeiffer et al. (2009b) introduced pseudo-code language to describe the relationship between decision strategies and IIMTs. An example for such an algorithmic description for the FRQ strategy is shown below.

Algorithm 1 FRQ with support of IIMT

// Activate the possibility to highlight attribute levels.
click $CALCULATE_{markings}$
// Compute utility of each alternative.
for $j = 1$ to n **do**
  for $i = 1$ to m **do**
    if a_{ij} is above the aspiration level **then**
      click $MARK_{manuallyPositive}$
    else if a_{ij} is below the aspiration level **then**
      click $MARK_{manuallyNegative}$
    end if
  end for
end for
choose the alternative with the highest score

With $CALCULATE_{markings}$, the user activates the possibility to mark attribute levels as either positive or negative (see Figure 3 (b), right box). The interface automatically sums up the positive and negative marks and displays the appropriate scores for each product in the top row. The users can thus choose the product with the highest score whenever they are finished with the mark assignments. The relationship between decision strategies and IIMTs is sometimes ambiguous because there might be different ways to use IIMTs to support the same decision strategy. For LEX, for example, a decision maker might sort the products hierarchically according to the most important attribute, for example, price (*SORT* ascendingly), and to the second most important attribute, for example display size (*SORT* descendingly). If two products share the same (cheapest) price, but one of them has a larger display, decision makers can easily identify their preferred product once the products are sorted:

Algorithm 2 LEX with support of IIMT, v1

// Process by attribute and eliminate alternative if necessary.
repeat
  retrieve preference order to choose next $attr_i$
  select $SORT_{hierarchically}$ for $attr_i$
until no alternatives are equivalent on considered attributes
choose most left alt

However, they might also consider the price without sorting and instead just remove (with $REMOVE_{alternative}$) all the products that are more expensive than the cheapest ones. They could then compare the remaining products according to display size and remove further alternatives:

Algorithm 3 LEX with support of IIMT, v2

// Process by attribute and eliminate alternative if necessary.
repeat
    retrieve preference order to choose next $attr_i$
    if a_{ij} is inferior to other attribute levels **then**
        click $REMOVE_{alternative}$ j
    end if
until no alternative is left
choose remaining alt

Obviously, both avenues for the application of LEX differ in their degree of cognitive effort. The second avenue implies that the decision maker identifies the relevant attributes and attribute levels on the basis of $REMOVE_{alternative}$ only, while $SORT_{hierarchically}$ would support the LEX strategy more completely.

In order to make the relationship between decision strategies and IIMTs as clear as possible, we assume that a decision maker's primary goal is the reduction of cognitive effort. Particularly in the case where several models exist for the same decision strategy, decision makers try to reduce cognitive effort as much as possible. Thus, in the above example, they would prefer the first version (v1). This assumption is in line with real-life decision-making processes because several experimental studies demonstrate that people consider reduction in cognitive effort to be very important (Todd and Benbasat 1991, 1992, 1994).

In the following section, we will describe how we can make use of these relationships, which were specified in pseudo-code notation in Pfeiffer et al. (2009b). Our approach with state machines translates the pseudo-code notation into an algorithmic concept that facilitates the inference of decision strategies from clickstream behavior.

4.3   State Machines for Interpretation of IIMT-Clickstreams

Finite-state machines (FSM) are a widely used concept in computer science. FSMs describe behavior models consisting of a finite number of states and transitions between those states. Depending on the input data, a state machine changes its state according to the specified transitions. The input data is processed one at a time without going backward.

Formally, a FSM is defined as a 5-tuple (I, S, s_0, δ, F) (Hopcroft 2006), where

- I specifies the input alphabet, a finite, non-empty set of symbols,
- S is a finite, non-empty set of states,
- $s_0 \in S$ is the initial state,
- $\delta: S \times \Sigma \rightarrow S$ the transition function, which returns a state depending on the input symbol and the current state, and
- $F \subseteq S$ is the (possibly empty) set of final states.

State machines can be used to represent processes and action/state conversions in a flexible and coherent way. By designing state machines which reflect the relationship between decision strategies and IIMTs, we are able to identify patterns in the clickstream data and trace those patterns back to the chosen strategy which led to the initial choice and use of the IIMT. The data analysis is performed in several steps:

1. preprocessing: data cleansing
2. creation of activation vectors for each state machine
3. postprocessing I: cleaning activation vectors from unfinished clickstreams
4. postprocessing II: finding the dominating activation vectors

Algorithm 4 (see below) outlines the process. In the first step, the obtained clickstream data is cleaned to remove user clicks that have no benefit to the decision process but might bias the state machine's activity. Examples are repeated clicks on the same button with no effect or undo-actions.

The cleaned data is then processed by a set of M finite state machines representing the decision strategies. In any state machine M_k, we represented the typical behavior of a user following strategy k. M_k consists of a set of states and corresponding transitions between the states.

Algorithm 4 Data analysis

// data preprocessing
clickstream ← clean(clickstream)
// create activation vectors
for all state machines M_k **do**
   $t ← 0$
   for all clicks in clickstream **do**
      $A_k^t ← M_k.process(click)$
      $t ← t + 1$
   end for
end for
// postprocessing I
for all activation vectors A_k **do**
   $A_k ←$ removeAbortedSequences(A_k)
   $A_k ←$ removeUnfinishedSequences(A_k)
end for
// postprocessing II
$t ← 0$
sequence ← []
while clickstream is not empty **do**
   sequence ← sequence + longestConsecutiveActivation(t)
   $t ← t +$ lengthOfLongestConsecutiveActivation(t)
end while

The behavior implemented for each state machine is based on the pseudo-code notation described in section 4.2. The original versions for each strategy as published in Pfeiffer et al. (2009b) were slightly adapted in the calibration phase. First, each state machine that reflected pairwise comparison decision strategies was configured to also process the alternative for which a SCOREattributeLevel was assigned. This approach captures cases where users do not explicitly apply the IIMT PAIRWISE COMPARISON, but instead just compare two alternatives one after the other. Second, if the user performs an action that clearly argues against the strategy k, a transition to the special ABORT state can be made, after which the state machine is reset. Third, one or many of the states can be end states, indicating that all necessary prerequisites for the successful application of the strategy have been fulfilled (e.g. clicking at least one MARKmanually and at least one REMOVEalternative). See Figures 4 and 5 for examples of state machines.

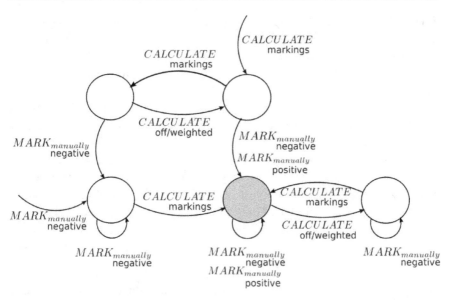

Figure 4   The state machine representing the FRQ strategy can be started by either click-
            ing the IIMTs $CALCULATE_{markings}$ (top right) or $MARK_{manuallyNegative}$ (bottom
            left). The state machine can only reach the final state (gray circle), if both the
            $CALCULATE$ radio button (see figure 3b) is set to the weighting mode markings
            (to display scores) and at least one mark (positive or negative) has been given.
            Note that giving negative marks is always possible, regardless of the state of the
            radio button.

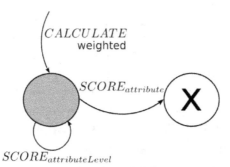

Figure 5   The state machine representing the EQW strategy can only be started by click-
            ing on the $CALCULATE_{weighted}$ button. It then accepts an arbitrary number of
            clicks on $SCORE_{attributeLevel}$ IIMTs (stars for attribute levels, e.g. "the attribute
            level '3' for the attribute 'megapixels of camera' equals to 4 stars"). If a $SCORE_{attribute}$ is clicked, the machine is aborted, because the user weighted an
            attribute and therefore clearly does not follow the equal weight strategy ("the
            attribute 'megapixels of camera' should be weighted with 5 stars").

The clickstream data of length l is represented by a sequence of input signals, where each I_t stands for a click on some IIMT at time t. A possible sequence of input signal might be (*FILTER, FILTER, MARK$_{negatively}$, REMOVE$_{markings}$*). Each state machine M_k decides whether it can process each input signal I_t ($a_t = 1$) or not ($a_t = 0$) and stores whether it is in a final state ($f_t = 1, if\ s_t \in F$) in an activation vector $A_k = ((a_1, f_1),\dots,(a_l, f_l)), a_t \in \{0,1\}, f \in \{0,1\}$. If I_t can be processed by M_k in the current state, a state change occurs and the successful transition is recorded by M_k in the activation vector. Furthermore, if the new state is a final state, this information is recorded. If I_t cannot be processed by M_k in its current state, the activation vector is assigned a 0 for a_t and the state of M_k remains unchanged. If the number of consecutive input symbols that cannot be processed rises over a threshold T, M_k is reset but the activation vector is retained. This prevents M_k from staying in an arbitrary state in case the user switches to another decision strategy within an ongoing decision process.

After all input signals I have been processed by all state machines M, the activation vectors A are postprocessed. In this step, all activation sequences preceding an ABORT state as well as all activation sequences that do not result in an end state (i.e. the prerequisites have not been fulfilled) are deleted.

The activation vectors A now represent the activity of the state machines M and thus the potential use of the strategies.

Since one IIMT is usually related to multiple decision strategies, it is likely that more than one state machine are active throughout the input sequence I (see Figure 6). Assuming that at each point in time t, a user follows only a single strategy, a dominant strategy for each t has to be identified. Let us define, $|A_k^t|$ as the length of consecutives ones for M_k in the activation sequence including and surrounding time t. For instance, if we have $A_k = ((1,0),(1,0),(0,0),(1,0),(1,1))$, then $|A_k^1| = 2, |A_k^2| = 2, |A_k^3| = 0, |A_k^4| = 2, |A_k^5| = 2$ and only the last state is an end state. The dominant strategy at each point in time t is the one with the largest $|A_k^t|$[4]. The dominating state machine in Figure 6 is highlighted in green.

While it dramatically reduces the complexity of the activation vectors, the applied domination principle has a disadvantage: it penalizes state machines that have successfully processed many clicks but show gaps in their activation pattern[5].

---

[4] Note that is possible that machine M_1 has a dominant activation of length l_1 at t_1 and machine M_2 has a dominant activation of length l_2 at $t_2 < t_1 + l_1$. Thus, the dominant strategies overlap at all t_n such that $t_2 < t_n < t_1 + t_n$. We preserved the full length of M_1 and M_2 in this case and accepted the overlap.

[5] These gaps can be due to several reasons, e.g. an incomplete definition of the state machine, experimental clicks by the user or incomplete data cleaning

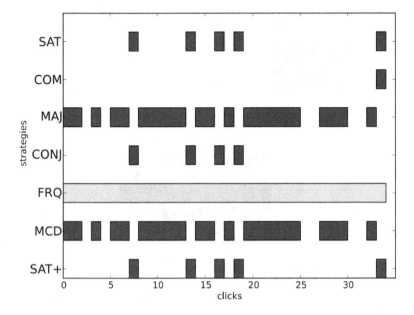

Figure 6   The state machine representing the FRQ strategy dominates the clickstream
              (longest uninterrupted activation).

5   Validation of State Machines with Empirical Data

We wanted to make sure that our algorithm detected the decision strategies actually used by decision makers. To this end, we conducted an empirical study with seventeen participants. The description of three different decision strategies (see descriptions in section 2 and in the appendix) was randomly assigned to each participant. The respondents were supposed to first get familiar with the user interface, including the different IIMTs. They were able to use all IIMTs as a test user and they also had the possibility to watch an introductory video which explained the functionality of the web page and each IIMT in detail. They were then asked to make three purchase decisions, using the three assigned decision strategies. In each purchase decision they were confronted with the same set of six cell phones described by sixteen different attributes. The cell phones and attributes were displayed in random order.

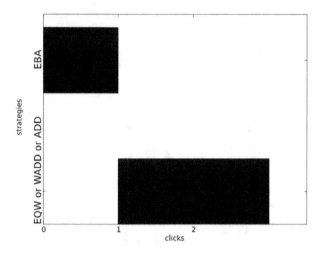

Figure 7   The dominating sequence of strategies is EBA, (EQW or WADD or ADD). In
                the first phase, a non-compensatory strategy is used, while in the second phase,
                the algorithm was unable to clearly distinguish between the three compensatory
                strategies.

One respondent only made two choices such that we collected a total data set of
50 decisions. Out of these 50 decisions, we had to delete one choice because of a
technical problem and six decisions because people reported that they hadn't understood the description of the decision strategy. Out of the remaining 43 decision
strategies, 20 decision strategies were fully identified by our algorithm and 8 had a
partial fit. We defined a partial fit as cases where the respondent used the supposed decision strategy but then used another strategy during a second decision-
making phase. For instance, if a respondent had first used a *FILTER* and then used
only $SCORE_{attribute}$, $SCORE_{attributeLevel}$ and $CALCULATE_{weighted}$, the algorithm would
identify a switch from an EBA to a WADD strategy. In the case where the respondent was supposed to use either EBA or WADD, this would be a partial fit. A
partial fit therefore does not mean that the algorithm assigned the wrong strategy,
rather it means that a respondent applied several strategies in a row instead of
sticking to the single one strategy he/she was assigned to. This happened because
the respondents were unfamiliar with the decision strategies before the experiment
and apparently sometimes had difficulties to fully understand the strategies.

The fact that respondents were unfamiliar with the decision strategies was also
reflected in 10 more choices. For these 10 choices, our algorithm classified an
EBA strategy although respondents were supposed to use CONJ (3 cases), COM
(1 case), DIS (3 cases), or SAT (3 cases). The latter four strategies are all charac-

terized by alternative-wise processing, while EBA is characterized by attribute-wise processing. Apparently it was not clear to respondents that applying a *FILTER* (indicating an EBA), which removes several alternatives at once from the matrix based on just one attribute, implies an attribute-wise comparison of alternatives and thus is not suitable to the application of any alternative-wise strategy.

The algorithm misclassified the remaining five choices. The five choices were interesting because the decision makers had understood the strategy and still deviated from the anticipated behavior. In two of these five choices, respondents were supposed to use a LEX strategy and the algorithm misclassified these decision processes as using an EBA strategy because of the usage of *FILTER*. Instead of *FILTER*, the LEX-state machine expects several $SORT_{hierarchically}$ because this is the IIMT that causes the least effort: a decision maker sorts the products according to the most important attribute. The product with the best attribute level for this attribute will appear in the leftmost column in the matrix. If there are ties, the decision maker sets a second sort criterion for the second most important attribute. The best product in terms of the two most important attributes will appear in the leftmost column. For these two misclassified choices, we encountered a special case. The two most important attributes for the two decision makers only had two attribute levels each. In this case, the effort to use *SORT* and *FILTER* is the same. When using *SORT,* the decision maker needs to select the most important attribute from a drop-down menu in the IIMT *SORT*. When using *FILTER*, the decision maker clicks the checkbox of the least preferred of the two attribute levels. Thus, for attributes with only two possible attribute levels (for instance, Bluetooth-yes, Bluetooth-no), the effort and the outcome for *FILTER* and *SORT* is comparable.

In one other case, the decision maker was supposed to use a WADD strategy. Instead of using $SCORE_{attributeLevel}$ and $SCORE_{attribute}$, which gives the user the possibility to assign up to 5 stars for each attribute and attribute level, this decision maker had very simple preferences and thus used a simplified version of a utility function. This simplified utility function was the same one that is assumed by FRQ. The decision maker used $MARK_{manually}$ to assign either 1 or 0 points to each attribute level and summed up the score of all attribute levels for each alternative. Furthermore, the decision maker did not weigh the importance of the attributes. Thus, in this case, the algorithm classified the behavior accurately as a FRQ strategy, which is the appropriate decision strategy describing this kind of simplified utility function.

In yet another case, a decision maker "misused" an IIMT. Although the decision maker was supposed to sum up negative attribute levels with $MARK_{manuallyNegative}$, she used $MARK_{manuallyPositive}$ instead. This had no effect on the final product chosen, but was unexpected by the state machine. More obviously distinguishing the design of the two IIMTs $MARK_{manuallyNegative}$ and $MARK_{manuallyPositive}$ might probably help to avoid this problem in future.

In the fifth of the five misclassified choices, a decision maker applied IIMT for SAT which causes much more effort than the behavior anticipated by the SAT-state machine. One might think about implementing several versions of possible IIMT-support for the same strategies and not just implementing the behavior that requires the least effort.

	Frequency
samples	49
incorrect use of strategy	16
full matches	20
partial matches	8
misclassifications	5

Table 2   Validation Results

To summarize, the algorithm correctly classified 20 of the 49 samples (see table 2). In eight other samples, the algorithm found mixed behavior where people applied an additional strategy to the one they were supposed to use. Thus, in these cases, the algorithm itself also correctly classified the choices, but the respondents failed to accurately follow the decision strategy. In total there were sixteen cases in which respondents had not correctly understood the strategy. It thus appears clear that a more elaborate description of strategies should be applied in future studies. In five other choices, respondents used IIMT in a way that caused more effort than the one implemented by the state machines and were thus misclassified. In sum, if we ignore all sixteen cases in which respondents had misunderstood the decision strategies, we get a hit rate of 85%.

6   Application

We conducted a second empirical study where 38 respondents had to, again, make three choices using the same settings as before (six cell phones described by sixteen attributes). This time, however, the respondents were not told to follow any particular decision strategy. Their task was just to purchase three different cell phones - one after the other - without any further instructions. Again, they were advised to watch the introductory video before they started their purchases. Our goal was to analyze real decision behavior and to test whether the state machines got meaningful results, in line with current research explaining how people decide.

Since in 12 choices respondents didn't use any IIMT at all and in one case, a respondent made four choices due to a technical error, we applied our algorithm to analyze the clickstream data of 102 choices.[6]

As expected, in some cases, people applied several decision strategies sequentially when making a choice (multiple-phased decision making). Respondents applied only one strategy in a single phase for 69 of the choice tasks. From these 69 strategies, EBA was the predominant strategy observed. In the remaining 33 choice tasks, respondents applied several decision strategies in subsequent phases, using on average three phases per choice. Thus in total, the state machines detected the application of 165 different phases. In 113 of the 165 phases, the algorithm infers a single strategy. In the rest of the phases, multiple strategies can be inferred from the clickstream. A common combination of strategies where the algorithm is unable to distinguish one strategy from another is WADD, ADD, EQW (see Figure 7). In sum, the high number of unambiguously identified strategies we found underlines the strength of our approach: despite the fact that only few IIMTs support so many different strategies, the algorithm succeeds in well differentiating between different decision strategies. Table 3 lists all decision strategies and their occurrences.

---

[6]   The pairs: LEX and LED as well as SAT and SAT+ are very closely related strategies and recovered by the same state machine. Hence, we count them as one single strategy.

Frequency	Strategy
10	ADD
5	ADD, DOM, MAJ, MCD
19	ADD, EQW, WADD
3	ADD, MCD
8	ADD, WADD
2	COM
4	COM,CONJ
2	COM, CONJ, DIS, SAT/SAT+
1	COM, CONJ, DOM, MAJ, MCD
1	CONJ
84	EBA
1	FRQ
4	LEX/LED
2	MCD
1	MCD, FRQ, MAJ
1	MCD, MAJ
9	SAT/SAT+
2	SAT/SAT+, CONJ
5	WADD
Sum: 165	

Table 3   Occurrences of Strategies

Finally, we analyzed whether the decision behavior inferred by the algorithm reflects the results which were found so far with process-tracing approaches. As a reminder, whenever people use not only one strategy but switch between several, studies have found that people first use non-compensatory strategies and then switch to compensatory strategies and that people tend to first use attribute-wise processing before switching to alternative-wise processing (see section 2). In the 33 cases with switching behavior, the switch between compensatory and non-compensatory strategies was observed in only 27 cases, while in 2 cases the switch occurred between two compensatory strategies and in 4 other cases, the switch occurred between two non-compensatory strategies. In 12 of the 27 cases, we found that people used the expected pattern: they first used non-compensatory strategies and then used compensatory strategies (see Table 4 and Figure 7). We observed unusual behavior in only 5 cases, where people switched from a compensatory to a non-compensatory strategy and in the remaining 10 cases they used mixed patterns, switching back and forth between compensatory and non-compensatory strategies. Within the 10 mixed-strategy choices, 7 started with the non-compensatory strategy EBA. Thus, in 19 of the 27 choices, respondents started with a non-compensatory strategy, which supports results from the literature.

Frequency	Phase 1	Phase 2	Phase 3
non-compensatory ⇒ compensatory			
1	SAT/SAT+	WADD	
2	LEX/LED	SAT,SAT+	ADD
1	EBA	MCD, DOM, ADD, MAJ	
7	EBA	EQW,ADD,WADD	
1	CONJ,COM	ADD,WADD	
compensatory ⇒ non-compensatory			
2	EQW, ADD, WADD	EBA	
1	WADD	EBA	
1	MCD,MAJ	CONJ,COM	EBA
1	MCD,DOM, ADD, MAJ	EBA	

Table 4   Occurrences of mixed strategies with a switch between non-compensatory and compensatory strategies.

We got very similar results when we analyzed the switch from attribute-wise to alternative-wise processing. In 75 of the 102 choices, decision makers applied only attribute-wise or alternative-wise decision strategies. In 12 of the remaining 27 choices, we observed the expected switch from attribute-wise to alternative wise processing and in only 5 cases the switch from alternative-wise to attribute-wise processing. In the remaining 10 cases, decision makers switched back and forth between attribute-wise and alternative-wise processing.

In sum, we found that the few mixed strategies observed in our studies were mostly in line with results from other studies. However, five respondents started with a compensatory strategy and then finished with a non-compensatory strategy. A possible explanation might be that they started with the more effortful EQW or WADD but gave up after some time to switch to a less effortful strategy. Furthermore, the question remains whether we are truly able to identify all types of mixed behavior when only analyzing the clicking data of IIMTs. It might be that people execute some decision phase in their mind without using any IIMT. Combining our analysis with eye tracking or some other process-tracing technique could reveal these mental processes and contribute relevant data to analyzing mixed behavior in more detail.

7   Conclusions and Future Work

In this work, we presented an algorithm which infers decision strategies from clickstreams. The main idea was to use a specific clickstream as input for the algorithm. The clickstream records the clicks on elements of a particular DSS, which in our case is an existing, prototypical implementation of IIMTs (Pfeiffer et al. (2010b)). IIMTs help consumers choose the preferred product when purchasing a good online. The algorithm is based on the concept of state machines. Each click on an IIMT triggers a set of state machines, where each state machine represents a particular decision strategy. After the state machines process the clickstream, the algorithm detects which of the activated state machines best explain the observed behavior. In the validation phase, we showed that the algorithm infers most of the strategies correctly. In a further empirical study, we analyzed the behavior of 38 respondents and showed that the inferred mix of decision strategies fits the behavior observed in literature so far. Until now, process-tracing approaches were only able to distinguish between general categories of strategies, such as between strategies with an overall alternative-wise or attribute wise information acquisition. In contrast to this, we were also able to determine the precise decision strategies that best explain the behavior.

The contribution of this work is threefold. First, we present a new process-tracing method that can be applied in decision-making research and goes beyond the limits of current approaches. Second, our concept can be applied to real-word online webstores that like to learn more about consumer decision-making behavior based on clickstreams. Finally, our algorithm is general enough to be easily applied to both research and real-world settings with other DSSs or other kinds of decision strategies. One has only to specify the relationship between single elements of the DSS and the decision strategies as well as design a state machine for each possible strategy.

In future work, we would like to compare other ways of finding the dominating activation vectors in the postprocessing phase. Furthermore, we would like to validate the state machines in an experiment where we ensure that each respondent has completely understood the decision strategies, which was the main disadvantage of the validation we presented in this work.

Appendix

DIS (disjunctive rule): The decision maker uses an alternative-wise approach. The alternative that satisfies the aspiration level for at least one relevant attribute is selected. If several alternatives fulfill this criterion, one of them is selected at random.

COM (compatibility rule): The decision maker uses an alternative-wise approach. The alternative that satisfies the aspiration levels on k attributes is selected. Parameter k is defined by the decision maker. k only defines how many attributes have to meet the aspiration level - the decision maker can consider different attributes for each alternative, as long as the number of considered attributes is equal to k for each alternative[7].

SAT (satisficing heuristic): The decision maker examines all alternatives alternative-wise and selects the first alternative that satisfies all aspiration levels. If no alternative satisfies all aspiration levels, nothing is selected.

ADD (additive difference rule): Attributes are compared two at a time. The decision maker evaluates all attributes and attribute levels with utility values. The overall utility of an alternative is the sum of all the weighted single utility values. A weighted single utility value is defined as the product of the utility value of the attribute level and the utility of the corresponding attribute. The utility value of an attribute allows the decision maker to rate some attributes as higher than others. The alternative with the highest overall utility value is compared with the next alternative. These pairwise comparisons are performed until only one alternative is left.

---

[7]   Note that for k=1 COM is equal to CONJ.

EQW (equal weights rule): The utility maximizing alternative is selected. The decision maker assigns attribute values to all attribute levels. The overall utility of an alternative is the sum of the attribute values. The strategy is called 'equal weight', since only attribute values vary, but attributes are weighted equally.

SAT+ (satisficing plus heuristic): The decision maker uses an alternative-wise approach in arbitrary order. The selected alternative is the one whose attribute levels meet the aspirations levels on all of the most important attributes first.

LED (minimum difference lexicographic rule): The alternative with the best attribute level for the most important attribute is selected. Alternatives that are only marginally worse are accepted. If several alternatives are equivalent for this attribute, then the second most important attribute is considered etc.

MAJ (majority rule): The decision maker defines the best attribute level for each attribute. The alternative that has the highest number of better attributes is selected.

References

Böckenholt, U., Albert, D., Aschenbrenner, M., and Schmalhofer, F. "The effects of attractiveness, dominance, and attribute differences on information acquisition in multiattribute binary choice," *Organizational Behavior and Human Decision Processes* (49:2), 1991, pp. 258–281.

Beach, L. *Image theory: Decision making in personal and organizational contexts.* Chichester, UK: Wiley, 1990.

Bettman, J., Johnson, E., Luce, M., and Payne, J. "Correlation, conflict, and choice," *Journal of Experimental Psychology: Learning, Memory, and Cognition*, 19, 1993, pp. 931–951.

Bettman, J., Johnson, E., and Payne, J. "A componential analysis of cognitive effort in choice," *Organizational Behavior and Human Decision Processes*, (45:1), 1990, pp. 111–139.

Bettman, J. and Park, C. W. "Effects of prior knowledge and experience and phase of the choice process on consumer decision processes: A protocol analysis," *Journal of Consumer Research*, 7, 1980, pp. 234–248.

Bröder, A. and Schiffer, S. "Bayesian strategy assessment in multi-attribute decision research," *Journal of Behavioral Decision Making*, 16, 2003, pp. 193–213.

Eisenfuhr, F. and Weber, M. *Rationales Entscheiden.* Springer, Berlin, Germany, 2002.

Fasolo, B., Misuaraca, R., and McClelland, G. "Individual differences in adaptive choice strategies," *Research in Economics*, (57:3), 2003, pp. 219–233.

Ford, J. K., Schmitt, N., Schechtman, S. L., Hults, B. M., and Doherty, M. L. "Process tracing methods: contributions, problems, and neglected research questions," *Organizational Behavior and Human Decision Processes*, (43:1), 1989, pp. 75–117.

Garbarino, E. C. and Edell, J. A. "Cognitive effort, affect, and choice," *Journal of Consumer Research*, (24:2), 1997, pp. 147–158.

Gilbride, T. and Allenby, G. "Estimating heteroogeneous eba and economic screening rule choice models," *Marketing Science*, (25:5), 2006, pp. 494–509.

Gilbride, T. J. and Allenby, G. M. "A choice model with conjunctive, disjunctive, and compensatory screening rules," *Marketing Science*, (23:3), 2004, pp. 391–406.

Gupta, P., Yadav, M. S., and Varadarajan, R. "How task-facilitative interactive tools foster buyers' trust in online retailers: A process view of trust development in the electronic marketplace," *Journal of Retailing*, (85:2), 2009, pp. 159–176.

Harte, J. M. and Koele, P. "Modelling and describing human judgement processes: The multiattribute evaluation case," *Thinking and Reasoning*, (7:7), 2001, pp. 29–49.

Hogarth, R. *Judgment and Choice* (2), Chichester, UK: Wiley, 1987.

Hopcroft, J. E., Motwani, R., and Ullman, J. D. *Introduction to Automata Theory, Languages, and Computation* (3). Addison-Wesley Longman Publishing Co., Inc., Boston, MA, USA, 2006.

Keeney, R. and Raiffa, H. *Decisions with multiple objectives: Preferences and value tradeoffs* (14), Wiley, 1993.

Klein, N. M. and Yadav, M. S. "Context effects on effort and accuracy in choice: An enquiry into adaptive decision making," *Journal of Consumer Research*, (15:4), 1989, pp. 411–421.

Lohse, G. and Johnson, E. "A comparison of two process tracing methods on choice tasks," *Organizational Behavior and Human Decision Processes*, (68:1), 1996, pp. 28–43.

Luce, M. F., Bettman, J. R., and Payne, J. W. "Choice processing in emotional difficult decisions," *Journal of Experimental Psychology: Learning, Memory, and Cognition*, (23:2), 1997, pp. 384–405.

Olshavsky, R. "Task complexity and contingent processing in decision making: A replication and extension," *Organizational Behavior and Human Performance*, 24, 1979, pp. 300–316.

Payne, J. "Task complexity and contingent processing in decision making: An information search and protocol analysis," *Organizational Behavior and Human Performance*, (16:2), 1976, pp. 366–387.

Payne, J., Bettman, J., and Johnson, E. "Adaptive strategy selection in decision making," *Journal of Experimental Psychology-Learning Memory and Cognition*, (14:3), 1988, pp. 534–552.

Payne, J., Bettman, J., and Johnson, E. *The Adaptive Decision Maker*. Cambridge University Press, Cambridge, UK, 1993.

Pfeiffer, J., Duzevik, D., Rothlauf, F., and Yamamoto, K. "A genetic algorithm for analyzing choice behavior with mixed decision strategies," In Raidl, G., editor, *Proceedings of the Genetic and Evolutionary Computation Conference*, Montreal, Canada. ACM Press, 2009a.

Pfeiffer, J., Meißner, M., Brandstätter, E., Riedl, R., and Rothlauf, F. "The influence of context-based complexity on human decision processes," Technical report, University of Mainz, University of Bielefeld, University of Linz, 2010a.

Pfeiffer, J., Riedl, R., and Rothlauf, F. "On the relationship between interactive decision aids and decision strategies: A theoretical analysis," In Hansen, H. R., Karagiannis, D., and Fill, H.-G., editors, *Proceedings of the 9th internationale Tagung Wirtschaftsinformatik*, 2009b.

Pfeiffer, J., Vogel, F., Stumpf, S., and Kiltz, C. "A theory-based approach for a modular system of interactive decision aids," In *Proceedings of the 16th Anmercias Conference on Information Systems (AMCIS)*, 2010b.

Reisen, N., Hoffrage, U., and Mast, F. W. "Identifying decision strategies in a consumer choice situation," *Judgment and Decision Making*, (3:8), 2008, pp. 641–658.

Riedl, R., Brandstätter, E., and Roithmayr, F. "Identifying decision strategies: A process and outcome-based classification method," *Behavior Research Methods*, (20:3), 2008, pp. 795–807.

Russo, J. and Dosher, B. "Strategies for multiattribute binary choice," *Journal of Experimental Psychology: Learning, Memory and Cognition*, (9:4), 1983, pp. 676–696.

Russo, J., Johnson, E., and Stephens, D. "The valdity of verbal protocols," *Memory and Cognition*, 17, 1989, pp. 759–769.

Russo, J. and Leclerc, F. "An eye-fixation analysis of choice processes for consumer non-durables," *The Journal of Consumer Research*, (21:2), 1994, pp. 274–290.

Russo, J. "Eye fixations can save the world: A critical evaluation and a comparison between eye fixations and other information processing methodologies," In Hunt, H. K., editor, *Advances in Consumer Research*, volume 21, pp. 561–570, Ann Arbor, MI. Association for Consumer Research, 1978.

Svenson, O. "Process descriptions of decision making," *Organizational Behavior and Human Performance*, 23, 1979, pp. 86–112.

Todd, P. and Benbasat, I. "An experimental investigation of the impact of computer based decision aids on decision making strategies," *Information Systems Research*, 2, 1991, pp. 87–115.

Todd, P. and Benbasat, I. "An experimental investigation of the impact of computer based decision aids on processing effort," *MIS Quarterly*, (16:3), 1992, pp. 373–393.

Todd, P. and Benbasat, I. "The influence of decision aids on choice strategies und conditions of high cognitive load," *IEEE Transactions on Systems Man and Cybernetics*, (24:4), 1994, pp. 537–547.

Tversky, A. "Intransitivity of preferences," *Psychological Review*, 76, 1969, pp. 31–48.

Tversky, A. "Elimination by aspects: A theory of choice," *Psychological Review*, 79, 1972, pp. 281–299.

A Research Model for Measuring IT Efficiency in German Hospitals[1]

Prof. Dr. Heiko Gewald

Neu-Ulm University of Applied Sciences, Wileystr. 21, 89231 Neu-Ulm, Germany, heiko.gewald@hs-neu-ulm.de

Prof. Dr. Heinz-Theo Wagner

German Graduate School of Management and Law, Bahnhofstr. 1, 74072 Heilbronn, Germany, heinz-theo.wagner@ggs.de

1 Introduction

More than 10% of the German gross domestic product is spent on health related services every year summing up to 263bn € in 2008 (Destatis 2010). A large proportion of these funds is invested into information technology (IT). Although solid empirical data on the allocation of these funds is scarce, the available studies offer interesting insights into the importance of IT in German health care: IT accounts for an estimated 2.9-3.7% of hospitals overall budget (VHitG 2010) and for an estimated ~14% of hospital investments (Blum and Schilz 2005).

IT in health care is used to lower the cost of health care delivery, to improve the quality of care for patients, to reduce medical errors and adverse patient events, thus improving health and well-being for the population (Devaraj and Kohli 2000).These outcomes are particularly salient in the current context of rising health care costs. The rising age of the population thus the increasing number of patients along with a declining number of medical doctors and nurses calls for efforts to optimally focus resources in this sector.

As mentioned above IT can support efforts to increase both efficiency e.g. in hospital processes by freeing up scarce human resources from administrative task and effectiveness, e.g. by providing means to improve the quality of care. However, health care presents a particularly difficult context for leveraging investments in IT, with highly decentralized structures, localized processes and specialized roles and skills becoming barriers to successfully deriving value from IT investments.

---

[1] Another version of this paper appeared as: Gewald, H., and Wagner, H.-T. "A Research Model for Measuring IT-Efficiency in German Hospitals", Proceedings of the 19th European Conference on Information Systems, Helsinki, Finland, 2011, pp. 1-8.

A. Heinzl et al. (eds.), *Theory-Guided Modeling and Empiricism in Information Systems Research*, DOI 10.1007/978-3-7908-2781-1_9, © Springer-Verlag Berlin Heidelberg 2011

Anecdotal evidence from expert discussions almost unanimously underlines a big potential to increase the value of IT often quoting inefficient usage of the deployed systems. This implies that even if the IT systems are the right ones (i.e. effective) the degree of usage is often suboptimal (i.e. inefficient). The role of IT usage as critical factor for leveraging IT investments has been shown in previous studies. In the context of hospitals - building on usage concepts of DeLone and McLean (1992) and Doll and Torkzadeh (1998) - Devaraj and Kohli (2003) identified IT usage as the missing link between investment into IT and performance effects.

If users refrain from using the provided IT systems[2] correctly as planned, inefficiencies are inevitable. The main concern in this kind of environment is that the actions of few have a big impact on the whole group of users mainly due to unavailability, inconsistency and incompleteness of data. In a patient care area incomplete or inconsistent data is virtually useless due to threats of malpractice.

Information systems (IS) research has investigated the factors influencing usage behavior in great detail, however, predominantly in contexts other than health care. For example, a large number of studies investigated usage behavior based on the Technology Acceptance Model (TAM) and its derivatives (DeLone and McLean 1992; DeLone and McLean 2003). Lately, the TAM and similar research models were consolidated, extended and reformulated as Unified Theory of Acceptance and Use of Technology (UTAUT) by Venkatesh et al. (2003). While studies using TAM or UTAUT focus on technology acceptance with special respect to IT, another more general theoretical perspective is rarely applied to the IT context: Social Cognitive Theory (Compeau and Higgins 1995) which explains usage behavior as influenced by psychological factors, e.g., individuals' beliefs about their abilities to handle IT systems, was shown to exert an influence on their usage behavior (Compeau and Higgins 1995) and in turn on the extent of IT usage.

In addition, we expect Perceived Risk Theory (PRT) (Bauer 1967) to play a vital role in our research context for the following argument: In health care doctors and nurses are liable for the actions they perform or chose not to perform on patients and may face lawsuits for malpractice in case of wrong decisions. The judgment whether a decision to perform certain action (or not) is appropriate, needs to be based on the information available at the time a certain decisions was made. It is important to recognize that IT systems like the electronic patient file provide quantitatively and qualitatively much more information than the old paper based file. This information needs to be taken into account for all patient related decisions in order to control liability issues.

---

[2]   There are multiple types of IT systems deployed within a hospital. This research focuses on the systems that support the major business process of a hospital (providing patient care). The systems associated to this process are administrative systems like electronic patient file. Specialized systems to analyze client health data, diagnostic or technical medical systems etc. as well as inter-organizational systems are not in scope.

Using these IT systems therefore involves two aspects that are considered by the users of these systems: (1) it becomes much easier to prove which information has been available at which point in time for diagnostic purposes, and (2) the doctor or nurse may face the allegation not to have taken all information into account which was available within the electronic file.

"Medical graphics" for example comprise the monitoring data and daily actions performed per patient by different nurses and doctors. In paper-based systems it is documented for which reason a patient is in hospital (main diagnosis). In electronic files issues as medication, body temperature, and blood pressure are documented additionally. Furthermore, new systems require the documentation of the complete anamnesis, e.g. patient often suffers from migraine but currently is in hospital because of heart insufficiency. In addition, issues as the registration of pain attacks (at which time, how long, which part of the body), nausea, appetite, and stool are required to be documented. Thus documentation is far more comprehensive than in the paper-based system and encompasses previously orally communicated issues when changing of shifts. Thus the use of these IT systems may subjectively increase the risk of malpractice lawsuits due to the vast amount of information per patient and the high degree of documentation and thus negatively influences IT usage (or foster resistance to use the system). Additionally, the system can document exactly at which time a doctor accessed which information, opening the door to delicate questions about personal prioritization of tasks. Therefore, PRT analyzing the risk a person subjectively associates with the consequences of a decision and its impact on the intention to perform the applicable action is also a relevant theory to incorporate.

Although there is a considerable amount of research in the IT usage context, the picture changes if it comes to the health care domain. The main issues are the influencing factors of IT usage rather than the IT usage construct itself. Devaraj and Kohli (2003) highlight the need for future research in particular for the following topics:

- Scrutinize factors influencing IT usage

- Determine key variables related to IT usage, and

- Investigate hospitals in different contexts.

Similarly, presenting one of the rare quantitative studies regarding the business value of IT in hospitals, Faehling et al. (2009) state that causal relationships are not sufficiently known and ask for further investigation.

In fact, research into IT usage in hospitals is indeed rare and insights into its antecedents are practically unknown. Regarding IT usage in German hospitals we were not able to locate academic research publications in this area. Given the importance as well as the anecdotal evidence regarding deficiencies in IT usage stated above it seems an obvious case for IS research to analyze user behavior in terms of systems acceptance and usage in a hospital environment and provide recommendations to increase efficiency.

To close this gap we formulate the main research question: What are the salient factors influencing the efficient usage of IT in hospitals?

To answer this question we built on previous research to propose a research model based on a combination of UTAUT, Social Cognitive Theory and PRT to provide a comprehensive basis for the analysis of usage. Furthermore, we refer to current research regarding the measurement of IT usage to measure the efficiency of IT in German hospitals. As outcome, we expect to provide a twofold theoretical contribution: (1) by using three rarely combined theoretical perspectives that all fit the research setting we expect to be able to more comprehensively explain IT usage in general and (2) by applying it to the health care sector we expect to deliver additional insights regarding IT usage, its antecedents and performance aspects in this research domain.

For practice, we aim to identify the levers influencing technology acceptance in the specific environment of public hospitals and to provide recommendation to increase user acceptance and thus overall efficiency.

To carry out this research project we engaged with two public hospitals (medium size and large) as well as a leading information technology provider with extensive experience in health care. We would be grateful for having the opportunity to discuss this proposal at ECIS 2011 with other researcher of this area in order to sharpen the model before we actually engage in the research project which is targeted to start in July 2011.

2   Related Literature

2.1   IT Business Value and IT Usage

The value contribution of IT is controversially discussed in theory and practice alike. Although some empirical studies demonstrate a positive relationship between IT and success variables (Bharadwaj, Bharadwaj, and Konsynski 1999; Brynjolfsson and Kemerer 1996; Devaraj and Kohli 2000; Dewan and Min 1997; Mukhopadhyay, Rajiv, and Srinivasan 1997) overall results are contradictive and result the so called "IT paradox" (Brynjolfsson, Hitt, and Yang 2002).

Recent studies address these contradictions and argue that the business value of IT is more indirect and characterized by a complex network of additional and moderating influence factors (Lee 2001). Melville et al. (2004) argue that both IT and organizational resources combined and orchestrated will create an output in the context of business processes which then affects the overall performance of a company.

One pivotal element found in studies dealing with the business value of IT is the "right" usage of provided information systems. In a study among US hospitals Devaraj and Kohli (2003) identify IT usage as the "missing link" to explain the business value of IT. They state that business value of IT accrues from IT usage and therefore, individual as well as organizational IT usage is crucial for exploiting e.g. the capacity of information systems.

Accordingly, many models have been developed to explain levels of usage. One of the most well-known models of usage at an individual level is the Technology Acceptance Model (TAM) and its derivatives investigating the effects of perceived usefulness and ease of use on user acceptance of IS (Lewis, Agarwal, and Sambamurthy 2003; Limayem and Hirt 2003; Taylor and Todd 1995; Venkatesh et al. 2003) as well as the enablers and inhibitors of technology adoption, acceptance, and usage (Cenfetelli 2004). Existing studies of IT usage mostly focus on the individual or task level (DeLone and McLean 2003; Doll and Torkzadeh 1998).

The extent to which IT is deployed can be measured along the four dimensions volume, diversity, breadth and depth that was proposed by Massetti and Zmud (1996) when examining EDI usage in complex organizations. Recently, Burton-Jones and Straub (2006) revised prior theoretical considerations on IT usage and propose measurement scales. Burton-Jones and Gallivan (2007) define a multi-level measurement of the IT usage construct.

This study builds on these insights of prior literature and addresses the IT usage context in hospitals.

2.2   IS Research in German Health Care

Given the importance of health care for the German economy and the relatively large role IT plays in it one wonders about the scarce body of research developed in this field to date. Research has not yet collected sufficient data, formulated the right research questions and developed adequate models to answer IS question in a hospital environment (Leimeister, Klapdor, Hoermann, and Krcmar 2008).

Amongst the few recent academic publications the work of Leimeister et al. ((Leimeister et al. 2008), (Faehling et al. 2009), (Koebler, Faehling, Leimeister, and Krcmar 2010)) based on a large scale quantitative empirical study is a rare exception. Leimeister et al. analyze questions of IT strategy, IT management practices and governance. However, they do not focus on IT efficiency and their outlook to further research explicitly calls for work on the causal connections determining the value of IT in hospitals.

Other research on IT in German hospitals focuses on budget related issues, methods to increase quality of patient treatment or the overarching question whether IT increases efficiency and effectiveness in hospitals. Koebler et al. (2010) provide a review of this literature. All these articles have one thing in common: although they focus on IT in German hospitals, none of them asks the question whether the IT is used efficiently.

3 Fundamental Research Model

The research approach is based on the assumption (backed by prior literature) that IT can generate more business value (e.g. by affecting business process performance) if the users, e.g. medical doctors, nurses, hospital administration, adopt and use the provided systems to a higher degree. Thus, human behavior is the key to efficient usage. For explaining IT usage we combine three theoretical perspectives all dealing with the explanation of usage behavior.

First, the well-known Technology Acceptance Model and its derivatives (e.g. DeLone and McLean 1992; DeLone and McLean 2003; Venkatesh et al. 2003) have been discussed and empirically tested in numerous studies covering several research domains.

Second, Social Cognitive Theory (Bandura 1977; Bandura 1978; Bandura 1982; Bandura 1984; Bandura 1986; Compeau and Higgins 1995) deals with the influence of psychological factors on usage behavior and complements of what we know from TAM and its derivatives.

Third, because case studies in the hospital context provide evidence for the importance of perceived risk and its influence on usage behavior, we also refer to Perceived Risk Theory (Bauer 1967). PRT analyses the risk a person subjectively associates with the consequences of a decision and its impact on the intention to perform the applicable action. PRT implies that, as long as the perceived benefits outweigh the perceived risks, the person has a positive attitude towards the particular decision. The perceived risk construct has been used to explain systems usage in areas where risk perception plays a vital role such as online banking or using online shops (e.g. (Cunningham, Gerlach, and Harper 2005)).

Combining these three theoretical perspectives into one research model we intend to get a more complete picture of the influencing factors of user behavior and in turn on IT usage.

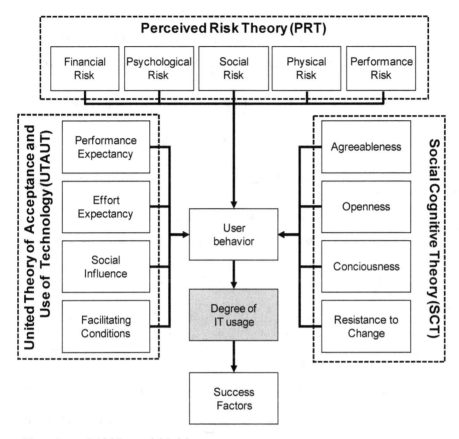

Figure 1:   Initial Research Model

In addition to the relationships amongst variables depicted in the research model we will also investigate cross-relationships between variables of one theory to variables of another one. E.g., variables of SCT might have influence on perceived risks.

4   Research Project Layout

In order to investigate the research questions described above the research project will focus on a primary business process in hospitals. There is strong evidence from literature to take on a business process perspective, because it is more appropriate to investigate the impact of IT factors on business outcomes (Barua, Kriebel, and Mukhopadhyay 1995; Tallon, Kraemer, and Gurbaxani 2000). One of the reasons to focus on business processes is to avoid a level of aggregation (such as analysis on firm level) that would lead to disguising the effects of IT by having too many influencing context factors.

The research project intends to deliver on following goals:

a) Develop instruments to quantitatively measure the efficiency of IT usage

b) Develop a research model to explain technology acceptance in a hospital context

c) Develop questionnaire to measure constructs included in the research model

d) Carrying-out pilot studies to test questionnaire and possibly adapt questionnaire

e) Empirically measure the status quo of IT usage (in participating hospitals)

f) Identify the enablers and inhibitors of efficient IT usage

g) Develop a framework to increase efficient IT usage (based on research model)

h) Apply framework in a real life project (action research within participating hospitals)

The scientific research work is supported by two publicly funded and administrated hospitals a very large and a medium sized organization. Additionally a globally leading provider of information technology and services to the health care industry joined the research group.

A project plan has been compiled consisting of measurable milestones to deliver the anticipated research goals in a three year time frame. Two fulltime research assistants are planned to work on the project supported by administrative staff. The project itself is scheduled to start in July 2011.

References

Bandura, A. "Self-Efficacy: Toward a Unifying Theory of Behavioral Change," *Psychological Review* (84:2), 1977, pp. 191-215.

Bandura, A. "Reflections on Self-Efficacy," In *Advances in Behavioral Research and Therapy* S. Rachman (Ed.), Pergamon Press, Oxford, 1978, pp. 237-269.

Bandura, A. "Self-Efficacy Mechanism in Human Agency," *American Psychologist*, (37:2), 1982, pp. 122-147.

Bandura, A. "Recycling Misconceptions of Perceived Self-efficacy," *Cognitive Therapy and Research* (8:3), 1984, pp. 231-255.

Bandura, A. Social Foundations of Thought and Action Prentice Hall, Englewood Cliffs, 1986.

Barua, A., Kriebel, C.H., and Mukhopadhyay, T. "Information Technologies and Business Value: An Analytical and Empirical Investigation," *Information Systems Research* (6:1), 1995, pp. 3-23.

Bauer, R. "Consumer Behavior as Risk Taking," In *Risk Taking and Information Handling in Consumer Behavior*, D.F. Cox (ed.), Harvard University Press, Cambridge, USA, 1967, pp. 21-33.

Bharadwaj, A.S., Bharadwaj, S.G., and Konsynski, B.R. "Information Technology Effects on Firm Performance as Measured by Tobin's q," *Management Science* (45:6), 1999, pp. 1008-1024.

Blum, K., and Schilz, P. "Krankenhaus Barometer 2005," Deutsches Krankenhaus Institut, 2005.

Brynjolfsson, E., Hitt, L.M., and Yang, S. "Intangible Assets: Computers and Organizational Capital," *Brookings Papers on Economic Activity* (1), 2002, pp. 137-181.

Brynjolfsson, E., and Kemerer, C.F. "Network Externalities in Microcomputer Software: An Economic of the Spreadsheet Market," *Management Science* (42), 1996, pp. 1627-1647.

Burton-Jones, A., and Gallivan, M.J. "Toward a Deeper Understanding of System Usage in Organizations: A Multilevel Perspective," *MIS Quarterly* (31:4), 2007, pp. 657-679.

Burton-Jones, A., and Straub, D.W. "Reconceptualizing System Usage: An Approach and Empirical Test," *Information Systems Research* (17:3), 2006, p 228-246.

Cenfetelli, R.T. "Inhibitors and Enablers as Dual Factor Concepts in Technology Usage," *Journal of the Association for Information Systems* (5:11-12), 2004, pp. 472-492.

Compeau, D.R., and Higgins, C.A. "Computer Self-Efficacy: Development of a Measure and Initial Test," *MIS Quarterly* (19:2), 1995, pp. 189-211.

Cunningham, L., Gerlach, J., and Harper, M. "Perceived risk and e-banking services: An analysis from the perspective of the consumer," *Journal of Financial Services Marketing* (10:2), 2005, pp. 165-178.

DeLone, W.H., and McLean, E.R. "Information Systems Success: The Quest for the Dependent Variable," *Information Systems Research* (3:1), 1992, pp. 60-95.

DeLone, W.H., and McLean, E.R. "The DeLone and McLean Model of Information System Success: A Ten-Year Update," *Journal of Management Information Systems* (19:4), 2003, pp. 9-30.

Destatis "2008: 263 Milliarden Euro fuer Gesundheit ausgegeben," Press Release Nr.126, 2010.

Devaraj, S., and Kohli, R. "Information Technology Payoff in the Health-Care Industry: A Longitudinal Study," *Journal of Management Information Systems* (16:4), 2000, pp. 41-67.

Devaraj, S., and Kohli, R. "Performance Impacts of Information Technology: Is Actual Usage the Missing Link?," *Management Science* (49:3), 2003, pp. 273-289.

Dewan, S., and Min, C.-k. "The Substitution of Information Technology for Other Factors of Production: A Firm Level Analysis," *Management Science* (43:12), 1997, pp. 1660-1675.

Doll, W.J., and Torkzadeh, G. "Developing a multidimensional measure of system-use in an organizational context," *Information & Management* (33:4), 1998, pp. 171-185.

Faehling, J., Koebler, F., Leimeister, J.-M., and Krcmar, H. "Wahrgenommener Wert von IT in Krankenhaeusern – eine empirische Studie," In *Business Services: Konzepte, Technologien, Anwendungen*, H.-R. Hansen, D. Karagiannis and H.-G. Fill (eds.), Oesterreichische Computer Gesellschaft, Wien, 2009, pp. 709-719.

Koebler, F., Faehling, J., Leimeister, J.-M., and Krcmar, H. "IT Governance and Types of IT Decision Makers in German Hospitals: An Empirical Study Among IT Decision Makers," *Business & Information Systems Engineering* (6), 2010, pp. 359-370.

Lee, C.S. "Modeling the business value of information technology," *Information & Management* (39:3), 2001, pp. 191-210.

Leimeister, J.-M., Klapdor, S., Hoermann, C., and Krcmar, H. *IT-Management in deutschen Krankenhaeusern: Eine empirische Untersuchung unter IT-Entscheidungstraegern*, Books on Demand, Norderstedt, 2008.

Lewis, W., Agarwal, R., and Sambamurthy, V. "Information Technology Use: An Empirical Study of Knowledge Workers," *MIS Quarterly* (27:4), 2003, pp. 657-678.

Limayem, M., and Hirt, S.G. "Force of Habit and Information Systems Usage: Theory and Initial Validation," *Journal of the Association for Information Systems* (4), 2003, pp. 65-97.

Massetti, B., and Zmud, R.W. "Measuring the Extent of EDI Usage in Complex Organizations: Strategies and Illustrative Examples," *MIS Quarterly* (20:3), 1996, pp. 331-345.

Melville, N., Kraemer, K.L., and Gurbaxani, V. "Information Technology and Organizational Performance: An Integrative Model of IT Business Value," *MIS Quarterly* (28:2), 2004, pp. 283-322.

Mukhopadhyay, T., Rajiv, S., and Srinivasan, K. "Information Technology Impact on Process Output and Quality," *Management Science* (43:12), 1997, pp. 1645-1659.

Tallon, P.P., Kraemer, K.L., and Gurbaxani, V. "Executives' Perceptions of the Business Value of Information Technology: A Process-Oriented Approach," *Journal of Management Information Systems* (16:4), 2000, pp. 145-173.

Taylor, S., and Todd, P. "Assessing IT Usage: The Role of Experience," *MIS Quarterly* (19:4), 1995, pp. 561-570.

Venkatesh, V., Morris, M.G., Davis, G.B., and Davis, F.D. "User Acceptance of Information Technology: Toward a Unified View," *MIS Quarterly* (27:3), 2003, pp. 425-478.

VHitG "Branchenbarometer 2010: Markterhebung zur Bewertung und Verteilung von IT in deutschen Gesundheitseinrichtungen.", 2010.

Managing the Impact of Differences in National Culture on Social Capital in Multinational IT Project Teams – A German Perspective[1]

Alexander von Stetten

Department of Information Systems and Services, University of Bamberg, Feldkirchenstr. 21, 96052 Bamberg, Germany, alexander.von-stetten@uni-bamberg.de

Dr. Daniel Beimborn

Department of Information Systems and Services, University of Bamberg, Feldkirchenstr. 21, 96052 Bamberg, Germany, daniel.beimborn@uni-bamberg.de

Prof. Dr. Tim Weitzel

Department of Information Systems and Services, University of Bamberg, Feldkirchenstr. 21, 96052 Bamberg, Germany, tim.weitzel@uni-bamberg.de

Zita Reiss

Department of Information Systems and Services, University of Bamberg, Feldkirchenstr. 21, 96052 Bamberg, Germany, zita.reiss@googlemail.com

1   Introduction

Social relationships within multinational teams are often burdened by cultural differences between the team members. Severe difficulties arising from such differences include conflict, mistrust, and miscommunication (Salk and Brannen,

---

[1]   Another version of this paper appeared as: von Stetten, Alexander, Beimborn, Daniel, Weitzel, Tim, and Reiss, Zita, "Managing the Impact of Differences in National Culture on Social Capital in Multinational IT Project Teams – A German Perspective," *Proceedings of the 19th European Conference on Information Systems (ECIS 2011)*.

A. Heinzl et al. (eds.), *Theory-Guided Modeling and Empiricism in Information Systems Research*, DOI 10.1007/978-3-7908-2781-1_10, © Springer-Verlag Berlin Heidelberg 2011

2000). This in turn hampers the creation of social capital within the team and thus leads to sub-optimal knowledge exchange, collaboration, and project performance. Consequently, numerous studies consider cultural differences in the context of multinational teams and propose various management actions that can be taken to overcome resulting problems in the network of relationships among team members (e.g., Carmel, 1999; Carmel and Agarwal, 2001; Earley and Mosakowski, 2000; Govindarajan and Gupta, 2001; Oshri et al., 2007; Sarker and Sarker, 2009; Walsham, 2002). However, in doing so, prior literature concentrates merely on the encompassing concept of cultural differences and remains silent about the impact of differences in particular dimensions of national culture. By contrast, we argue that elaborating on the specific cultural dimensions in which general cultural differences are rooted would significantly contribute to better understand and manage negative effects of such differences on intra-team relationships in multinational teams. Consequently, our research questions (RQ) are:

RQ1: *What are negative consequences of cultural differences on social capital in multinational IT project teams and in which particular dimensions of national culture are these differences rooted?*

RQ2: *Which management measures can be applied to handle these differences in particular dimensions of national culture that had been identified within RQ1?*

By answering these questions, this paper covers the three waves of culture research mentioned by Leidner (2010). First, cultural differences between team members are identified, second, the identified cultural differences are explained drawing on the concept of cultural dimensions, and third, activities for managing the negative effects of these differences are proposed. However, answering culture-related research questions is always contingent on the culture(s) of the objects of empirical analysis. For this paper, we have conducted case studies in firms headquartered in Germany; therefore the answers to the research questions given by this paper solely reflect a German perspective.

The remainder of this paper is structured as follows: Section 2 forms the conceptual basis for our research model. Section 3 introduces the applied research approach before chapter 4 presents and analyzes the results. Finally, section 5 draws a conclusion.

2   Theoretical Background and Model Development

2.1   Dimensions of (National) Culture

Driven by the rising globalization in the IT industry, national culture and resulting cultural differences have received much attention in IS research for several years. Sarker et al. (2010) just recently stated that cultural differences constitute a key issue in global software development projects.

Serving as a theoretical basis for our research work, the GLOBE project defines culture as "shared motives, values, beliefs, identities, and interpretations or meanings of significant events that result from common experiences of members of collectives and are transmitted across age generations" (House et al., 2004, p. 57). GLOBE is a comprehensive study examining the relationship between cultural values, practices, and leadership, as well as organizational and societal effectiveness in 62 societies and was initiated in 1991 (House et al., 2004). Having extensively analyzed numerous cultural dimensions developed in prior scientific literature, the authors identified nine cultural dimensions (cf. Table 1) that were measured in terms of practices ("the way things are") and values ("the way things should be").

Uncertainty Avoidance (UA)	the extent to which members of a society strive to avoid uncertainty by relying on established social norms, rules or bureaucratic practices
Power Distance (PD)	the degree to which members of an organization or society expect and agree that power should be stratified and concentrated at higher levels of an organization or government
Institutional Collectivism (I/C 1)	the degree to which organizational and societal institutional practices encourage and reward collective distribution of resources and collective action
In-group Collectivism (I/C 2)	the degree to which individuals express pride, loyalty, and cohesiveness in their organization or families
Gender Egalitarianism (GE)	the degree to which an organization or a society minimizes gender role differences while promoting gender equality
Assertiveness (AS)	the degree to which individuals in organizations or societies are assertive, confrontational, and aggressive in social relationships
Future Orientation (FO)	the degree to which individuals in organizations or societies engage in future-oriented behaviors such as planning, investing in the future, and delaying individual or collective gratification
Performance Orientation (PO)	the degree to which an organization or society encourages and rewards group members for performance improvement and excellence
Humane Orientation (HO)	the degree to which individuals in organizations or societies encourage and reward individuals for being fair, altruistic, friendly, generous, caring, and kind to others

Table 1:   Definitions of the Cultural Dimensions of House et al. (2004)

2.2   Social Capital

Our research objective is to analyze negative consequences of differences in particular dimensions of national culture on social relationships in multinational IT
project teams. We conceptualize social relationships in a team context by drawing
on the social capital concept. Although the current literature lacks agreement on a
precise definition of social capital, of its measurement and its interpretation, there
is a broad consensus among the researchers in different disciplines about the significance of inter-personal relationships as a resource for social action (Yang et al.,
2009) and the ability of actors to secure benefits by virtue of membership in social
networks or other social structures (Portes, 1998). Nahapiet and Ghoshal (1998),
who provided one of the most commonly used conceptualizations of social capital
in organizational research (cf. Robert Jr. et al., 2008), define it as "the sum of the
actual and potential resources embedded within, available through, and derived
from the network of relationships possessed by an individual or social unit" (Nahapiet and Ghoshal, 1998, p. 243). They specified three dimensions of social capital: the structural, the cognitive and the relational dimension.

The structural dimension is defined as "the impersonal configuration of linkages
between people or units […] [or] the overall pattern of connections between actors" (Nahapiet and Ghoshal, 1998, p. 244) and refers to the ties among actors and
reflects the potential resources accruing to an individual or a group from those ties
(e.g., "who knows whom" and "how do you reach him"). The cognitive dimension
of social capital describes "those resources providing shared representations, interpretations, and systems of meaning among parties" (Nahapiet and Ghoshal,
1998, p. 244) and is embodied in attributes that facilitate common understanding
of collective goals and proper ways of acting in a social system. In this context,
shared representations, interpretations, and systems of meaning serve as a bonding
system and can reduce inter-partner conflict and facilitate the negotiation and
establishment of common goals (Tsai and Ghoshal, 1998). The cognitive dimension can be divided into the subcomponents shared language and codes as well as
shared narratives. The third dimension, labeled "the relational dimension", corresponds to "the kind of personal relationships people have developed with each
other through a history of interactions" (Nahapiet and Ghoshal, 1998, p. 244) and
relates to the nature and quality of relationships among people and how those
relationships affect their behavior. The relational dimension of social capital can
be divided into the subcomponents trust, norms, obligations and expectations, and
identification.

Several works have shown the applicability of the social capital concept on the
team level (e.g., Oh et al., 2004; Reagans and Zuckerman, 2001; Robert Jr. et al.,
2008). Elaborating on the influence of national culture on subcomponents of social

capital in a multinational team context, existing literature revealed that cultural diversity hampers the efficient development of a shared understanding as well as commonality among teammates (Carmel, 1999; DeSanctis and Poole, 1997; Vallaster, 2005). DeLone et al. (2005) quote that cultural differences based on divergent values affect team cognition encompassing shared beliefs, shared knowledge, and the development of trust in global IS development projects. Particularly, trust building is highly influenced by differences in national culture as this process strongly depends upon the societal norms and values that guide people's behavior and beliefs (Doney et al., 1998; Huff and Kelley, 2003). Earley and Mosakowski (2000) confirm that team identity is affected by the nationality of the team members, and Paul and Ray (2009) report a negative relationship between cultural differences and team social integration in this context.

2.3   Management Measures to Overcome the Negative Impact of Cultural Differences on Social Capital in Multinational Project Teams

To overcome the negative effects of cultural differences on social capital, certain management practices have to be applied. Examples how management can react to problems arising from cultural differences, include cross-cultural education and training (e.g., Carmel, 1999; DeLone et al., 2005; Walsham, 2002), clearly specifying roles and coordination mechanisms (Winkler et al., 2008), setting up (periodic) face-to-face meetings (e.g., Carmel, 1999; Kotlarsky and Oshri, 2005; Oshri et al., 2007), selecting global team leaders who exhibit high levels of cultural awareness (e.g., Carmel and Agarwal, 2001; Govindarajan and Gupta, 2001; Kayworth and Leidner, 2000), language training (e.g., DeLone et al., 2005; Govindarajan and Gupta, 2001), creating a hybrid team culture (Earley and Mosakowski, 2000), or instilling a sense of cultural awareness (Kayworth and Leidner, 2000). A comprehensive range of such measures, applied to manage cross-cultural differences in IS offshoring relationships, is provided by Gregory (2010).

3   Research Approach

Prior literature shows that cultural differences have an impact on social capital and that this impact is – to a certain degree – manageable. However, these studies usually talk about cultural differences in general but do not amplify the cultural dimensions in which the cultural differences are rooted. To address this lack, we did an exploratory case study analysis. This analysis was guided by a baseline model (cf. Figure 1) which explicates possible relationships between (differences in) all dimensions of national culture and the three dimensions of social capital and which also takes into account the impact which different management measures have on those relationships. First, our exploratory case study approach intends to reduce this baseline model to those relationships between culture dimensions and social capital dimensions that could *indeed* be explored in our interviews (i.e., answer to RQ1). Second, it is our goal to identify those management measures that reduce or dampen those negative effects of cultural differences on social capital which were uncovered in the first step of the analysis (i.e., answer to RQ2)[2].

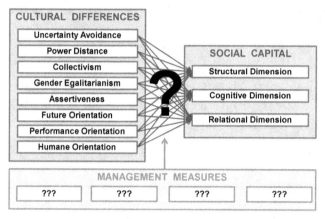

Figure 1:   Baseline Model

Kaplan and Duchon (1988, p. 15) assert that case studies provide "a source of well grounded, rich descriptions and explanations of processes occurring in local contexts" making them well suited for investigating emergent phenomena. In line with Kaplan and Duchon (1988), Yin (2009) points out that case studies are ideally suited when "how" or "why" research questions are posed, when the investigator has limited control over events and boundaries of a contemporary, complex social phenomenon (i.e., cultural differences and social capital) within its real-life context (i.e., multinational IT project teams), and when the phenomenon and the context in which it is investigated are unclear or closely related. Challenges of understanding the relationships between the particular dimensions of national culture and the dimensions of social capital within multinational IT project teams as well as the critical question how to manage this relationship meet these criteria.

---

[2]   Since Figure 1 looks like a causal model, we want to clarify that we follow a purely exploratory approach. This baseline model does not reflect a derived theory to be tested but serves as the starting point of our exploratory case analysis.

Since "theory building from multiple cases typically yields more robust, genera-lizable, and testable theory than single-case research" (Eisenhardt and Graebner, 2007, p. 27), we adopted a multiple-case study design within this research work. Two case selection criteria were applied. First, the chosen IT project team had to consist of members from at least two different nationalities. Second, we chose cases with both successful and unsuccessful projects because Flyvbjerg (2006) and Eisenhardt (1989) recommend maximum variation cases and extreme situations to be appropriate to obtain information about the significance of various circums-tances. We collected data from six different IT projects by interviewing 8 key informants (with one of them comparing two of the projects). The projects belong to four companies from different industries, and the companies as well as the project teams vary in size. The subsequent tables summarize context information about the case study partner firms, the investigated projects, and the interviewees. The IT projects ranged from software development to replacement and roll-out of ERP systems.

	Company A	Company B
Industry	construction	manufacturer of specialized technical components
Turnover	1-5 bn €	< 1 bn €
Employees	5,000-10,000	< 5,000
	Company C	Company D
Industry	IT	consulting
Turnover	5-15 bn €	> 15 bn €
Employees	10,000-50,000	> 50,000

Table 2:   Case Study Partner Firms (no Exact Numbers Given to Ensure the Firms' Anonymity)

	Project 1 (Company A)	Project 2 (Company B)	Project 3 (Company C)
project type	replacement of legacy ERP system by ERP standard software in a plant in the Czech Republic	replacement of legacy ERP system by ERP standard software in a plant in the Czech Republic	ongoing software development project with release cycles of 3 months
initiator	German parent company	German sister company	-
geograhically distributed?	team distributed between Germany and the Czech Republic	team distributed between Germany and the Czech Republic	team distributed betw. Germany and India (since summer 2008)
team configuration	15 team members (9 Czechs, 6 Germans)	23-29 team members (16-22 Czechs, 7 Germans)	10 team members (5 Indian, 5 German)
project start	beginning of 2008	April 2007	project start: 1998; start of staff distribution: summer 2008
project success	project still in progress; time delays	project successfully (in time) completed in March 2008	project still in progress; distribution of the project was stopped by the end of 2008; relocation on-site back to Germany due to time and quality problems

	Project 4 (Company C)	Project 5 (Company C)	Project 6 (Company D)
project type	ongoing software development project with release cycles of 6 months	software development project	software development project for client firm (finance industry)
initiator	-	-	-
geograhically distributed?	team distributed between Canada and India	team distributed between Germany and India	team distributed between Switzerland and India
team configuration	about 50 team members, organized in 5 sub-teams; 4 sub-teams located in Canada (members from various countries); 1 sub-team located in India (consisting of 10 Indian team members)	4 team members (3 Indian, 1 German)	62 team members, organized in several sub-teams in Switzerland (in total consisting of 17 Swiss consultants from Company D, 30 Swiss employees of the client company, and 1 German project manager) and one sub-team in India (consisting of 14 Indians)
project start	beginning of 2007	summer 2009	November 2009
project success	project still in progress	project successfully (in time) completed in spring 2010	project still in progress; project completion planned in 2011

Table 3:   Case Study Projects

A team of two researchers (same persons in all interviews) conducted eight semi-structured interviews (cf. Table 4) following the recommendations from Myers and Newman (2007). Each interview lasted between one and two hours and was recorded and fully transcribed. Regarding 3 projects, we were able to get two perspectives from different managers involved.

	Mr. A	Mr. B	Mr. C	Mr. D
interview	face-to-face	face-to-face	face-to-face	face-to-face
company	A	A	B	C
project	1	1	2	3
nationality	German	German	German	German
job location	Germany	Germany	Germany	Germany
job title	head of department for international business	member of department for international business	team manager sales, logistics, and international information management	software developer
role within the project	advisory activity within the project	project manager (German side)	manager of sub-project (sales order process)	project team member
intercultural experience before the project	broad experience; several job-related trips to several foreign countries	broad experience; several job-related trips to several foreign countries	broad experience; several job-related trips to several foreign countries	no experience
	Mr. E	Mr. F	Mr. G	Mr. H
interview	telephone	face-to-face	face-to-face	telephone
company	C	C	C	D
project	4	5	3 & 5	6
nationality	German	German	German	German
job location	Canada (since 2005)	Germany	Germany	Switzerland
job title	quality program engineer/ software developer	software developer	software development manager	senior technology architect
role within the project	project team member with coordination function	project team member	manager of several project teams including projects 3 and 5	overall project manager
intercultural experience before the project	broad experience; several job-related trips to several foreign countries	no experience	broad experience; several job-related trips to India	broad experience; several job-related trips to several foreign countries

Table 4:   Interviewees

Within the data analysis, we applied both qualitative and quantitative methods of transcript analysis. However, consistent with Yin (2009), the primary purpose of conducting this case study is to create theory by exploration from qualitative content analysis. Thus, quantitative data analysis (i.e., frequency analysis) merely served to further substantiate and to illustrate the results gathered from the qualitative data analysis. Data analysis was conducted by using MAXQDA (www.maxqda.com). Qualitative data analysis occurred by systematically structuring the transcribed material into categories and to generate hypotheses (Brodbeck et al., 2007; Kohlbacher, 2005). Quantitative data analysis was carried out by frequency analysis (Brodbeck et al., 2007; Kohlbacher, 2005).

Cultural differences and social capital were coded based on the cultural dimensions of House (2004) and on the conceptualization of social capital according to Nahapiet and Ghoshal (1998). With the first goal being to explore the impact of cultural differences on social capital, relationship categories were created, linking differences in cultural dimensions to the components of social capital. Further, inductive category development (open coding) was applied to extract management measures – fitting to the context of our research model – from the interviews (Brodbeck et al., 2007). Within a feedback loop between the researchers, the identified measures were revised and checked with respect to their reliability. Eventually, they were categorized in higher-order categories.

4   Results

Projects 1 and 2 face cultural differences between team members from the Czech Republic and Germany while projects 3 to 6 consist of team members from India and various Western nations (mostly Germany, Switzerland, and Canada). These different settings provided two different groups of results which are treated separately in the following. Thereby, all of our results are limited to a German perspective as we only had German interview partners.

Elaborating on projects 3 to 6, our five German interviewees reported almost the same typical characteristics of Indian colleagues which resulted in relationship problems within the team. Summarizing the interviews, we identified two India-specific patterns with regard to negative effects of cultural differences on subcomponents of social capital and pattern-specific as well as general management measures that were employed to address such effects (cf. Figure 2). These two patterns, displayed in Figure 2, result from reducing the baseline model (cf. Figure 1) to all relationships uncovered from analyzing the Indian-German IT project teams. We did not identify any other relationships between culture dimensions and social capital dimensions in these cases.

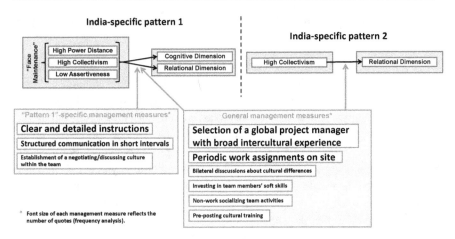

Figure 2:   Identified Relationships between Culture Differences and Social Capital
              (India-specific)

In the first pattern (left) cultural differences are rooted in a combination of relatively higher Power Distance, higher Collectivism, and lower Assertiveness of
Indian team members compared to their German respectively Western colleagues.
These three dimensions and their characteristics on the Indian side were highly
interdependent. Thus, we were not able to analyze each dimension's impact on
social capital separately and therefore treated them as a combined concept. This
combination of high Power Distance, high Collectivism, and low Assertiveness
results in a certain code of conduct on the Indian side, which was observed repeatedly by our interviewees. Typical characteristics of this code of conduct include a
tendency to say yes, to express oneself in an indirect and concealing way, and to
avoid criticism. Referring to Ting-Toomey and Cole (1990), this observation can
be labeled as "Face Maintenance". Pointing in the same direction, House et al.
(2004, p. 131) bring "Face Saving" into relation with avoiding negatives and being
indirect and evasive. Investigating the impact of the characteristics of these three
cultural dimensions in a joint manner seems to be appropriate against the chosen
theoretical background as the observed traits cannot be clearly assigned to only
one cultural dimension when following the GLOBE study (House et al., 2004).
For instance, indirect communication indicates both low Assertiveness (House et
al., 2004, p. 405) and high Collectivism (House et al., 2004, pp. 452, 454). Furthermore, Dibbern et al. (2008, p. 358) bring up Power Distance in the same context by claiming that "the high level of power distance in India [is] reflected in
certain behaviors [...] such as a high level of conformism (tendency to say yes)".
With regard to social capital, we identified a negative impact of "Face Maintenance" on the cognitive and most of all on the relational dimension. In contrast, we

did not identify any relationship between "Face Maintenance" and the structural dimension of social capital.

Elaborating on the relational dimension, trust was the subcomponent which has repeatedly been reported to be negatively affected by "Face Maintenance". The interview partners D to H had more or less difficulties to trust their Indian colleagues for quality reasons as they never asked for assistance even if they had serious trouble when accomplishing work and because they would not raise concerns against anything or admit not to be able to fulfill a given task. For instance, Mr. D mentioned: "You cannot rely on each spoken word. If you ask them something like 'Are you able to do this?' they will always reply 'Yes' no matter if they are able or if they are not. [...] When it then comes to a milestone or a deadline, we discovered too often that they had not been able to handle their workload". Mr. H takes a similar line: "If they are not able to fulfill a task, they usually won't ask another colleague even if they are pretty sure that one of their colleagues knows how to fulfill this particular task. They will try on their own again and again even if they go round in circles. [...] I am always a bit skeptical concerning the results". With regard to the contrary direction, all our (German) interview partners D to H felt that the Indian colleagues trusted them. However, this trust is highly vulnerable when it comes to criticism: "In their culture, criticism is never expressed openly and directly. If you do so, they won't complain or anything alike but become even quieter as they already are. [...] Their confidence in the person criticizing will decline. [...] If you want to criticize them you have to be very cautious because we seem offensive to them quite fast" (Mr. F).

Concerning the cognitive dimension of social capital, creating a shared understanding between Indian team members and their foreign colleagues is problematical due to the Indians' indirect and convoluted enunciation: "Sometimes, words spoken by an Indian colleague don't mean the same what we understand by these words. [...] You have to realize that 'Yes' could mean anything. It could actually mean 'Yes' or it could mean 'No' or 'Maybe' or anything else. [...] Building up a common understanding of what a spoken word really means is difficult" (Mr. E). Another example is given by Mr. F: "You have to learn to interpret what they say. For instance, if it exceptionally happens at one point that an Indian colleague remarks something about a very small issue concerning the task to be accomplished, it means that he has absolutely no idea about how to accomplish this task and that it will never be accomplished in time".

To overcome the abovementioned difficulties particularly arising from "Face Maintenance", companies employed certain specific management measures. In this context, giving clear and detailed instructions was most frequently mentioned and also most emphasized within the interviews (highlighted by larger font size in

Figure 2). A typical statement has been given by Mr. H who explains that "[the Indian colleagues] require highly detailed and perfectly clear instructions as they would not inquire if something is ambiguous". Further on, it is suggested to introduce structured communication in short intervals: "Regular meetings in short intervals - if possible in a daily rhythm – enhance transparency and thus trust on our side as they give us the opportunity to check the work progress and address possible issues promptly" (Mr. F). Within those meetings, interviewees underline that monologues of the German team members are not very helpful. Everything is about real discussions all team members participate in. To achieve this, an open and discussion-oriented culture has to be established: "The first thing is, not to give them the opportunity to answer with 'Yes' or 'No'. To get a real discussion started you have to ask something like 'What has changed since our last conversation?' or 'What do you think about the progress against the background of the next milestone?" (Mr. F). Another advice is given by Mr. G who underlined "to over and over again encourage and ask them to give their own opinion. However, this will not result in an Indian colleague saying anything like 'No, it is not possible', but at least an expression of opinions like 'Yes, but...' is realistic. [...] However, it is definitely not our goal to have Indian colleagues behaving like Germans. But if both sides approach each other a little bit, different interpretations and systems of meaning are better understood, and misunderstandings become less likely".

This first India-specific pattern, revealing the negative effect of "Face Maintenance" on the relational and the cognitive dimension of social capital has been confirmed implicitly by each of our German interviewees D to H. They claimed that it is of utmost importance to manage the negative consequences of what we labeled "Face Maintenance".

The second identified India-specific pattern was also raised by each of our German interview partners. However, it has been rated as less important compared to the first pattern. It is about the negative influence of relatively higher Collectivism of Indians as compared to Germans on the relational dimension of social capital. In this context, high Collectivism on the Indian side means a very strong relationship to the wider family circle. Such a strong relationship for instance results in Indian team members travelling thousands of kilometers overnight in case of (not even seriously) illness of a more or less closely related family member and staying there until the ill relative feels better, completely neglecting any urgent project deadline or something alike. As a consequence, some distrust exists on the German side if important deadlines or milestones are imminent since it is always possible that an Indian team member stays away from work some days without prior warning because of any family reason. Mr. H comments on this issue as follows: "If there is any problem in the wider family, they are gone. From one day to the next. They say they need a four week time-out or so and then they just leave. [...] As a consequence, skepticism on our side is rising the closer a deadline comes. [...] Yes, possibly this could also result in declining confidence on our side". However, our German interview partners did not report any management measures that had been employed especially with regard to this second pattern. One possible reason for this is given by Mr. H: "In my view there is nothing you can do. [...] You have to learn to get used to it". Learning how to deal with such cultural differences between German and Indian colleagues implies to become more familiar with the other culture. This again is indispensable for any kind of cultural management which always pursues the objective to manage cultural differences and not to reduce them. To create such a comprehensive awareness of the other culture and to better understand it, companies employ several general management measures beside the pattern-specific ones which were presented before. Two of these general measures were mentioned by each interviewee and deemed absolutely crucial. The first is to select a global project manager with broad intercultural experience who takes a mediating role and operates as a global bridgehead; the second are periodic (if possible bidirectional) work assignments on site. Such assignments enable to gain insight in the colleagues' foreign culture and clearly contribute to better understanding each other. The interview partners emphasize that – for a certain time – on-site employment in India and vice versa is indispensable regardless of the costs. Further measures that were less frequently mentioned and considered reasonable include the investment in team members' soft skills (to be able to better react to unpredictable situations or behavior), intercultural training, bilateral discussions about cultural differences within the team (in group or in confidence), and non-work socializing team activities during on-site visits.

After having presented the India-specific results of our exploratory case study, we dwell on the Czech-specific results (cf. Figure 3) gained within the three interviews (projects 1 and 2) with members of the Czech-German IT project teams. Extracting links from culture dimensions to social capital dimensions (cf. Figure 1) from these three interviews resulted in Figure 3. Other relationships than the ones displayed here could not be identified by the researchers.

Czech-specific pattern

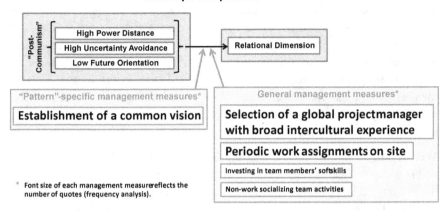

Figure 3:   Identified Relationships between Culture Differences and Social Capital
                 (Czech-specific)

In general, our German interview partners (Mr. A, Mr. B, and Mr. C) reported cultural differences between Czech and German team members but also under-lined that those differences are in most cases not big enough to cause serious prob-lems within the team. However, they indicated negative effects of a characteristic we labeled "Post-Communism". This concept can be described by a combination of high Power Distance, high Uncertainty Avoidance, and low Future Orientation. Indicating high Power Distance and high Uncertainty Avoidance, Mr. A mentions: "In the Czech Republic, everything is very formal. Nothing will happen without the signature of the superior. Everything needs to be signed or at least stamped. [...] Documents which are signed by an apprentice here in Germany have to be signed by an executive in the Czech Republic". Low Future Orientation is evi-denced by lacking acceptance of certain projects: "Most of the Czech team mem-bers didn't see the necessity of a system change. They wanted to keep the old system. [...] As they didn't consider the system implementation as necessary they became very passive. [...] Individual initiative was rare" (Mr. C). However, not surprisingly, the interviewees stated "Post-Communism" being apparent only at older Czech colleagues, who had witnessed the respective political system, but not at the younger ones. Consequently, "Post-Communism" has a negative impact on the relationships not only between German and Czech team members but also between old and young Czechs. Building trust was hindered by the older Czech team members' rejection of the project respectively by their general resistance to change and by continuous time delays which again were caused by the much more distinct formality on the Czech side as compared to the German side. Moreover, the older Czechs' resistance to change impeded the creation of shared norms and objectives. To respond to this specific difficulty, the German interviewees emphasized the importance to establish a common vision within the project team – and if this is not accomplished – to even draw staffing consequences: "Every team member should be involved in the project from the very beginning, be aware of the project objectives and agree to them. [...] If someone in the team does absolutely not agree with the project s/he has to be removed from the team. Otherwise serious problems are to be expected. We experienced exactly such a case. A Czech member did not agree to the necessity of the project and constantly put obstacles into the way. Eventually, he was removed from the team. From that point, the project ran smoothly" (Mr. B).

With regard to further general management measures that had been employed within projects 1 and 2, results are comparable with the India-specific results. The highest importance is again assigned to the selection of a global project manager with broad intercultural experience and to periodic (if possible bidirectional) work assignments on-site. Moreover, the interview partners recommended non-work socializing team activities and to invest in team members' soft skills.

5   Conclusion

This work contributes to research on multicultural teams by presenting three typical patterns revealing how differences in particular dimensions of national culture have a negative impact on team-internal social capital and thus affect project performance. Within two of these patterns, we identified certain cultural dimensions to be closely interrelated resulting in two concepts labeled "Face Maintenance" (India-specific) and "Post-Communism" (Czech-specific) which negatively affect social capital in multinational teams. Within the third pattern (India-specific), high Collectivism solely was found to negatively influence the relational dimension of social capital. In addition, we presented sets of situation-specific and general management measures which had been employed to better deal with culture-driven negative consequences.

However, we cannot claim our results to be exhaustive. Of course, other cultural dimensions than the ones identified are imaginable to negatively affect social capital within multicultural teams as well. Further, with regard to our results revealing a negative impact of "Face Maintenance" on trust, we have to remark that trust in this context rather means trust in the output quality than trust among persons. Consequently, it is questionable if trust in the sense of social capital is fitting here; nevertheless, there is interdependence and overlap between trust in a person and trust in his/her actions and deliverables. Further, our results are limited to cultural differences between the Czech Republic and Germany on the one hand

and between India and Germany (and other Western countries) on the other; and we observed only the German perspective since we only had German interview partners. As Dibbern et al. (2008) as well as Gregory et al. (2009) showed, there can be strongly diverging perceptions of cultural characteristics being an issue or not if you ask the different sides. Another potential issue refers to the question whether the observed negative consequences on social relationships within the multinational teams are indeed a result of the cultural differences between the two sides (e.g., German and Indian team members) or of the characteristics of the cultural dimensions per se (e.g., high Power Distance, high Collectivism, and low Assertiveness respectively "Face Maintenance" in India). Unfortunately, we are not able to provide a data-driven answer to this question as we only had German interview partners. Interviews with Indian team members would have been necessary to investigate if "Face Maintenance" might cause the same problems in a purely Indian team as it does between Indians and Germans in a multinational team. We believe that "Face Maintenance" leads to some problems in a purely Indian team as well. However, these problems will not be as critical as in multinational teams because Indians know "how to play the game" around "Face Maintenance" since it is an integral part of their culture. In contrast, people from Western cultures will be faced with much larger problems from our point of view because they naturally do not know how to deal with such "foreign" phenomena like "Face Maintenance".

In our future research, we will conduct further interviews with team members from India and Eastern Europe to better conceptualize and elaborate on "Face Maintenance" and "Post-Communism". By uncovering the relationships between both national cultural differences and social capital in terms of particular dimensions, research can deliver more in-depth and better structured insights to the relevance of cultural differences and how to manage them in order to achieve superior project performance.

References

Brodbeck, F.C., Chhokar, J.S., and House, R.J. "Culture and Leadership across the World: The Globe Book of in-Depth Studies of 25 Societies," Lawrence Erlbaum Associates, 2007.

Carmel, E. "Global Software Teams: Collaborating across Borders and Time Zones," Prentice Hall PTR, 1999.

Carmel, E. and Agarwal, R. "Tactical Approaches for Alleviating Distance in Global Software Development," *IEEE Software* (18:2), 2001, pp. 22-29.

DeLone, W., Espinosa, J.A., Lee, G., and Carmel, E. "Bridging Global Boundaries for IS Project Success," *Proceedings of the 38th Hawaii International Conference on System Sciences*, 2005.

De Sanctis, G. and Poole, M.S. "Transitions in Teamwork in New Organizational Forms," *Advances in Group Processes* (14), 1997, pp. 157-176.

Dibbern, J., Winkler, J., and Heinzl, A. "Explaining Variations in Client Extra Costs between Software Projects Offshored to India," *MIS Quarterly* (32:2), 2008, pp. 333-366.

Doney, P.M., Cannon, J.P., and Mullen, M.R. "Understanding the Influence of National Culture on the Development of Trust," *Academy of Management Review* (23:3), 1998, pp. 601-620.

Earley, P.C. and Mosakowski, E. "Creating Hybrid Team Cultures: An Empirical Test of Transnational Team Functioning," *Academy of Management Journal* (43:1), 2000, pp. 26-49.

Eisenhardt, K.M. "Building Theories from Case Study Research," *Academy of Management Review* (14:4), 1989, pp. 532-550.

Eisenhardt, K.M. and Graebner, M.E. "Theory Building from Cases: Opportunities and Challenges," *Academy of Management Journal* (50:1), 2007, pp. 25-32.

Flyvbjerg, B. "Five Misunderstandings About Case Study Research," *Qualitative Inquiry* (12:2), 2006, pp. 219-245.

Govindarajan, V. and Gupta, A.K. "Building an Effective Global Business Team," *MIT Sloan Management Review* (42:2), 2001, pp. 63-71.

House, R.J., Hanges, P.J., Javidan, M., Dorfman, P.W., and Gupta, V. "Culture, Leadership, and Organizations: The Globe Study of 62 Societies," Sage Publications, 2004.

Huff, L. and Kelley, L. "Levels of Organizational Trust in Individualist Versus Collectivist Societies: A Seven-Nation Study," *Organization Science* (14:1), 2003, pp. 81-90.

Kaplan, B. and Duchon, D. "Combining Qualitative and Quantitative Methods in Information Systems Research: A Case Study," *MIS Quarterly* (12:4), 1988, pp. 571-586.

Kayworth, T.R. and Leidner, D.E. "The Global Virtual Manager: A Prescription for Success," *European Management Journal* (18:2), 2000, pp. 183-194.

Kohlbacher, F. "The Use of Qualitative Content Analysis in Case Study Research," *Qualitative Social Research* (7:1), 2005, pp. 1-23.

Kotlarsky, J. and Oshri, I. "Social Ties, Knowledge Sharing and Successful Collaboration in Globally Distributed System Development Projects," *European Journal of Information Systems* (14:1), 2005, pp. 37-48.

Leidner, D.E. "Globalization, Culture, and Information: Towards Global Knowledge Transparency," *Journal of Strategic Information Systems* (19:2), 2010, pp. 69-77.

Maznevski, M.L. and Chudoba, K.M. "Bridging Space over Time: Global Virtual Team Dynamics and Effectiveness," *Organization Science* (11:5), 2000, pp. 473-492.

Myers, M.D. and Newman, M. "The Qualitative Interview in IS Research: Examining the Craft," *Information and Organization* (17:1), 2007, pp. 2-26.

Nahapiet, J. and Ghoshal, S. "Social Capital, Intellectual Capital and the Organizational Advantage," *Academy of Management Review* (23:2), 1998, pp. 242-266.

Oh, H., Chung, M., and Labianca, G. "Group Social Capital and Group Effectiveness: The Role of Informal Socializing Ties," *Academy of Management Journal* (47:6), 2004, pp. 860-875.

Oshri, I., Kotlarsky, J., and Willcocks, L.P. "Global Software Development: Exploring Socialization and Face-to-Face Meetings in Distributed Strategic Projects," *Journal of Strategic Information Systems* (16:1), 2007, pp. 25-49.

Paul, S. and Ray, S. "Cultural Diversity, Perception of Work Atmosphere, and Task Conflict in Collaboration Technology Supported Global Virtual Teams: Findings from a Laboratory Experiment," *Proceedings of the 42nd Hawaii International Conference on System Sciences*, 2009.

Portes, A. "Social Capital: Its Origins and Applications in Modern Sociology," *Annual Review of Sociology* (24:1), 1998, pp. 1-24.

Reagans, R. and Zuckerman, E.W. "Networks, Diversity, and Productivity: The Social Capital of Corporate R&D Teams," *Organization Science* (12:4), 2001, pp. 502-517.

Robert Jr., L.P., Dennis, A.R., and Ahuja, M.K. "Social Capital and Knowledge Integration in Digitally Enabled Teams," *Information Systems Research* (19:3), 2008, pp. 314-334.

Salk, J.E. and Brannen, M.Y. "National Culture, Networks, and Individual Influence in a Multinational Management Team," *Academy of Management Journal* (43:2), 2000, pp. 191-202.

Sarker, S. and Sarker, S. "Exploring Agility in Distributed Information Systems Development Teams: An Interpretive Study in an Offshoring Context," *Information Systems Research* (20:3), 2009, pp. 440-461.

Sarker, S., Sarker, S., and Jana, D. "The Impact of the Nature of Globally Distributed Work Arrangement on Work–Life Conflict and Valence: The Indian GSD Professionals' Perspective," *European Journal of Information Systems* (19:2), 2010, pp. 209-222.

Ting-Toomey, S. and Cole, M. "Intergroup Diplomatic Communication: A Face-Negotiation Perspective," In: Korzenny, F. and Ting-Toomey, S. (eds.) Communicating for Peace: Diplomacy and Negotiation, Sage Publications, 1990.

Tsai, W. and Ghoshal, S. "Social Capital and Value Creation: The Role of Intrafirm Networks," *Academy of Management Journal* (41:4), 1998, pp. 464-476.

Vallaster, C. "Cultural Diversity and its Impact on Social Interactive Processes: Implications from an Empirical Study," *International Journal of Cross Cultural Management* (5:2), 2005, pp. 139-163.

Walsham, G. "Cross-Cultural Software Production and Use: A Structurational Analysis," *MIS Quarterly* (26:4), 2002, pp. 359-380.

Winkler, J.K., Dibbern, J., and Heinzl, A. "The Impact of Cultural Differences in Offshore Outsourcing - Case Study Results from German-Indian Application Development Projects," *Information Systems Frontiers* (10:2), 2008, pp. 243-258.

Yang, S., Lee, H., and Kurnia, S. "Social Capital in Information and Communications Technology Research: Past, Present, and Future," *Communications of the Association for Information Systems* (25), 2009, pp. 183-220.

Yin, R.K. "Case Study Research: Design and Methods," SAGE Publications, 2009.

Towards an IT-based Planning Process Alignment: Integrated Route and Location Planning for Small Package Shippers[1]

Andreas Stenger

IT-based Logistics, Institute of Information Systems, Goethe University Frankfurt, Grüneburgplatz 1, 60323 Frankfurt, Germany, stenger@wiwi.uni-frankfurt.de

Michael Schneider

Chair of Business Information Systems & Operations Research, Technical University Kaiserslautern, Erwin-Schrödinger-Straße, 67663 Kaiserslautern, Germany, schneider@wiwi.uni-kl.de

Prof. Dr. Oliver Wendt

Chair of Business Information Systems & Operations Research, Technical University Kaiserslautern, Erwin-Schrödinger-Straße, 67663 Kaiserslautern, Germany, wendt@wiwi.uni-kl.de

1 Introduction

Competition in the logistics sector significantly increases driven by high cost pressure and new legal regulations. In particular, the new rules for CO_2 emissions increase the pressure on logistics companies to improve their network efficiency. On the strategic level, the network efficiency of small package shippers (SPS) mainly depends on the locations of hubs and depots. Since customer demand as well as customer locations vary within the planning horizon of a strategic decision, which is about 10-15 years, a reasonable approximation of those values and a powerful planning tool are required. Concerning these strategic decisions, a huge

---

[1] Another version of this paper appeared as: Stenger, Andreas; Schneider, Michael and Oliver Wendt, "Towards an IT-based Planning Process Alignment: Integrated Route and Location Planning for Small Package Shippers," *in: Proceedings of the 17th Americas Conference on Information Systems (AMCIS 2011)*.

A. Heinzl et al. (eds.), *Theory-Guided Modeling and Empiricism in Information Systems Research*, DOI 10.1007/978-3-7908-2781-1_11, © Springer-Verlag Berlin Heidelberg 2011

body of solution methods for Location Routing Problems (LRP) have been proposed in literature to determine the optimal number and location of depots while considering the underlying vehicle routing.

However, existing approaches neglect an important trend: SPS involve subcontractors in the delivery of packages in order to increase the cost efficiency. In detail, two types of subcontracting are common for SPS: 1) long-term subcontraction of unprofitable delivery areas and 2) subcontraction of single customers on a daily basis in order to tackle demand peaks and to avoid deliveries to unprofitable customers. Thus, on the strategic level, depots of subcontractors must be considered in the LRP such that the assignment of unprofitable delivery areas to a specific subcontractor is simultaneously decided with the planning of the self-owned depots since those decisions are clearly related.

On the operational level, an efficient allocation of customers to vehicles and the related delivery sequences have to be determined, considering practical aspects such as customer time windows. The routing operations of SPS have several additional characteristics that have to be considered in the planning process. On the one hand, subcontracting options should be included into the applied planning model, i.e., the model should allow to subcontract single customers if this leads to a cost reduction. On the other hand, the explicit exploitation of driver familiarity with routes and customers plays a prominent role in SPS routing operations. If customers or neighborhoods are repeatedly visited by the same driver, the driver becomes acquainted with the territory and the customer locations therein and thus both service quality and driver efficiency can be increased (Smilowitz et al. 2009). Moreover, service consistency creates a bond between customer and driver that not only enhances the customer's loyalty but may also improve the reputation of the package shipping company (Smilowitz et al. 2009; Christofides 1971). Any solution method to achieve these benefits has to aim at repeatedly assigning each driver to the same customers and regions within the whole depot area, thus enabling the driver to gain enhanced experience in servicing its regular customers.

Furthermore, business processes for strategic decision making are not well-structured in most SPS companies and do not yet make use of the potential cost savings, which could be generated by an IT-based support infrastructure. Such an IT-platform integrates decision making and planning not only along the supply chain, but also across the mutually dependent layers of strategic, tactical and operational planning. As strategic decisions set the constraints for short-term planning, a suitable IT platform supporting strategic business processes should anticipate their impact on a wide range of subsequent operational problems not by "guessing" this impact based on crude abstractions. Instead, simulations based on realistic assumptions and the constraints imposed should be performed. Whereas the pursuit of such an integration might have been too ambitious 10 years ago, the ongoing decline of the cost of computational resources on the one hand and the ongoing rise in cost of physical logistics on the other hand makes it obvious that an optimal alignment will require (and has to solve) models of increasing integration and complexity.

In this paper, we present a framework for an integrated logistics planning tool. Its main focus lies on the tools that allow the determination of optimal numbers and locations of depots while paying attention to the currently established network structure, as well as daily delivery tours. The underlying optimization models are tailored to consider the practically relevant aspects described above, such as the existence of subcontractors and the exploitation of driver knowledge. To this end, the framework makes use of the logistics information system used by carriers to collect data of daily deliveries. Appropriate tools are designed to analyze collected data including customer demand, customer locations, flow within the network etc. in order to approximate the future development in the delivery areas. Furthermore, results of the data analysis support the SPS by identifying general problems in the delivery organization, such as unused depot capacity or unbalanced routes. To the best of our knowledge, we are the first designing such a framework including various location and route planning tools based on recently developed, state-of-the-art heuristic solution methods.

The remainder of the paper is structured as follows. First, we provide a brief overview of literature related to route and location planning of SPS. Subsequent, we describe the general design of our framework and detail the characteristics and functionality of the associated tools with special emphasis on the location and route planning tools. Finally, we give a short conclusion.

2 Preliminaries and Literature

In this section, we give a brief overview of the relevant location planning literature, give a short introduction to route planning models and provide a review of the literature addressing the industry considerations that are central to this work: driver learning and subcontracting.

2.1 Location Planning

The following works are relevant to our paper because they present the currently best-performing methods for solving basic LRPs, which form the core of our problem at hand. We refer the reader to Min et al. (1998) and Nagy and Salhi (2007) for a more extensive literature review on LRP.

Prins et al. (2007) present a cooperative metaheuristic based on lagrangian relaxation and granular tabu search (TS). In the location phase, they solve a Facility Location Problem to form supercustomers out of each route. Subsequently, the vehicle routes are optimized by means of the granular TS heuristic. The algorithm alternates between the two phases, which collect information about the most promising edges in order to use them in the next iterations. The heuristic proposed in Duhamel et al. (2010) adapts an evolutionary local search (ELS) to optimize the initial solution found by a multi-start Greedy Randomized Adaptive Search Procedure (GRASP), based on an extended Clarke and Wright algorithm (Clarke and Wright 1964). ELS starts with building giant traveling salesman tours, which are split into LRP solutions and are then further improved.

2.2   Route Planning

The Vehicle Routing Problem (VRP) is one of the oldest and most discussed optimization problems in the Operations Research literature. The goal of the VRP is to find a set of minimum-cost vehicle routes that cover a set of nodes (customers) so that each route starts and ends at a central depot and each customer is serviced. Among the numerous variants of VRP that have evolved over the years, the VRP with time windows (VRPTW) is probably the most important and most studied. It requires that each customer is serviced within an individual time window and it can be used to model many real-world distribution management problems, like parcel deliveries in various industries or solid waste collection. Due to its computational complexity, VRPTW can only be solved by exact methods for moderate-sized instances, a fact that has given rise to a large number of successful (meta-)heuristic solution methods that are able to produce high-quality solutions for instances of reasonable size in limited time (Bräysy and Gendreau 2005a;b; Gendreau et al. 2008).

2.2.1   Routing with Driver Learning Aspects

As described in the first section, routing in SPS companies pays attention to the available drivers' local knowledge. The following works addressing this aspect are mostly based on fixed or partially fixed service territories. Such a preassignment of drivers to service territories not only yields driver familiarity benefits in a straightforward manner but also simplifies the daily vehicle routing operations to a great extent.

Wong and Beasley (1984) divide the complete depot area into a number of fixed delivery areas based on historical demand data, each of which is visited by a single driver. Due to this preassignment of the drivers to territory, the VRP to solve becomes a traveling salesman problem, which greatly simplifies the operational planning. The disadvantage of such an approach is the flexibility forfeited by having fixed driver assignments, which makes it difficult to absorb daily workload fluctuations and thus yields route configurations that are suboptimal concerning the total traveled distance.

This tradeoff between driver familiarity benefits and routing flexibility is investigated in comprehensive simulation studies by Haughton (2008). He studies the effect of exclusive territory assignment on route design efficiencies as compared to non-exclusive assignment, where drivers are assigned flexibly based on the day-to-day demand situation.

Zhong et al. (2007) pool customers into "cells" and, based on historical demand data, assign only a given proportion of all cells to fixed "core areas", which are always visited by the same driver. Customers located in the "flex zone" around the depot are not assigned to core areas but assigned flexibly to different drivers depending on their workload because they can be reached by practically every route without making long detours. The remaining customers, which are located in the space between the core areas are also assigned on a daily basis.

Haugland et al. (2007) present a two-stage approach to the districting problem for the VRP. In the first stage, a number of service territories, called "districts", are designed. In the second stage, the order of delivery of the customers within each district is optimized for each day of delivery by means of a local search heuristic which basically moves border customers from one district to another until the objective function cannot be improved any further.

2.2.2   Routing with Subcontracting Options

Besides fixed subcontracted delivery areas, SPS additionally assign customers to subcontractors in a flexible manner if the available vehicle capacity is not sufficient. The VRP with private fleet and common carriers (VRPPC) represents this practical problem. In a VRPPC, deliveries to customers can either be performed by a vehicle of the private fleet located at the depot, or be assigned to a subcontractor. In general, a fixed price for subcontracting a customer is assumed which depends on the demand (Bolduc et al. 2008).

Available heuristics to solve the VRPPC are quite scarce. Bolduc et al. (2008) propose a perturbation metaheuristic and present a large set of benchmark instances with up to 483 customers on which the solution method is tested. Côté and Potvin (2009) use an adapted TS heuristic, originally proposed by Cordeau et al. (1997), to solve the VRPPC which outperforms the approach of Bolduc et al. (2008) on benchmark instances in terms of solution quality. However, similar to the currently best-performing heuristic, a TS with ejection chains (Potvin and Naud 2010), total computation times are quite high.

3 Routing and Location Planning Framework

In practice, big SPS companies require a sizeable IT infrastructure to manage business from administrative processes to the tracking and tracing of packages. Every day millions of incoming packages, each assigned to a specific customer, are scanned and delivered. From these processes, SPS companies retrieve and collect all data relevant for the strategic and operational decisions. The data collection is performed continuously and information about customers served, such as address, package volume, delivery date and time, number of delivery attempts, etc. are stored.

On the strategic level, data collected over several years builds the basis for location decisions. Here, sophisticated data analysis methods are applied to, e.g., forecast the distribution of customers within the areas of interest and the future customer demand. Subsequent, location problems specifically tailored to the practical problem at hand are solved with the approximated values. On the operational level, data collected about the routes performed in the past are, e.g., used to estimate a driver's familiarity with customers. This information is considered when constructing delivery regions as well as in the daily routing.

Our Route and Location Planning (RLP) framework and the associated modules are illustrated in Figure 1.

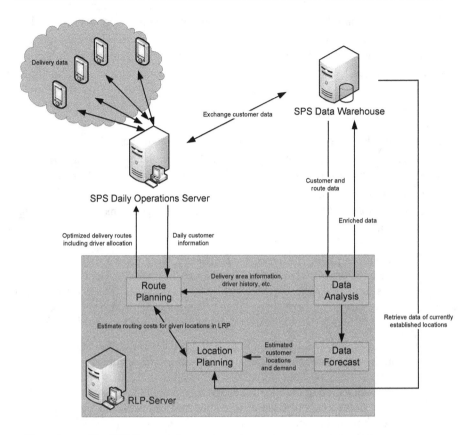

Figure 1:   The RLP-Framework

The RLP-Server is directly connected to the SPS Daily Operations Server (DOS) of the SPS as well as to the SPS Data Warehouse (DW). The DOS transfers the daily delivery routes to the handhelds of the drivers in the morning, and collects all delivery information such as customer signatures, failed deliveries, performed routes etc. in the evening. This information is stored on the DW. From there, the RLP-Server retrieves the data and a Data Analysis module preprocesses and stores the relevant information. Furthermore, the module performs a number of simple tests and analyses to enrich the data, which serves as input to the Route Planning and the Data Forecast module.

Route Planning considers the current day's customer set and package volumes as well as information gathered from Data Analysis, such as delivery histories of drivers and possibly established delivery areas. The determined delivery routes and the drivers' allocation to the routes are transmitted to the DOS in order to feed the drivers' handhelds.

The Location Planning module works on approximated customer data provided by the Data Forecast. Additional information about currently established locations is retrieved from the DW. For estimating the routing costs resulting from a given network structure, Location Planning cooperates with the Route Planning module.

3.1   Data Analysis

The Data Analysis module processes all information about customers served, such as address, package volume, delivery date and time, number of delivery attempts, routes on which deliveries are performed, the associated driver and vehicle used. Based on this data, Data Analysis performs preliminary tests to detect fundamental problems with the network organization and delivery operations as the following examples show:

- When comparing the average total package volume of a route and the capacity of the vehicle used, a high amount of unused capacity signals that reassigning vehicles to routes might be beneficial. Results might also show that some routes exceed the maximum allowed travel time while other drivers return to the depot one or two hours before finishing time.

- Unprofitable depot locations are indicated by the following two measures. First, the degree of capacity utilization is determined by comparing average daily package volume to the maximum number of packages that can be handled in the depot. Second, the average distance of the depot to all customers can be used as a simple measure to indicate the quality of the chosen location within a delivery area. If the average distance is clearly higher than the average over all depots, a relocation might be reasonable.

Moreover, Data Analysis enriches stored data, e.g. by analyzing delivery patterns of customers. For example, if delivery to a regular customer is only successful in the evening, the customer is assigned a time window. Thus, the information is integrated in the future tour planning in order to reduce the number of delivery attempts.

Another important task of Data Analysis is the examination of performed vehicle routes in order to record for each driver the set of visited customers as well as for each of these customers the visiting frequency and the days of the visits. Together with an estimation of daily demand for each customer, this information is vital for the Route Planning module to be able to consider driver knowledge in the generation of service territories and daily routes.

3.2 Data Forecast

A reliable forecast is of great importance to strategic decisions like location planning that involve high investments. Due to the large amount of collected data and the high number of analyses performed by the Data Analysis module, the information basis for forecasting future customer demand values and the customers' geographic distribution is sufficiently large. In addition to the data collected by Data Analysis, the Data Forecast module incorporates demographic information published by the government, such as official figures about, e.g., the growth of population in the concerned regions. In order to reduce the complexity, Data Forecast aggregates customer into clusters, and determines forecast values for the average number of stops as well as the average package volume per day in those areas.

3.3 Location Planning

Depot location decisions are of high strategical importance since they strongly influence the efficiency of daily route operations as well as the total network and thus the company's profitability. Based on a good approximation of the changes in customer locations and package volume, we use an LRP to determine optimal number and locations of depots of an SPS. Our Location Planning module bases on a model extending the classical LRP. Since the currently established network exists, we consider relocation aspects within the optimization process (Stenger et al. 2010a). In detail, we use the current network as initial solution and consider fixed costs of establishing and closing depot locations during the optimization process. Furthermore, we also include subcontracted depots in the LRP which helps to decide with which subcontractor a delivery contract should be closed (Stenger et al. 2010c). By doing so, delivery areas are fixedly assigned to a subcontractor in the long term. The simultaneous consideration of all these aspects in combination with reasonable forecast values ensures that resulting depot locations are close to the optimum for real-world applications.

The solution method proposed for the LRP with subcontracting options (LRPSO) iterates between a location and a routing phase. In the location phase, a simulated annealing heuristic, combined with a tabu list (TL) to avoid cycling, determines which depots to open, close or swap as well as which depots to switch from self-operation to subcontracting and vice versa. The influence of all moves on the routing costs is quickly evaluated by means of the savings algorithm. In order to reduce the complexity, we introduce the Adjustable Area of Influence (AAOI) concept which restricts the recalculation of routing costs on a small area around the depot modification. In the subsequent routing phase, given a fixed depot location setting, a Variable Neighborhood Search (VNS) algorithm based on CROSS-exchange neighborhoods is used to solve the underlying Multi-Depot VRP

(MDVRP). An overview of the algorithm is depicted in Figure 2. The solution method proved its competitiveness against state-of-the art methods on benchmark sets available for the standard LRP.

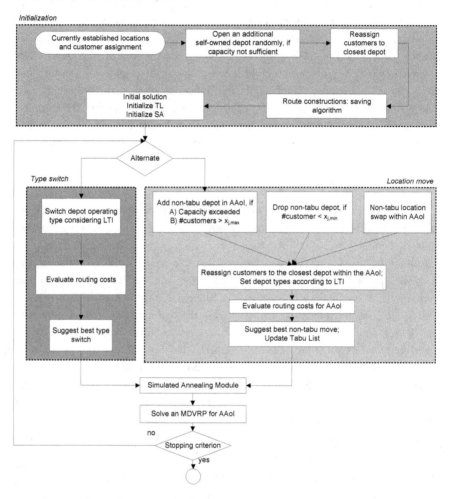

Figure 2:   Overview of the combined SA and VNS solution method for the LRPSO

3.4   Route Planning

On the operational level, delivery tours from given depots to the daily set of customers have to be determined. For this task, the Route Planning module incorporates algorithms for several VRPs that differ in the characteristics of the planning problem. For optimizing the delivery routes of one single depot and a given set of vehicles, we use an Ant Colony Optimization (ACO) algorithm which proves able to find high-quality solutions to VRPTW in reasonable time (Schneider et al. 2010b). Due to the large size of real-world problem instances, we make use of graph sparsification methods in order to reduce the complexity and to achieve short computation times (Doppstadt et al. 2011). To incorporate relevant practical considerations, Route Planning offers two methods addressing driver familiarity aspects and one method studying subcontracting options. These are detailed in the following sections.

3.4.1   Driver Learning

All of the above described works considering driver learning aspects neglect the existence of time windows. However, up to 60% of the orders of our industry partner are time-definite, which is also consistent with the industry statistics given in Campbell and Thomas (2009). If time windows are considered, routing flexibility is not only needed to achieve distance-efficient route configurations but also to fulfill customer delivery time requirements. Thus, the value of routing flexibility increases, which is likely to have significant negative effect on the solution quality of any approach based on fixed delivery areas.

Therefore, Route Planning incorporates an approach that forgoes any fixing of delivery areas. Instead, it accounts for delivery consistency by using driver specific travel and service times and thus explicitly considering driver knowledge. In this way, drivers have an incentive to stay in familiar areas due to shorter driving and service times while still maintaining their flexibility (Schneider et al. 2010a). Route Planning uses an ACO algorithm as solution method: Each ant represents a single driver and creates a route dependent on driver-specific heuristic information and pheromone values that are traded off against each other. The ACO procedure, the complementary local search method and all parameter settings are described in Schneider et al. (2010b).

To address the common fixed area approach of SPS, Route Planning also offers an intelligent method for generating partially fixed service territories (and performing the resulting daily routing). As described above, this procedure is relevant because 1) strong driver familiarity benefits can be achieved by this straightforward method, 2) it is implemented in one form or the other in most SPS companies, and 3) the simplification of daily routing operations achieved by a preassignment of drivers to service territories, i.e., route optimization based on fixed areas is much easier since a TSP has to be solved instead of a VRP. This makes it possible to concentrate on other relevant real-world constraints and characteristics, such as lunch breaks for drivers, route duration issues, etc. within the routing problem.

Route Planning's method for routing with "fixed" areas bases on the work of Wong and Beasley (1984). Instead of completely fixing the delivery areas, which results in significant problems if demand varies strongly or if time windows are to be considered, we design fixed service territories which only include a predefined proportion of customers (cf. Zhong et al. 2007). In order to balance the tradeoff between familiarity effects and routing flexibility, the remaining flexible customers are integrated into the routes that serve the fixed service territories based on the actual workload on each particular day.

The solution approach can be divided into three basic phases, which are illustrated in Figure 3 (cf. Schneider et al. 2010c).

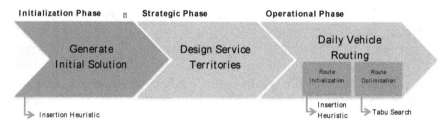

Figure 3:   Three-phase approach to solve a VRP with fixed service territories

1. Similar to Wong and Beasley (1984), our initialization phase generates independent solutions for a number of sample days, on which a VRPTW is solved without considering consistency requirements. For the routing in this phase, we implement a simple insertion heuristic to quickly generate solutions for the sample days. We adopt the objective function and the time window handling introduced by Nagata et al. (2010), which allows the temporary violation of time window and capacity constraints.

2. In the strategic phase, we design a number of fixed service territories based on the initial solutions created in the previous phase. The aim of this strategic phase is to generate a subdivision of the delivery area which is robust with respect to both consistency and flexibility requirements. The building of service territories has to rely on historical data from the initialization phase, because the demand in the consecutive operational phase is not known in advance.

3. In the operational phase, daily routing is conducted on the basis of the fixed service territories developed in the strategic phase. The generated service territories contain a predefined percentage of all customers and are exclusively visited by a single driver. The remaining customers are assigned to the service territories on a daily basis. Thus, the problem to

be solved in this operational phase is a VRPTW with the additional feature, that part of the customers are preassigned to a specific driver. As solution method, a TS heuristic based on the intra-route optimization method Or-opt and a simple relocation heuristic for the inter-route exchange of customers is used. In order to ensure that feasible routes are generated in the daily routing phase, we permit the exceptional expulsion of individual customers from their service territory.

3.4.2 Subcontracting

If the SPS outsources parts of its daily deliveries to subcontractors, the underlying VRP model significantly changes to a VRPPC, where customers can either be served by owned vehicles or by a subcontractor. In this case, we apply a VNS heuristic based on cyclic-exchange neighborhoods (Stenger et al. 2010b). Compared to the state-of-the-art approaches, the heuristic proves able to significantly reduce the computing times without a significant loss in solution quality. This is highly relevant for practical purposes, where the time available for determining daily route plans is tightly restricted. Furthermore, we extended the VRPPC to multiple depots, in order to decide to which subcontractor a customer should be assigned or from which self-owned depot it should be served. The resulting problem is called Multi-Depot VRP with Private Fleet and Common Carriers (MDVRPPC) (Stenger et al. 2010b).

4 Conclusion

In this paper, we described an integrated logistics planning framework which is designed to meet crucial requirements of the small package shipping industry. The framework incorporates a data analysis and forecast tool as well as tools for location and route planning. The information obtained from the analysis and forecast tools serves as input for the planning tools. Concerning the route planning, we identified the integration of subcontractors as well as the consideration of driver familiarity as crucial factors. We presented two intelligent approaches to deal with driver familiarity – an approach with semi-fixed delivery areas solved with a TS heuristic and an ACO approach with driver specific travel and service times. In order to incorporate subcontractors in the daily routing, we described the multi-depot extension of the VRP with private fleet and common carriers. Additionally, considering subcontractors is also highly relevant making depot location decisions. In order to simultaneously determine optimal depot locations as well as the assignment of delivery areas to subcontractors, we presented an LRP with Subcontracting Option (LRPSO) that extends the classical LRP.

References

Bolduc, M.-C., Renaud, J., Boctor, F. and Laporte, G. "A perturbation metaheuristic for the vehicle routing problem with private fleet and common carriers," *International Journal of the Operational Research Society* (59:6), 2008, pp. 776-787.

Bräysy, O. and Gendreau, M. "Vehicle routing problem with time windows, Part I: Route construction and local search algorithms," *Transportation Science* (39:1), 2005a, pp. 104-118.

Bräysy, O. and Gendreau, M. "Vehicle routing problem with time windows, Part II: Meta-heuristics," *Transportation Science* (39:1), 2005b, pp. 119-139.

Campbell, A. M. and Thomas, B. W. "Runtime reduction techniques for the probabilistic traveling salesman problem with deadlines," *Computers & Operations Research* (36:4), 2009, pp. 1231-1248.

Christofides, N. "Fixed routes and areas for delivery operations," *International Journal of Physical Distribution & Logistics Management* (1:2), 1971, pp. 87–92.

Clarke, G. and Wright, J. W. "Scheduling of vehicles from a central depot to a number of delivery points," *Operations Research* (12:4), 1964, pp. 568-581.

Cordeau, J.-F., Gendreau, M. and Laporte, G. "A tabu search heuristic for periodic and multi- depot vehicle routing problems," *Networks* (30:2), 1997, pp. 105-119.

Côté, J.-F. and Potvin, J.-Y. "A tabu search heuristic for the vehicle routing problem with private fleet and common carrier," *European Journal of Operational Research* (198:2), 2009, pp. 464- 469.

Doppstadt, C., Schneider, M., Stenger, A., Sand, B., Vigo, D. and Schwind, M. "Graph sparsification for the vehicle routing problem with time windows," in Hu, B., Morasch, K., Pickl, S. and Siegle, M. (Eds.): *Operations Research Proceedings 2010*, Springer, 2011.

Duhamel, C., Lacomme, P., Prins, C. and Prodhon, C. "A GRASPxELS approach for the capacitated location-routing problem," *Computers & Operations Research* (37:11), 2010, pp. 1912-1923.

Gendreau, M., Potvin, J.-Y., Bräysy, O., Hasle, G. and Løkketangen, A. "Metaheuristics for the vehicle routing problem and its extensions: A categorized bibliography," in: Bruce L. Golden (Ed.): *The Vehicle Routing Problem: Latest Advances and New Challenges*, Springer, 2008, pp. 143-169.

Haughton, M. A. "The efficacy of exclusive territory assignments to delivery vehicle drivers," *European Journal of Operational Research* (184:1), 2008, pp. 24-38.

Haugland, D., Ho, S. C. and Laporte, G. "Designing delivery districts for the vehicle routing problem with stochastic demands," *European Journal of Operational Research* (180:3), 2007, pp. 997-1010.

Min, H., Jayaraman, V. and Srivastava, R. "Combined location-routing problems: A synthesis and future research directions," *European Journal of Operational Research* (108:1), 1998, pp. 1-15.

Nagata, Y. Bräysy, O. and Dullaert, W. "A penalty-based edge assembly memetic algorithm for the vehicle routing problem with time windows," *Computers & Operations Research* (37:4), 2010, pp. 724-737.

Nagy, G. and Salhi, S. "Location-routing: Issues, models and methods," *European Journal of Operational Research* (177:2), 2007, pp. 649-672.

Potvin, J.-Y. and Naud, M.-A. "Tabu search with ejection chains for the vehicle routing problem with private fleet and common carrier," to appear in: *International Journal of the Operational Research Society,* 2010.

Prins, C., Prodhon, C., Ruiz, A., Soriano, P. and Wolfler Calvo, R. "Solving the capacitated location-routing problem by a cooperative lagrangean relaxation-granular tabu search heuristic, " *Transportation Science* (41:4), 2007, pp. 470-483.

Schneider, M., Doppstadt, C. Sand, B., Stenger, A. and Schwind, M. "A vehicle routing problem with time windows and driver familiarity," in: *Seventh Triennial Symposium on Transportation Analysis*, Tromsø, Norway, 2010a.

Schneider, M., Doppstadt, C., Stenger, A. and Schwind, M. "Ant colony optimization for a stochastic vehicle routing problem with driver learning," in: *Proceedings of the IEEE Congress on Evolutionary Computation (IEEE CEC)*, Barcelona, Spain, 2010b.

Schneider, M., Stenger, A. and Lagemann, H. "Vehicle routing problem with driver learning aspects – a solution approach based on fixed service territories." Technical report, Chair of Business Information Systems and Operations Research, Technical University Kaiserslautern, Germany, 2010c.

Smilowitz, K., Nowak, M. and Jiang, T. "Workforce management in periodic delivery operations," Working Paper No. 09-004, 2009.

Stenger, A., Schneider, M. and Schwind, M. "Decision support for location routing with relocation aspects," in: *Proceedings of the Multikonferenz Wirtschaftsinformatik 2010*, 2010a, pp. 1949–1959.

Stenger, A., Vigo, D., Enz, S. and Schwind, M. "A variable neighborhood search algorithm for a vehicle routing problem arising in small package shipping." Technical report 02/2010, IT-based Logistics, Institute of Information Systems, Goethe University, Frankfurt, Germany, 2010b.

Stenger, A., Schneider, M. and Schwind, M. "A combined simulated annealing and variable neighborhood search heuristic for a location routing problem with subcontracting option, " Technical report 01/2010, IT-based Logistics, Institute of Information Systems, Goethe University, Frankfurt, Germany, 2010c.

Wong, K. F. and Beasley, J. E. "Vehicle routing using fixed delivery areas," *Omega* (12:6), 1984, pp. 591-600.

Zhong, H., Hall, R. W. and Dessouky. M. "Territory planning and vehicle dispatching with driver learning," *Transportation Science* (41:1), 2007, pp. 74-89.

Where is the "I" in "IS Research"? The Quest for a Coherent Research Stream in the Context of Human Information Behavior

Erik Hemmer

Business School, University of Mannheim, L15, 1-6, 68161 Mannheim, Germany,
erik.hemmer@uni-mannheim.de

Prof. Dr. Armin Heinzl

Business School, University of Mannheim, L15, 1-6, 68161 Mannheim, Germany,
heinzl@uni-mannheim.de

1   Introduction

The amount of information produced by and available to every member of today's society grows at a stunning pace. Driven by the importance of an efficient information distribution, a large field of heterogeneous research streams has developed in the course of the last four decades in various scientific domains. Major and important contributions have been created with respect to the behavior of organizations, groups and individuals towards the acquisition and processing of information. Furthermore, the outcome effects of these activities such as decision-making and sense-making have been investigated. This article focuses on literature dealing with the exploration and explanation of specific behavioral patterns occurring when individuals interact with information in computer-mediated contexts. Following the terminology of the neighboring discipline *Information Science*, we call this field of research "human information behavior" (HIB), defined as "the totality of human behavior in relation to sources and channels of information, including both active and passive information seeking, and information use" (Wilson 2000, p. 49). Therefore, HIB can be understood as an overarching research trajectory trying to offer generalizable predictions about and explanations of behavioral phenomena observable when humans acquire and process information. Thus, it is not limited to the isolated consideration of a specific type of tasks such as decision-making. Instead, it can be interpreted as a boundary spanner serving as a frame for IS research uncovering the aforementioned phenomena in computer-mediated settings.

The Information Systems (IS) discipline has been trying primarily to provide explanations of organizational and human behavior with respect to IT artifacts and their integration into organizational contexts. Therefore, it seems to be a promising source of knowledge when it comes to the examination of human information seeking and processing activities. An analysis of existing literature in the IS domain reveals that valuable recommendations have been generated regarding the design of information systems supporting business users in information-related processes. Surprisingly, however, research is largely fragmented and lacks a concerted effort to bridge the boundaries of various disciplines and combine the results in a holistic way. Propelled by an article by McKinney Jr. and Yoos II (2010) in which the authors summarize that the Information Systems disciplines lacks a clear understanding of its central entity "information", this study's objectives are

- the creation and application of a coherent framework for analyzing and categorizing prior work dealing with the relationship between human beings and information in the IS domain, and

- the identification of trends in literature and the discovery of promising fields and opportunities within the IS discipline resulting in suggestions for future research and in doing so, showing the importance of this broad topic for both theory and practice.

In this article literature on information-related topics is reviewed while setting a strong focus on the IS discipline. Articles from non-IS journals are integrated into the analysis to complement and extend the findings. Thus, the major contribution consists in the creation of synthesized inter-textual coherence by drawing connections between "streams not typically cited together to suggest the existence of undeveloped research areas" (Locke and Golden-Biddle 1997, p. 1030). First, following the approach of Webster and Watson (2002), the relevant IS literature is collected, then the strengths and weaknesses of the existing discourse are discussed, and finally open research questions are deduced. The result is a conceptual article concentrating on the discovery of new ideas and the synthesis of well-established constructs with the overarching goal of advancing theory development (Yadav 2010).

In chapter 2 the research design is introduced and a conceptual framework is derived. This framework serves as a means for structuring the subsequent literature review on 49 articles from the IS domain presented in chapter 3. In chapter 4 open research questions are formulated with the goal of offering advice on how to develop the field with respect to research in human information behavior from an Information Systems perspective, before the findings are summarized in chapter 5.

2   Research Approach and Conceptual Framework

Webster and Watson (2002) provide the fundamental guidelines for structuring this review article. The literature review required (1) the definition of a search scope, (2) guidelines for analyzing and clustering the selected articles, and (3) a strategy for identifying relevant publications.

Consequently, in a first step, following the recommendations of the "AIS Senior Scholars' Basket of Journals"[1], the search was restricted to publications in the six major top-ranked IS outlets and covered all issues before 2011 as shown in table 1. The goal was to realize a maximum coverage of the most relevant and influential IS literature over several decades, which allows for additional longitudinal investigations.

In a second step, an analytical framework for clustering the articles was developed. Since a coherent and parsimonious theory of human information behavior is not yet existent, publications in the field of information science were screened. In this domain, there is a long tradition of models describing behavioral patterns of humans who are seeking for information. Wilson (1999) provides a profound overview of existing models which were used as a guiding pattern for crafting an analytical framework suitable for structuring the literature analysis. Due to its high degree of generalizability and its strong process character Wilson's model of information behavior (Wilson 1999, p. 251) was integrated into a model proposed by Gemünden (1993, p. 848) which resulted in the analytical framework presented in Figure 1. It contains the basic steps in computer-mediated information acquisition processes in sequential order.

The coding of the various studies investigated in this literature review follows the logic of the proposed framework which can therefore be regarded as an instrument for structuring this review article. The model is not claiming to be complete in the sense of covering all aspects of information acquisition and processing but to represent an adequate means for clustering the literature along major dimensions. According to the proposed model, a sequence of information-seeking activities is initiated by the awareness of a problem which requires the collection of information from the problem domain. Based on this *ex-ante information need*, an adequate information channel is selected, i. e. the question of *where* to get the information is answered. Restricted by the specific properties of the chosen information channel, the information need is amended resulting in an *actual*, i. e. "realized" information request. After this interaction with the information system, the human

---

[1]   http://home.aisnet.org/displaycommon.cfm?an=1&subarticlenbr=346
       [download: 2011/06/07]

information seeker has to decide on *how* to process and evaluate the resulting information. Therefore, the seeker has to choose from various cognitive strategies culminating in the termination of the process or a reiteration.

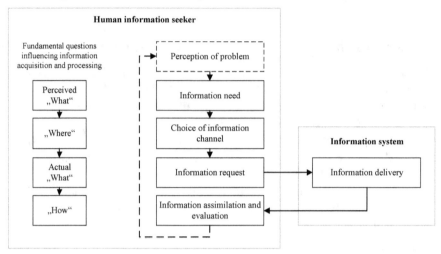

Figure 1:   Conceptual framework (based on Gemünden (1993) and Wilson (1991))

In addition to the aforementioned clustering the reviewed articles were divided according to their underlying research approaches. Following the understanding of Dibbern et al. (2004) we interpret the term "research approach" in a general sense consisting of several dimensions. Consequently, we analyzed if the articles belong to an *empirical* or a *non-empirical* stream of research and subsequently differentiated between the epistemological foundations *interpretive* and *positivist*. The non-empirical articles were classified as *conceptual* or *mathematical / axiomatic* (Dibbern et al. 2004). In order to get a better understanding of the predominant research methods employed in past information behavior research, the papers' techniques for acquiring empirical data were further qualified as *survey / interview*, *case study* and *laboratory experiment*. Thereby, the full range of the knowledge-accrual triangle proposed by Bonoma (1985) is covered which groups those methods according to their internal and external validity. Finally, the level of analysis was extracted ranging from *individual* over *group* to *organization*.

In a third step, the relevant journals and databases (ABI/INFORM and Business Source Premier) were browsed based on a list of suitable key words which had been created beforehand. Since there is no common terminology yet, applicable to the field of information behavior in the IS context, a top-down approach had to be combined with a bottom-up approach, i. e. potential key words were deduced from existing information behavior models and compared with the terms used in the IS domain. Therefore, a software tool was developed which contains all articles that appeared in the journal *MIS Quarterly* as it is the journal in the sample with the longest tradition. Every word of all articles was classified with computer-linguistic methods as noun, verb, and adjective. In a last step, ranked lists of the different types of words occurring next to the term "information" were generated and analyzed. Based on this approach, it was possible to amend and extend the key word list by synonyms which had not been identified before and which significantly improve the coverage of the literature review. For example, the analysis revealed that the term "information need" is often substituted by "information requirement" in IS literature. Finally, the bibliographies of the identified articles were scanned in order to detect further papers which were not included in the key word search.

Title of journal	Abbreviation	Coverage	Selected articles
European Journal of Information Systems	EJIS	1993 – 2010	6
Information Systems Journal	ISJ	1998 – 2010	2
Information Systems Research	ISR	1990 – 2010	12
Journal of AIS	JAIS	2003 – 2010	3
Journal of MIS	JMIS	1984 – 2010	9
MIS Quarterly	MISQ	1977 – 2010	17
		Sum	**49**

Table 1:   Reviewed IS top journals and number of articles selected

3   Literature Review and Analysis

Following the framework outlined in Figure 1 the selected articles were assigned to the corresponding steps in the information acquisition process they mainly contribute to. A detailed list of these assignments is given in Table 2 (Appendix) which is supplemented by an analysis of the employed research approach, research method, and level of analysis. In the following paragraphs, the major streams of research are extracted and presented in a clustered format.

3.1   Perception of Problem and Information Need

Research in the information science field intensively discussed factors which initiate the process of acquiring information and identified the broad concept of an "anomalous state of knowledge" as a main driver (Belkin 1980). In this understanding, a lack of information acts as a trigger for bridging the gap between a complex situation and a desired outcome (Wilson 1999). More specifically, information acquisition is usually not an "end in itself", but is embedded into goal-oriented activities such as decision-making or making sense of a situation in order to fulfill a given task. In organizational settings, Vandenbosch (1997) further differentiates between focused (active) search and scanning for information. While the former behavior is exercised to improve organizational efficiency by fine-tuning operations and verifying assumptions, the latter approach is intended to improve organizational effectiveness by challenging fundamental managerial assumptions.

When taking a detailed look at the existing IS literature it becomes apparent that the prevailing literature is very task-centered and almost exclusively investigates phenomena from the focused search domain (Specht 1986, Wetherbe 1991, Melville and Ramirez 2008). Consequently, the authors predominantly try to derive objective, i. e. ex-ante perceived information needs from organizational tasks. By doing so, they largely neglect information seekers' individual differences such as personality traits, prior experience, existing knowledge, and mental capabilities. These differences, however, might lead to contrary perceptions of the seekers' subjective information needs. A reason for neglecting these aspects in IS research might be the findings of an article by Huber (1983) in which he claims that cognitive styles do not necessarily affect Management Information Systems (MIS) success due to a low amount of variance explained in the outcomes. Mendelson and Pillai (1998) contrast this task-driven approach of determining information needs with the concept of bounded rationality and show that growing task-induced information needs lead to excessive demands with respect to human information processing capacities. In doing so, they are able to create a multi-level analysis combining the organizational perspective based on the information processing view of the firm with an individual level perspective rooted in the assumptions of bounded rationality.

Besides the aforementioned endogenous activation mechanisms, recent IS literature also covers exogenous factors triggering information processing in web environments. Dou et al. (2010) build on the schema theory from the field of cognitive psychology in order to show that by priming users of e-commerce websites, the operators of such platforms can indirectly influence the way users browse through the web page and seek for information. Similar studies of exogenous activation factors can be found in the marketing literature with respect to the effect of advertisements on the willingness of its viewers to gather more information about the advertised product or service (MacInnis and Jaworski 1989, Meyers-Levy and Malaviya 1999).

3.2   Choice of Information Channel

The large variety of information systems that can be used to satisfy a specific information need motivates a separate research stream within the IS domain. The corresponding articles deal with determinants influencing the choice of information channels depending on their specific properties. The majority of IS articles addressing such research questions concentrates on the support of organizational decision-making (Jones et al. 1993, Mennecke and Valacich 1998) and collaboration tasks (Watson-Manheim and Bélanger 2007, Dennis et al. 2008). The articles strongly focus on computer-mediated communication, i. e. information-seeking is operationalized as a process of acquiring information from other human beings. As a consequence, there is a long tradition of research relying on the concept of media richness (Daft et al. 1987) for explaining humans' media choices and effectiveness of decision-making in group collaboration as a dependent variable. Dennis et al. (2008), however, provide a comprehensive overview over former media choice research and challenge the basic assumption of media richness which consists in the idea that face-to-face communication has the highest degree of naturalness and, consequently, richer media will be used for equivocal tasks. Subsequently, they develop a theory of media synchronicity arguing that communication processes can be divided into convergence and conveyance processes which strongly determine the choice of communication media. Thus, they develop a more fine-grained set of media properties which influence the selection process.

The common denominator of the aforementioned research stream is the focus on computer-mediated information acquisition while the source of information is another human being. Wang and Benbasat (2009) take a completely different perspective and explain the factors influencing the choice of interactive decision aids on websites which can be regarded as means for acquiring information in buying processes. Thus, the source of information is not a human being but a purely artificial recommendation system. By extending the effort-accuracy framework of cognition (Payne 1982), which holds that information seekers minimize their effort to get as accurate information as possible, they show that especially the degree of restrictiveness of the decision aids has an impact on the choice of those systems. In this terminology, a decision aid is restrictive when the desired decision processes or strategies are not supported. By illustrating that an increased perceived restrictiveness of the decision aid leads to a decreasing intention to use this tool, they contribute to existing cognitive fit and task-technology fit theories (Vessey and Galletta 1991, Goodhue and Thompson 1995) and show that users generally prefer information channels which are in line with their mental representations of the problem.

In the marketing domain, Murray (1991) analyzes the differences in consumer behavior depending on the type of decision the consumer has to make and concludes that subjects have more confidence in personal sources of information when making decisions on services compared to goods. This finding is justified by the idea of services being perceived as riskier than goods and thereby directly influencing the choice of appropriate information channels.

3.3   Information Request

The category *information request* contains all articles which are concerned with the actual act of acquiring information from a specific information system. Therefore, it is significantly different from the *information need* concept since the latter comprises ex-ante assumptions about required information.

The common theme emerging from the literature is a distinction between search strategies on a macro and on a micro level. Research focused on the *macro level search strategies* abstracts from the immediate interaction between the user and an information system and sheds light on broader concepts such as the quantity and quality of information requested in order to fulfill a certain task (Todd and Benbasat 1992, Pitts and Browne 2004). In this context, the idea of information overload is mentioned in several articles to explain why humans do not necessarily request all available information. This phenomenon is due to limited mental capacities and the goal of minimizing the search effort, even if the consequences manifest in a decreasing information and decision quality (Jones et al. 2004, Liang et al. 2006). However, in a comprehensive study on the concept of information overload in organization science, accounting, marketing, and MIS the authors conclude that "[s]urprisingly, MIS has not been the discipline that has dealt with information overload in the most extensive manner" (Eppler and Mengis 2004, p. 339).

Pitts and Browne (2004) and Browne et al. (2007) significantly extend this stream of research by investigating human stopping behavior in information systems design and online search scenarios. They show that the application of various cognitive stopping rules such as *mental list* or *magnitude threshold* highly depends on the task which has to be performed. Cognitive stopping rules have been investigated in other disciplines before entering the IS domain and might be a valuable basis for explaining differences in the actual quantity and quality of information requested in computer-mediated decision-making and problem solving scenarios. Prabha et al. (2007) give an extensive overview of stopping rule-related literature in the Information Science domain and conclude that also in this discipline "[it has been] neglected to study how individuals decide what and how much information is enough to meet their [the information seekers'] needs or goals" (p. 75). Economics complement this literature by research relying on expected-utility maximization assuming that humans behave rationally during information seeking in that they are able to quantify the cost of getting additional information and compare it with the expected value of this information in decision tasks (Schunk 2009). A similar stance is taken by marketing researchers trying to explain consumer search behavior in sequential search processes. The major conclusion consists in the observation that under certain conditions subjects searched for too much information. This finding challenges the existing marketing literature claiming that "consumers either do not search enough or search just the right amount" (Zwick et al. 2003, p. 517).

Literature on behavioral and technical aspects focusing on the immediate interaction between the user and a specific information system is classified as *micro level search strategies*. For example, Gordon and Moore (1999) concentrate on the problem of document retrieval and propose a formal language for describing documents. Another stream of research addresses semantics to develop more accurate retrieval mechanisms which match the users' natural language use (Arazy and Woo 2007, Storey et al. 2008).

3.4   Information Delivery (through an Information System)

The two major topics emerging when looking at the role of information systems in the information acquisition process comprise (1) the visualization of information with the goal of establishing a cognitive fit between task, user and technology, and (2) the issue of personalization in order to account for contextual and social information.

The differing impacts of various forms of information visualization on the efficiency and effectiveness of information systems use have been broadly and extensively analyzed in the past, especially with regard to decision support systems. Starting with the effect of numerical, textual, and relational representations (Robey and Taggart 1982) the field matured and intensified the research beyond the classical graph versus table discussions of the past. Vessey and Galletta (1991) formalize the concept of cognitive fit by including the human information seeker and calling for an adequate support of human information seeking and problem-solving strategies. Based on the information processing theory, they assume that only a fit between problem solving task and problem representation leads to a consistent mental representation which is the prerequisite for reducing the effort in acquiring information. Lin et al. (1999) complement these findings by measuring improvements in human recall and precision when information is visualized in self-organizing maps. Such maps cluster terms of a specific domain such that the size of a cluster correlates with its relative importance. In more recent research, Hong et al. (2004) examine the effect of flash animations on online users' performance in search scenarios drawing on theories from cognitive psychology, the central capacity theory, and the associative network model. Chung et al. (2005) eventually develop new web visualization methods for facilitating mental model building in exploratory information-seeking processes.

Starting in 2005, more and more articles elaborate on the personalization aspect especially in web environments. They cover various topics such as trust in recommendation agents conceptualized as "social actors" with human characteristics (Wang and Benbasat 2005), or the effect of personalization on user satisfaction and perceived information overload (Liang et al. 2006). The reduction of information load in organizational settings by presenting customized content is also addressed (Scheepers 2006) as well as users' perceptions of personalized information in decision-making contexts (Tam and Ho 2006).

In summary, the articles grouped in this category predominantly use data from *classical* laboratory experiments. In the early 1980s, Ives (1982) and Robey and Taggart (1982) suggested to get a better understanding of the human brain in order to be able to design information systems which address both functionally different brain hemispheres. This aspect, however, was largely neglected in the following three decades. Riedl et al. (2010) use modern brain imaging techniques for the first time in the IS domain in a laboratory experiment. Thus, they advance the field by introducing new approaches for measuring complex mental phenomena which might also substantially propel research in human information behavior.

3.5   Information Assimilation and Evaluation of Information

Following the analytical framework, all these articles were clustered into the category *information assimilation and evaluation of information* which deal with
behavioral and mental processes that take part after the act of requesting specific
information from an information system.

Literature in the IS domain is mainly concerned with (1) the integration of information into mental models and – with a strong focus – (2) the analysis of the
trade-off between effort of information-acquisition and the quality of information
eventually used for decision-making or problem-solving.

Vandenbosch and Higgins (1996) take a cognitive learning perspective to investigate the relationship between information acquisition and learning in the context
of executive support systems. They primarily differentiate between mental model
building and mental model maintenance. While the former is conceptualized as a
change of an existing mental model in order to integrate new information, the
latter represents a confirmation mechanism in which new information fits into the
prevalent mental model. The organizational impact of these differing behavioral
patterns is illustrated by the assumption that executives, who are scanning information, challenge fundamental assumptions and therefore build new mental models while executives who are answering specific questions verify assumptions and
therefore maintain existing mental models (Vandenbosch 1997). Dou et al. (2010)
extend this research and show – based on the schema theory – that information,
evaluated as being incongruent with the searcher's basic assumptions about how
the world works, is more memorable and thereby make recommendations for the
design of search engine marketing campaigns.

The aspect of effort minimization in information acquisition tasks has been discussed by many authors and is regularly seen as a consequence of the limited
information processing capabilities of human problem-solvers (Mendelson and
Pillai 1998, Liang et al. 2006). Hong et al. (2004) focus on active suppression of
information, while Browne et al. (2007) take the opposite stance and analyze various mechanisms which help to judge the sufficiency of information acquisition
based on cognitive heuristics. The phenomenon of sacrificing information quality
for the sake of reduced effort in acquiring that information is brought up by Liang
et al. (2006) and Wang and Benbasat (2009), however, without setting a focus on
the exploration of that phenomenon.

3.6   Comparison of Research Designs

In addition to a content analysis which will be discussed in more detail later, the
research approaches, research methods, and levels of analysis employed in the
reviewed articles were extracted. As expected, most papers build their line of
argumentation around an individual or a group of individuals interacting with an
information system. While the high ratio of empirical positivist research approaches is equally less surprising, it is noticeable that there seems to be a wave of
non empirical mathematical / axiomatic research in the 1990s that tries to formal-

ize behavior and normatively deduce implications for IS design which is in contrast to the premise of bounded rationality underlying most of the remaining articles. In combination with the high proportion of papers using laboratory experiments to verify assumptions, it becomes obvious that there is a strong dominance of research belonging to the category of artificial reconstruction of object reality (Meredith et al. 1989) which is commonly characterized by a high degree of internal but rather low levels of external validity.

4   Discussion and Implications

Although a two-digit number of articles could be identified, which deal with various aspects of human information behavior, it was not possible to provide evidence for a coherent cumulative research tradition in the IS domain. On the contrary, the existing literature is multifaceted and focuses on specific sub-dimensions of information behavior in a rather isolated way. At the same time, the articles follow the common objective of increasing organizational performance by aligning behavioral patterns in information acquisition and processing with the amount, quality, and nature of information provided by technical systems. This can be interpreted as a clear indication for the aforementioned topic's general importance in IS research.

From our analysis of the existing literature regarding human information behavior in the IS domain, we summarize a set of key findings and deduce avenues for further research:

Interdependencies between information acquisition and information processing steps

The literature review reveals that there is no publication integrating all stages of an information acquisition process and thereby covering the topic holistically. Especially remarkable is the fact that a systematic examination of the differences between a priori defined subjective information needs, information actually requested from an information system, and information finally assimilated by the human seeker is not existent. It seems reasonable to assume that an initial information need explicated by the seeker will not translate identically into the set of information which is finally used by the person to make a decision or to solve a problem, since the seeker can usually (in non-routine tasks) not determine a priori if the available information channels will provide information in the quantity, quality, and nature (e.g. form of presentation) in which he expects them to appear and therefore changes his strategy during the seeking process. From the perspective of information systems designers it is highly relevant to get a more profound understanding of the determinants leading to such changes in seeking strategies. Thus, they would be able to create software artifacts that systematically guide and streamline the seeking process with the goal of maximizing organizational performance.

Since decision processes are typically highly information intensive it would be helpful to derive information seeking strategies from research in the aforementioned field and to combine it with studies dealing with stopping behavior and the effort-accuracy theory. Thus, it would be possible to gain insights into the question why humans stop seeking for information under some circumstances in immature states due to factors such as a high subjective mental workload induced by an information overload as proposed by Browne et al. (2007).

Determinants of information channel choice

From our synopsis we found that there is especially a lack of literature addressing both determinants of information channel choice and the consequences with regard to subsequent behavioral patterns. A promising research question consists in the amalgamation of the path dependency theory with information channel choice presuming that the selection of a specific information channel restricts the set of information channels which are used in later phases of the information acquisition.

Another viable way of addressing information channel choice more holistically is the instantiation of information acquisition as a communication process between a human information seeker and a human *or* artificial information source. Especially driven by the emergence of fundamentally new communication technologies there might be new variables influencing the choice of information channels as for example the degree of social presence (Short et al. 1976) which is conveyed by that channel and which might be important constituents of a theory of information channel choice that does not exist yet.

Impact of disruptive technological innovations on information behavior

About one third of all articles published between 2000 and 2010 is concerned with aspects of human information behavior in the context of web environments. This is a clear indicator for the urgent need of a more comprehensive knowledge base addressing the specific characteristics of these technologies and their impact on information-seeking behavior. At the same time, the research in this field is rather eclectic in that it incorporates a wide range of different topics such as trust (Wang and Benbasat 2005), satisfaction (Liang et al. 2006), information saturation (Browne et al. 2007), or different ways of visualizing information (Hong et al. 2004, Chung et al. 2005).

Promising research projects could, for example, explore the influence of social networking websites or modern forms of communication such as microblogging on users' seeking behavior, their problem-solving efficiency, or perceived degree of cognitive effort in using and integrating these technologies into traditional seeking strategies. Social capital theory delivers valuable insights into the underlying cause-effect relationships leveraging the success of those technologies with regard to every-day information-seeking and problem-solving, especially in organizational contexts. Among other things, the theory comprises the concept of weak ties between members of social networks facilitating "privileged access to information and to opportunities" (Nahapiet and Ghoshal 1998, p. 243) as one important and potential factor to explain the success of the aforementioned technologies in information-seeking scenarios. Furthermore, those technologies might have the potential to act as a substitute for immediate face-to-face information seeking. Thus, it would be possible to extend and update the research by Murray (1991) who observes differences in consumers' information channel choice behavior depending on the type of decision, subjects have to make, i. e., if they have to buy a service or a good. E. g., from the perspective of producers of Software-as-a-Service solutions it is highly relevant to clearly understand prospective customers' information requirements in order to effectively reduce uncertainties arising from the service characteristics of this type of software.

The current success of social software technologies mentioned above particularly among young people might have consequences for the design of future organizational information systems. Those people who grew up "entirely networked" might have developed different techniques for seeking information, integrating more and more computer-mediated information from their social environment. Those tendencies could be thoroughly investigated in future research with the goal of designing information systems meeting the fundamentally different requirements of the generation of people who will soon enter the job market.

5   Conclusion

McKinney Jr. and Yoos II (2010) were able to show convincingly that over the last decades, the Information Systems discipline failed to clearly define its understanding of the central term "information" which they consider as a major barrier to realizing advances in theory development and propose a framework for classifying different views on information. Kettinger and Li (2010) go into the same direction by stating that data, information, and knowledge are core to the Information Systems domain, but still a completely satisfying definition is missing which hinders a cumulative tradition. Research in the IS domain is intensely concerned with the explanation of human behavior with respect to information technology, e. g., in the form of adoption and diffusion studies. Thus, we assumed that there is a comprehensive body of knowledge dealing with the interrelationship between the discipline's core entity – information – and the behavior humans exert in order to acquire it to fulfill tasks in computer-mediated business scenarios. From our perspective, fundamental research in this field, which we call – following the research tradition in the Information Science domain – "human information behavior", is a necessary prerequisite for designing information systems that adequately fit the evolutionary, social, and experience-shaped information-seeking patterns (Kock 2009).

Surprisingly, questions conceptualizing human information behavior in computer-mediated settings have not yet been researched explicitly and coherently in the IS domain. However, based on the papers included in our review, there is evidence for the topic's importance in general, a fact that calls for concentrated and incremental interdisciplinary research endeavors in the future. Therefore, possible avenues for future work were presented. Nevertheless, they should not be misunderstood as a complete enumeration of open research questions but as suggestions on how the field can be developed. Besides the dedicated topics mentioned above, it would be desirable to shed light on human information behavior holistically, i. e., to investigate all phases of the conceptual framework introduced in Figure 1 in one research project. Thus, it would be possible to identify path-dependencies within the information-seeking process and detect changes in a user's information needs during an isolated information-seeking activity which has a high potential not only for Information Systems theorizing but also for managers. These would be able to specify more clearly what future organizational information systems should look like or how e-commerce platforms should be designed in order to support and guide customers during their information-seeking activities in such a way as to increase the probability for their prospective customers' buying intentions being translated into an actual customer order.

Human information behavior research in the IS context has the potential to substantially refine existing theories and therefore satisfy the call of Benbasat and Barki (2007) who ask for additional research concerning the antecedents of information systems' usefulness with the goal of being able to give more design-oriented advices. Therefore, they propose to create an augmented task-technology fit model. Our vision is the extension of that idea towards a "human-task-technology fit model" considering the specific characteristics of human information seeking activities.

Appendix: Research in Human Information Behavior

Journal	Study	Information need	Choice of information channel	Information request	Information delivery	Information assim. and evaluation	Interpretive (Empirical)	Positivist (Empirical)	Conceptual (Non empirical)	Mathematical / axiomatic (Non empirical)	Survey / interview	Case study	Lab. experiment	Individual	Group	Organization
MISQ	Ives (1982)	X			X				X					X		
MISQ	Robey and Taggart (1982)				X	X			X						X	
MISQ	Huber (1984)	X			X				X					X		
MISQ	Specht (1986)							X				X		X		
JMIS	Sviokla (1989)						X					X				X
Total	**Total 1980–1989**	2	0	0	3	1	1	1	3	0	0	2	0	3	1	1
ISR	Vessey and Galletta (1991)				X	X		X					X	X		
MISQ	Wetherbe (1991)	X							X					X		
MISQ	Todd and Benbasat (1992)			X		X		X			X			X		
ISR	De et al. (1993)									X						
EJIS	Hertzum et al. (1993)				X				X			X				
EJIS	Jones et al. (1993)		X					X						X		
MISQ	Dennis (1996)					X		X					X		X	
EJIS	Rudy (1996)								X						X	
ISR	Vandenbosch and Higgins (1996)	X			X	X		X			X			X		
MISQ	Choudhury and Sampler (1997)			X					X	X						X
ISR	Moore et al. (1997)					X		X			X			X		
ISR	Mendelson and Pillai (1998)	X			X	X							X			X
JMIS	Mennecke and Valacich (1998)		X		X								X		X	
ISR	Gordon and Moore (1999)			X	X					X						X
JMIS	Grisé and Gallupe (1999)				X								X	X		
JMIS	Lin et al. (1999)					X				X			X	X		
Total	**Total 1990–1999**	3	2	3	7	7	0	6	4	4	3	1	5	8	3	3

Table 2: Research in Human Information Behavior (Part 1 of 3)

Journal	Study	Information need	Choice of information channel	Information request	Information delivery	Information assim. and evaluation	Interpretive	Positivist	Conceptual	Mathematical / axiomatic	Survey / interview	Case study	Lab. experiment	Individual	Group	Organization
		Stages in information acquisition process					**Research approach — Empirical**		**Non empirical**		**Research method**			**Level of analysis**		
ISR	Bordetsky and Mark (2000)	×				×			×					×		
EJIS	Edwards et al. (2000)	×						×					×	×		
ISJ	Sheizaf and Gilad (2003)			×	×								×		×	
ISR	Hong et al. (2004)			×	×	×		×					×	×		
ISR	Jones et al. (2004)		×	×		×		×					×	×		
JMIS	Pitts and Browne (2004)					×		×				×		×		
ISR	Schultze and Orlikowski (2004)			×	×		×					×				
JMIS	Chung et al. (2005)				×				×					×		
ISR	Jiang et al. (2005)			×	×				×					×		
JMIS	Nelson et al. (2005)	×			×			×			×			×		
JAIS	Wang and Benbasat (2005)	×						×					×	×		
EJIS	Hovorka and Larsen (2006)						×					×				
MISQ	Kuechler and Vaishnavi (2006)				×	×			×				×	×		
JAIS	Li and Kettinger (2006)	×		×	×	×		×					×	×		
JMIS	Liang et al. (2006)			×	×	×		×					×	×		
EJIS	Scheepers (2006)				×				×			×		×		
MISQ	Tam and Ho (2006)				×			×				×		×		
MISQ	Arazy and Woo (2007)			×	×			×					×			×
MISQ	Browne and Pitts (2007)			×		×		×					×	×		
MISQ	Watson-Manheim and Bélanger (2007)		×					×				×		×		
MISQ	Dennis et al. (2008)		×						×					×		
ISJ	Melville and Ramirez (2008)	×			×			×			×					×

Table 2: Research in Human Information Behavior (Part 2 of 3)

Journal	Study	Level of analysis			Research method			Research approach — Non empirical		Research approach — Empirical		Stages in information acquisition process				
		Organization	Group	Individual	Lab. experiment	Case study	Survey / interview	Mathematical / axiomatic	Conceptual	Positivist	Interpretive	Information assim. and evaluation	Information delivery	Information request	Choice of information channel	Information need
JMIS	Ren et al. (2008)		×			×					×					×
ISR	Storey et al. (2008)								×				×	×		
JAIS	Zhang and Watts (2008)			×			×			×					×	
MISQ	Wang and Benbasat (2009)			×	×							×	×			
MISQ	Dou et al. (2010)			×	×					×		×	×			×
MISQ	Mani and Barua (2010)	×					×			×		×	×			×
Total	Total 2000–2010	3	3	19	13	8	4	0	7	18	3	11	16	11	4	8
Sum	Sum 1980–2010	3	7	30	18	11	7	4	14	25	4	19	26	14	6	13

Table 2: Research in Human Information Behavior (Part 3 of 3)

References

Arazy, O. and Woo, C. "Enhancing Information Retrieval Through Statistical Natural Language Processing: A Study of Collocation Indexing," *MIS Quarterly* (31:3), 2007, pp. 525-546.

Belkin, N. J. "Anomalous states of knowledge as a basis for information retrieval," *The Canadian journal of information science* (5), 1980, pp. 133-143.

Benbasat, I. and Barki, H. "Quo vadis, TAM," *Journal of the Association for Information Systems* (8:4), 2007, pp. 211–218.

Bonoma, T. V. "Case Research in Marketing: Opportunities, Problems, and a Process," *Journal of Marketing Research* (22:2), 1985, pp. 199-208.

Bordetsky, A. and Mark, G. "Memory-Based Feedback Controls to Support Groupware Coordination," *Information Systems Research* (11:4), 2000, pp. 366-385.

Browne, G. J., Pitts, M. G. and Wetherbe, J. C "Cognitive Stopping Rules for Terminating Information Search in Online Tasks," *MIS Quarterly* (31:1), 2007, pp. 89-104.

Choudhury, V. and Sampler, J. L. "Information Specificity and Environmental Scanning: An Economic Perspective," *MIS Quarterly* (21:1), 1997, pp. 25-53.

Chung, W., Chen, H. and Nunamaker Jr., J. F. "A Visual Framework for Knowledge Discovery on the Web: An Empirical Study of Business Intelligence Exploration," *Journal of Management Information Systems* (21:4), 2005, pp. 57-84.

Daft, R. L., Lengel, R. H. and Trevnio, L. K. "Message Equivocality, Media Selection, and Manager Performance: Implications for Information Systems," *MIS Quarterly* (11:3), 1987, pp. 355-366.

De, P., Jacob, V. S. and Pakath, R. "A Formal Approach for Designing Distributed Expert Problem-solving Systems," *Information Systems Research* (4:2), 1993, pp. 141-165.

Dennis, A. R. "Information Exchange and Use in Group Decision Making: You Can Lead a Group to Information, but You Can't Make It Think," *MIS Quarterly* (20:4), 1996, pp. 433-457.

Dennis, A. R., Fuller, R. M. and Valacich, J. S. "Media, Tasks, and Communication Processes: A Theory of Media Synchronicity," *MIS Quarterly* (32:3), 2008, pp. 575-600.

Dibbern, J., Goles, T., Hirschheim, R. and Jayatilaka, B. "Information Systems Outsourcing: A Survey and Analysis of the Literature," *The DATA BASE for Advances in Information Systems* (35:4), 2004, pp. 6-102.

Dou, W., Lim, K. H., Su, C., Zhou, N. and Cui, N. "Brand Positioning Strategy Using Search Engine Marketing," *MIS Quarterly* (34:2), 2010, pp. 261-A4.

Edwards, J. S., Duan, Y. and C, R. P. "An analysis of expert systems for business decision making at different levels and in different roles," *European Journal of Information Systems* (9:1), 2000, pp. 36-46.

Eppler, M. J. and Mengis, J. "The Concept of Information Overload: A Review of Literature from Organization Science, Accounting, Marketing, MIS, and Related Disciplines," *The Information Society* (20), 2004, pp. 325-344.

Gemünden, H. G. "Informationsverhalten" Schäffer-Poeschel, Stuttgart, 1993.

Goodhue, D. L. and Thompson, R. L. "Task-Technology Fit and Individual Performance," *MIS Quarterly* (19:2), 1995, pp. 213-236.

Gordon, M. D. and Moore, S. A. "Depicting the Use and Purpose of Documents to Improve Information Retrieval," *Information Systems Research* (10:1), 1999, pp. 23-37.

Grisé, M.-L. and Gallupe, R. B. "Information Overload: Addressing the Productivity Paradox in Face-to-Face Electronic Meetings," *Journal of Management Information Systems* (16:3), 1999, pp. 157-185.

Hertzum, M., Soes, H. and Frokjaer, E. "Information retrieval systems for professionals: A case study of computer supported legal research," *European Journal of Information Systems* (2:4), 1993, pp. 296-303.

Hong, W., Thong, J. Y. L. and Tam, K. Y. "Does Animation Attract Online Users' Attention? The Effects of Flash on Information Search Performance and Perceptions," *Information Systems Research* (15:1), 2004, pp. 60-86.

Hovorka, D. S. and Larsen, K. R. "Enabling agile adoption practices through network organizations," *European Journal of Information Systems* (15:2), 2006, pp. 159-168.

Huber, G. P. "Cognitive Style as a Basis for MIS and DSS Designs: Much ado about Nothing?," *Management Science* (29:5), 1983, pp. 567-579.

Huber, G. P. "Issues in the Design of Group Decision Support Systems," *MIS Quarterly* (8:3), 1984, pp. 195-204.

Ives, B. "Graphical User Interfaces for Business Information Systems," *MIS Quarterly* (6:Special Issue), 1982, pp. 15-47.

Jiang, Z., Mookerjee, V. S. and Sarkar, S. "Lying on the Web: Implications for Expert Systems Redesign," *Information Systems Research* (16:2), 2005, pp. 131-148.

Jones, J. W., Saunders, C. and McLeod, R. J. "Media usage and velocity in executive information acquisition: An exploratory study," *European Journal of Information Systems* (2:4), 1993, pp. 260.

Jones, Q., Ravid, G. and Rafaeli, S. "Information Overload and the Message Dynamics of Online Interaction Spaces: A Theoretical Model and Empirical Exploration," *Information Systems Research* (15:2), 2004, pp. 194-210.

Kettinger, W. J. and Li, Y. "The infological equation extended: towards conceptual clarity in the relationship between data, information and knowledge," *European Journal of Information Systems* (19:4), 2010, pp. 409-421.

Kock, N. "Information Systems Theorizing Based on Evolutionary Psychology: An Interdisciplinary Review and Theory Integration Framework," *MIS Quarterly* (33:2), 2009, pp. 395-418.

Kuechler, W. L. and Vaishnavi, V. "So, Talk to Me, The Effect of Explicit Goals on the Comprehension of Business Process Narratives," *MIS Quarterly* (30:4), 2006, pp. 961-A16.

Li, Y. and Kettinger, W. J. "An Evolutionary Information-Processing Theory of Knowledge Creation," *Journal of the Association for Information Systems* (7:9), 2006, pp. 593-616.

Liang, T.-P., Lai, H.-J. and Ku, Y.-C. "Personalized Content Recommendation and User Satisfaction: Theoretical Synthesis and Empirical Findings," *Journal of Management Information Systems* (23:3), 2006, pp. 45-70.

Lin, C., Chen, H. and Nunamaker, J. F. "Verifying the Proximity and Size Hypothesis for Self-Organizing Maps," *Journal of Management Information Systems* (16:3), 1999, pp. 57-70.

Locke, K. and Golden-Biddle, K. "Constructing Opportunities for Contribution: Structuring Intertextual Coherence and "Problematizing" in Organizational Studies," *Academy of Management Journal* (40:5), 1997, pp. 1023-1062.

MacInnis, D. J. and Jaworski, B. J. "Information Processing from Advertisements: Toward an Integrative Framework," *Journal of Marketing* (53:4), 1989, pp. 1-23.

Mani, D. and Barua, A. "An Empirical Analysis of the Impact of Information Capabilities Design on Business Process Outsourcing Performance," *MIS Quarterly* (34:1), 2010, pp. 39-62.

McKinney Jr., E. H. and Yoos II, C. J. "Information About Information: A Taxonomy of Views," *MIS Quarterly* (34:2), 2010, pp. 329-A5.

Melville, N. and Ramirez, R. "Information technology innovation diffusion: an information requirements paradigm," *Information Systems Journal* (18:3), 2008, pp. 247-273.

Mendelson, H. and Pillai, R. R. "Clockspeed and Informational Response: Evidence from the Information Technology Industry," *Information Systems Research* (9:4), 1998, pp. 415-433.

Mennecke, B. E. and Valacich, J. S. "Information Is What You Make of It: The Influence of Group History and Computer Support on Information Sharing, Decision Quality, and Member Perceptions," *Journal of Management Information Systems* (15:2), 1998, pp. 173-197.

Meredith, J. R., Raturi, A., Amoako-Gyampah, K. and Kaplan, B. "Alternative Research Paradigms in Operations," *Journal of Operations Management* (8:4), 1989, pp. 297-326.

Meyers-Levy, J. and Malaviya, P. "Consumers' Processing of Persuasive Advertisements: An Integrative Framework of Persuasion Theories," *Journal of Marketing* (63:4), 1999, pp. 45-60.

Moore, J. C., Rao, H. R., Whinston, A., Nam, K. and Raghu, T. S. "Information Acquisition Policies for Resource Allocation Among Multiple Agents," *Information Systems Research* (8:2), 1997, pp. 151-170.

Murray, K. B. "A test of services marketing theory: Consumer information acquisition activities," *Journal of Marketing* (55:1), 1991, pp. 10-25.

Nahapiet, J. and Ghoshal, S. "Social Capital, Intellectual Capital, and the Organizational Advantage," *The Academy of Management Review* (23:2), 1998, pp. 242-266.

Nelson, R. R., Todd, P. A. and Wixom, B. H. "Antecedents of Information and System Quality: An Empirical Examination Within the Context of Data Warehousing," *Journal of Management Information Systems* (21:4), 2005, pp. 199-235.

Payne, J. W. "Contingent Decision Behavior," *Psychological Bulletin* (92:2), 1982, pp. 382-402.

Pitts, M. G. and Browne, G. J. "Stopping Behavior of Systems Analysts During Information Requirements Elicitation," *Journal of Management Information Systems* (21:1), 2004, pp. 203-226.

Prabha, C., Connaway, L. S., Olszewski, L. and Jenkins, L. R. "What is enough? Satisficing information needs," *Journal of Documentation* (63:1), 2007, pp. 74-89.

Ren, Y., Kiesler, S. and Fussell, S. R. "Multiple Group Coordination in Complex and Dynamic Task Environments: Interruptions, Coping Mechanisms, and Technology Recommendations," *Journal of Management Information Systems* (25:1), 2008, pp. 105-130.

Riedl, R., Hubert, M. and Kenning, P. "Are there neural gender differences in online trust? An fMRI study on the perceived trustworthiness of eBay offers," *MIS Quarterly* (34:2), 2010, pp. 397-428.

Robey, D. and Taggart, W. "Human Information Processing in Information and Decision Support Systems," *MIS Quarterly* (6:2), 1982, pp. 61-73.

Rudy, I. A. "A critical review of research on electronic mail," *European Journal of Information Systems* (4:4), 1996, pp. 198.

Scheepers, R. "A conceptual framework for the implementation of enterprise information portals in large organizations," *European Journal of Information Systems* (15:6), 2006, pp. 635.

Schultze, U. and Orlikowski, W. J. "A Practice Perspective on Technology-Mediated Network Relations:The Use of Internet-Based Self-Serve Technologies," *Information Systems Research* (15:1), 2004, pp. 87-106.

Schunk, D. "Behavioral heterogeneity in dynamic search situations: Theory and experimental evidence," *Journal of Economic Dynamics & Control* (33), 2009, pp. 1719-1738.

Sheizaf, R. and Gilad, R. "Information sharing as enabler for the virtual team: an experimental approach to assessing the role of electronic mail in disintermediation," *Information Systems Journal* (13:2), 2003, pp. 191-206.

Short, J., Williams, E. and Christie, B. "The Social Psychology of Telecommunications, " Wiley, London, 1976.

Specht, P. H. "Job Characteristics as Indicants of CBIS Data Requirements," *MIS Quarterly* (10:3), 1986, pp. 271-287

Storey, V. C., Burton-Jones, A., Sugumaran, V. and Purao, S. "CONQUER: A Methodology for Context-Aware Query Processing on the World Wide Web," *Information Systems Research* (19:1), 2008, pp. 2-25.

Sviokla, J. J. "Expert Systems and Their Impact on the Firm: The Effects of PlanPower Use on the Information Processing Capacity of the Financial Collaborative," *Journal of Management Information Systems* (6:3), 1989, pp. 65-84.

Tam, K. Y. and Ho, S. Y. "Understanding the Impact of Web Personalization on User Information Processing and Decision Outcomes," *MIS Quarterly* (30:4), 2006, pp. 865-890.

Todd, P. and Benbasat, I. "The Use of Information in Decision Making: An Experimental Investigation of the Impact of Computer-Based Decision Aids," *MIS Quarterly* (16:3), 1992, pp. 373-393.

Vandenbosch, B. "Searching and Scanning: How Executives Obtain Information from Executive Information Systems," *MIS Quarterly* (21:1), 1997, pp. 81-107.

Vandenbosch, B. and Higgins, C. "Information Acquisition and Mental Models: An Investigation into the Relationship Between Behaviour and Learning," *Information Systems Research* (7:2), 1996, pp. 198-214.

Vessey, I. and Galletta, D. "Cognitive Fit: An Empirical Study of Information Acquisition," *Information Systems Research* (2:1), 1991, pp. 63-84.

Wang, W. and Benbasat, I. "Trust in and Adoption of Online Recommendation Agents," *Journal of the Association for Information Systems* (6:3), 2005, pp. 72-101.

Wang, W. and Benbasat, I. "Interactive Decision Aids for Consumer Decision Making in E-Commerce: The Influence of Perceived Strategy Restrictiveness," *MIS Quarterly* (33:2), 2009, pp. 293-320.

Watson-Manheim, M. B. and Bélanger, F. "Communication Media Repertoires: Dealing with the Multiplicity of Media Choices," *MIS Quarterly* (31:2), 2007, pp. 267-293.

Webster, J. and Watson, R. T. "Analyzing the Past to Prepare for the Future: Writing a Literature Review," *MIS Quarterly* (26:2), 2002, pp. xiii-xxiii.

Wetherbe, J. C. "Executive Information Requirements: Getting It Right," *MIS Quarterly* (15:1), 1991, pp. 51-65.

Wilson, T. D. "Models in Information Behaviour Research," *Journal of Documentation* (55:3), 1999, pp. 249-270.

Wilson, T. D. "Human Information Behavior," *Informing Science* (3:2), 2000, pp. 49-55.

Yadav, M. S. "The Decline of Conceptual Articles and Implications for Knowledge Development," *Journal of Marketing* (74:1), 2010, pp. 1-19.

Zhang, W. and Watts, S. A. "Capitalizing on Content: Information Adoption in Two Online communities," *Journal of the Association for Information Systems* (9:2), 2008, pp. 72-93.

Zwick, R., Rapoport, A., Lo, A. K. C. and Muthukrishnan, A. V. "Consumer Sequential Search - Not Enough or Too Much?," *Marketing Science* (22:4), 2003, pp. 503-519.

„Meine Investition. Meine Entscheidung. Mein Erfolg."

Sie wollen Ihr Unternehmen fit für die Zukunft machen. Gut, wenn Sie dabei einen Partner haben, der Investitionen erleichtert. Die Deutsche Leasing kann dieser Partner für Sie sein. Denn sie bietet Ihnen weltweit höchste Seriosität und Zuverlässigkeit – und damit das gute Gefühl, die richtige Entscheidung getroffen zu haben. **www.deutsche-leasing.com**

Curriculum Vitae Prof. Dr. Wolfgang König

1970	High-school diploma (Abitur) at the Einhard-Gymnasium, Seligenstadt
1975	Masters Diploma in Business Administration (Diplom-Kaufmann) at the Johann Wolfgang Goethe University, Frankfurt am Main (summa cum laude; majors: Information Systems, Industrial Management, Operations Research)
1975	Masters Diploma in Business Pedagogics (Diplom-Wirtschaftspädagoge) at the Johann Wolfgang Goethe University (summa cum laude)
1979	Doctorate in Business Administration at the Johann Wolfgang Goethe University in Frankfurt (topic: "Hardware-based Parallelisation of Corporate Planning Systems"; Committee: Prof. Dr. Joachim Niedereichholz, Prof. Dr. Gerriet Müller)
1980	Assistant Professor (Hochschulassistent) at the Johann Wolfgang Goethe University
1981 - 1982	Visiting researcher at IBM Research Center in San Jose, California for the project: "Extending System R* for technical applications, especially chip design"
1985	Habilitation at the Johann Wolfgang Goethe University (topic: "Strategic Planning for Corporate Information Processing")
1985	Chair of Business Administration, especially Information Systems and Information Management at Koblenz Corporate School of Management - Otto Beisheim School

A. Heinzl et al. (eds.), *Theory-Guided Modeling and Empiricism in Information Systems Research*, DOI 10.1007/978-3-7908-2781-1, © Springer-Verlag Berlin Heidelberg 2011

| 1986 - 1989 | Rector at the Koblenz Corporate School of Management - Otto Beisheim School |

| 1987 | Visiting researcher at the Kellogg Graduate School of Management, Evanston/Chicago for the project: "Strategic Planning of the Information Processing Function" |

| 1990 | Visiting researcher at the IBM Watson Research Center in Yorktown Heights, New York for the project: "Expert Systems for Mainframe Allocation Planning" |

| 1991 | Chair of Business Administration, especially Information Systems and Information Management at Johann Wolfgang Goethe University in Frankfurt (declined offers from Cologne, Essen and Saarbrücken) |

| 1992-1997 | Originator and spokesperson of the focused research initiative of the German Science foundation (DFG-Schwerpunktprogramm) on "Distributed DP-Systems in Business Administration" |

| 1993 | Visiting researcher at the Haas School of Business at the University of California at Berkeley for the project: "The future of the IS function" |

| 1994 | Co-editor of the journal WIRTSCHAFTSINFORMATIK |

| 1995 - 2000 | Originator and spokesperson of the special research initiative of the German Science Foundation (DFG-Sonderforschungsbereich) on "Networks and competitive adavantage exemplified with the Rhein-Main Region" |

1998 - 2008   Editor in chief of the journal WIRTSCHAFTSINFORMATIK

2001   Visiting researcher at University of Hawaii in Manoa for the project: "IS Education in MBA Programs"

2002   Founder and chairman of the board of the E-Finance Lab e.V., a public private research partnership

2004 - 2006   Dean of the Faculty of Economics and Business Administration at the Johann Wolfgang Goethe University

2005   IBM Faculty Award for research on "Risk Mitigation in the Context of Business Process Outsourcing"

2007   Visiting researcher at City University of Hong Kong for the project: "IS Research and Education in Hong Kong and in Mainland China"

2007   Visiting researcher at IBM Almaden Research Center in San Jose for the project: „Service Industry"

2008   Co-founder and executive director of the House of Finance at the Johann Wolfgang Goethe University

Professor König has published his research in many scientific journals including MIS Quarterly, Information Systems Frontiers, Journal of Global Information Management and BISE/WIRTSCHAFTSINFORMATIK.

He served on the editorial board or as reviewer for journals including European Journal of Information Systems and Information Systems and E-Business Management and as Chair, co-chair or reviewer for national and international conferences including International Conference on Information Systems, European Conference on Information Systems, the biennial International Conference Wirtschaftsinformatik and the annual conferences of the E-Finance Lab. Wolfgang König is also a referee for the German Science Foundation (Deutsche Forschungsgemeinschaft), Federal Ministry of Education and Research (Bundesministerium für Bildung und Forschung), the European Union and the Federal State of Hesse.

His current research interests are E-Finance, Information Systems in human resource processes, open publishing and systemic risks in finance and raw materials. Wolfgang König was or is member of the supervisory boards or advisor at various firms including Veritas AG, Gelnhausen, and Deufol AG, Wallau. He is also chairman of the corporate advisory board of the DZ Bank.

Wofgang König has accepted a multitude of honorary appointments and volunteers for the scientific advisory board of Offis e. V., Oldenburg, as member of the board of trustees of the Hochschule der Sparkassen, Bonn, and as chairman for various associations promoting and advancing the Rhine-Main area and its academic infrastructure like the Frankfurter Institut für Risikomanagement und Regulierung (FIRM), Frankfurt Main Finance and Digital Hub Frankfurt Rhein-Main.

Index

GPSR Compliance
The European Union's (EU) General Product Safety Regulation (GPSR) is a set
of rules that requires consumer products to be safe and our obligations to
ensure this.

If you have any concerns about our products, you can contact us on

ProductSafety@springernature.com

In case Publisher is established outside the EU, the EU authorized
representative is:

Springer Nature Customer Service Center GmbH
Europaplatz 3
69115 Heidelberg, Germany